PUT ON A
HAPPY FACE

PUT ON A
HAPPY FACE

A BROADWAY MEMOIR

Charles Strouse

Emmy®, Grammy®, and Tony® Award–winning
composer of *Annie* and *Bye Bye Birdie*

UNION SQUARE PRESS
An imprint of Sterling Publishing Co., Inc.

New York / London
www.sterlingpublishing.com

STERLING and the distinctive Sterling logo are
registered trademarks of Sterling Publishing Co., Inc.

Library of Congress Cataloging-in-Publication Data Available

10 9 8 7 6 5 4 3 2 1

Published by Sterling Publishing Co., Inc.
387 Park Avenue South, New York, NY 10016
© 2008 by Charles Strouse
Distributed in Canada by Sterling Publishing
c/o Canadian Manda Group, 165 Dufferin Street
Toronto, Ontario, Canada M6K 3H6
Distributed in the United Kingdom by GMC Distribution Services
Castle Place, 166 High Street, Lewes, East Sussex, England BN7 1XU
Distributed in Australia by Capricorn Link (Australia) Pty. Ltd.
P.O. Box 704, Windsor, NSW 2756, Australia

Book design and layout by *T. Reitzle/Oxygen Design*

Sterling ISBN 978-1-4027-5889-8

For information about custom editions, special sales, premium and
corporate purchases, please contact Sterling Special Sales Department at
800-805-5489 or specialsales@sterlingpublishing.com.

Who else? For Barbara

Contents

Take off that gloomy mask of tragedy,

It's not your style;

You'll look so good that you'll be glad y'dee-

-cided to smile.

LEE ADAMS

Overture

COMPOSING IS FRIGHTENING. My finger may inadvertently land on a note, and then, as in a dream, continue in an unexpected way. I've begun to learn: Let it happen—later it may turn into something meaningful. Or surprising. Funny. Or beautiful.

Or not.

Is it the same writing words? I've never attempted a memoir before—never flattered myself that anyone other than my wife and children would be interested—

Liar, you've already planned a book signing party at the Mvsevm of Natvral History.

(Private joke: This New York institution, around which I spent my early life, had every letter "u" chiseled into the front of the building as a "v.")

I imagine my book signing party will be held there, a laughter-filled gathering beneath the great blue whale on the main floor.

Look, there's Elliott Carter dancing with Arthur Carter and Arthur Laurents and Arthur Kopit. And isn't that Hal Prince chatting with Prince Littler? See Carolyn Leigh and Carol Burnett? And there's Michael Feinstein with Sidney Michaels; (faster) and Warren Lyons and Margo Lion tête-á-tête with Lenny Bernstein. And there's Stephen Sondheim tangoing with Stephen Schwartz. (Faster and faster!) And Kander and Ebb and Maltby and Shire and Leiber and Stoller and David Merrick and David Diamond and Dr. Droller and . . . (music stops!)

Dr. Droller! How did he get into this?

1

He just removed your prostate—wake up!
What are the reviews like?
"A very assertive cancer." The *New York Times*.
"Needs cutting." *Variety*.
Write this all down!
What else can you do at Mount Sinai, anyway?

𝄢

The next morning, I look at what I've written. Almost immediately, I hate it. As with my music, only if others like it will I come around. I have no mind of my own.

I'm wary of the ghosts that appear: expected and obvious or senseless and unconnected. Funny thing is, if I can pin them down—like my preserved butterflies at summer camp—they begin to swarm over the page by themselves. Not art; just easy. Quick is good. Why is it that once something is down on paper, I enjoy twisting and shaping it? It's just like with music: I keep at it until the notes I've put down find their own way, dividing and multiplying like a cell, separating as a child does from its parent.

It seems I'm sentenced to spend the rest of my life trying to make this happen with notes. This twisting and shaping drowns out the sound of my brother David's coughing, of my parents arguing, and of my own inner voice screaming, so I keep at it until, finally, I can't and don't want to do anything *but* compose. But now other ghosts I hadn't expected are turning up.

Mozart said, "It's God, not I, who writes the notes."

I'm not religious, but I know what he means.

CHAPTER ONE

A Lot of Living

IT WAS 1962. Over in England, an unknown group of Liverpool boys needing haircuts auditioned and were rejected by Decca Records, before being picked up by a manager named Brian Epstein. In another part of the UK, Mick Jagger and his friend Keith Richards met Brian Jones. Pop sparks flew across the sea as the '60s took hold in a rock-and-roll way. Meanwhile, back in Hollywood, aging gossip columnist Louella Parsons reported that Columbia Pictures had purchased the rights to a little Broadway show that satirized rock and roll called *Bye Bye Birdie* for more than one million dollars, at the time the highest price paid for a musical.

But then *Bye Bye Birdie* wasn't just any musical. When it opened on April 14, 1960, to mostly rave reviews, it was the sleeper hit of the season. There were no names involved, and no one expected anything of the show, so boy, was everyone surprised when the papers loved it! It ran for 607 performances and won the Tony Award for Best Musical. In 1961, it was produced in London and now, one million dollars later, Hollywood.

A small squib in *Variety*, the show biz bible, read, COLUMBIA JETS 'BIRDIE' BOYS TO COAST TO PEN NEW TITLE SONG.

The "Birdie Boys" were lyricist Lee Adams and I. The Hollywood studio system was barely hanging on by its fingernails, but walking into the lobby of the Beverly Hills Hotel made me wish it would go on forever.

My room was what might be called "opulent tropical." The wallpaper had large green leaves spread against a pink-and-white background. The windows were dressed in shutters of dark mahogany. There were fresh flowers and a bottle of wine on the table. Near them was a basket of fruit in hermetically sealed cellophane. The card read, "Welcome, Columbia Pictures." And, in the bathroom, a roll of toilet paper was folded neatly into a point at the end of the roll.

My mother would have loved it.

I tumbled backward onto the bed (expensive mattress) and looked at the ceiling. I couldn't think of what to do. I was on complete disconnect.

Of course, the pool! There would be starlets there and, this way, when I returned to New York, I'd not only have a new title song called "Bye Bye Birdie," but I'd also have a great tan. That was nothing to be sneezed at on the Upper West Side in the winter. I grabbed sunglasses, a book, and my Pall Malls (we all smoked back then) and doffed swim trunks, a Yankees cap, and my DeWitt Clinton High School T-shirt (to remain true to my New York roots). I purchased some overpriced French coconut oil at a pink-and-green drugstore (and signed for it—the studio was paying for everything, oh happy day!), and hopped into a pink-and-green elevator where the elevator operator—also done up in pink and green (I was starting to notice a theme here)—paid absolutely no attention to me.

Arriving at the pool, I gave a casual nod to the perfectly tanned, bleached-blond pool boy in tight white shorts with an equally tight ass, looking older than he thought he did. He spread a towel with practiced flair on the best-positioned chaise at the pool—or so his conspiratorial wink told me. I settled myself poolside and picked up my hardcover book, which I only had so that I could glance up from it and surreptitiously observe the beautiful starlets.

And then—I kid you not—over the loudspeaker came Tony Bennett, telling one and all to "Put on a Happy Face."

And that's just what I did.

By the time Tony got to "wipe off the clouds and cheer up," my thoughts were spinning.

My mother would have loved sitting among the celebrities at the Beverly Hills Hotel swimming pool. At least I had that in common with Stravinsky and Ravel, Beethoven and Boulez: We all wanted to make Mommy proud.

I napped intermittently as Tony Bennett's jazzy tones were interrupted by disembodied voices summoning important people to urgent telephone calls.

"Call for Fernando Lamas. Please dial extension 268."

"Call for Lucille Ball. Please dial 234."

Was she here? In my sun-drenched stupor, I supposed that my call would come soon as well.

Now, Lee's lyrics are good, but I was never the type to listen to what a popular song told me. I never walked on the sunny side of the street or danced all night. But today, with all that Beverly Hills sunshine being spread on me like butter, well . . . could it be that Charles was actually happy?

"I knew a girl so gloomy, she wouldn't laugh or sing," Tony continued as I opened my eyes to see a fat little boy with a round face and dark circles under his eyes. He was inappropriately dressed for a hot California day by the pool in a sweater and knickers. I judged him to be about ten.

"You should have tipped the pool boy when he brought you the chaise," he said.

Was the sun playing tricks on me?

"She wouldn't listen to me, now she's a mean old thing!" Tony continued.

The boy seemed familiar somehow.

"I know, I know—you don't have a pocket in your swim trunks," the fat kid sneered, anticipating my excuse. "You could have put a couple of bucks in that lousy book you're not even reading. Phony cheapskate!"

I closed my eyes again, focusing on the song again and hoping this rude, obnoxious kid would go back to his mother.

"So spread sunshine all over the place . . ."

But when I opened them again, he was still there. He was eating a big sloppy tuna fish sandwich. "You should check out now," he continued. "You don't belong here. Remember it was Gower Champion's staging and not your music that made the show a success."

I shut my eyes again to make him go away, and when I opened them, he was gone and Tony Bennett had turned into Lena Horne singing "Stormy Weather."

The next day, my lawyer, Bella Linden, turned to the president of Columbia Pictures, Abe Schneider, whose office we'd been sitting in for nearly an hour, and said, "Don't you think we should begin the meeting?"

I thought this was a good idea. Lee and I had already filled up on the buffet in Schneider's office. Now there were important matters to deal with.

"I think we should wait until the composer gets here," Schneider responded.

"I'm the composer," I whispered.

Columbia Pictures had paid us the largest amount of money ever paid for motion picture rights, and the president didn't even know who I was.

"I thought your name was Buddy. Everyone's calling you Buddy," he said in surprise.

"It's a nickname. I'm really Charles."

He seemed confused.

Suddenly I remembered the fat little boy at the pool telling me his name.

It was Buddy.

CHAPTER TWO

A Healthy, Normal American Boy

I'VE BEEN CALLED BUDDY for as long as I can remember. My mother told me that it was my older brother David who actually gave me my nickname. When I was still in diapers, his childish mispronunciation of "brother" or "brudder" came out of his three-year-old mouth as "Buddy." And so, Charles was called Buddy by one and all.

I was a depression baby. Maybe things would have been different if the stock market crash of 1929 hadn't come when I was one-and-a-half years old, but I doubt it, because the depression in my house wasn't brought on by the crash. The "great depression" at 120 West Seventieth Street was my mother, Ethel, a woman of many mood swings. If I got an A in some class (which I usually did because school came easily to me), we would celebrate with chocolate ice cream sodas. Then Mom would become depressed because she had enjoyed the treat and was becoming fat. I realize now her mood swings (they didn't have a name for manic-depression or bi-polar disorder then) must have been as hard on my father as it was on my brother and me. But my father, Ira, was a traveling salesman dealing in shade-grown tobacco (the kind used to wrap cigars), and he was often away, leaving my roller coaster of a mom to take care of us.

Like many other people who lived through these times, the Depression outside of our house affected my parents (and consequently me) for the rest of their lives. They were forever frugal and my father's love of gambling didn't help the matter. Pop would spend untold hours playing gin rummy and bridge at the Friars Club. His old friend, vaudevillian Harry Delf (who, besides writing plays and the first three sound-on-film talkies ever made, also penned special material for the Dolly Sisters), had become the Dean of the Friars, and let Pop in. Pop loved the card tables, but even more he loved hobnobbing with the big name entertainers who frequented that hallowed show business club.

To add to everyone's woes, Pop's health was always precarious. We all learned to be fearful of his chronic cough (which would often manage to dislodge his false teeth at the dinner table), his diabetes, and his periodic heart attacks. Pop was also hard of hearing but refused to wear a hearing aid. I always figured he just didn't want to hear Mom's constant *kvetching*.

Although Mom was frightened of life, she was also smart and observant and had a terrific sense of humor. And I loved her—maybe too much. In fact, I loved her so much that I unconsciously began to take on some of her qualities, both good and bad. If Mom could never take a compliment, neither could I. If Mom worried about the butcher cheating her, I would help her count the pennies in her change purse. We always had a special connection and because she was down a lot, I quickly learned to protect her feelings and help her in the kitchen or around the house. She and I shared a love of Shirley Temple, which embarrassed me at the time.

All of these "sensitive" ways of mine resulted in my older brother, David, making fun of me. This hurt, especially because I was crazy about my brother. He was the one who took care of me as he dreamed of becoming a doctor, even though he never did as well in school as I did. It was probably clear to him that I was Mom's favorite, her little shadow, the good little boy who supported her against the world; while if David sought some physical affection from her, Mom would push him away because he hugged her too hard. Is it any wonder he locked me in a steamer trunk when I was five or six?

But Mom, with her constant threats of suicide, needed me. I always made her laugh, and when she wasn't depressed, she made me laugh in turn. When, inevitably, her depression returned, it was my job to dispel her despair. No one else seemed interested or had the knack. So Buddy dutifully accepted the assignment—which turned out to be a lifelong one.

We also shared music.

Like many women of her generation, my mother played piano. When she was growing up in Brooklyn in the early part of the twentieth century, most households had a piano as their key source of home entertainment. Radio didn't really come into popular fashion until the 1920s, and television was an unheard-of fantasy. Hell, movies didn't even talk yet, so families gathered around the piano to play and sing the latest popular songs, most from Broadway shows. We were the proud owners of a piano Mom went all the way to Brooklyn to buy. (She never trusted Manhattan merchants, lawyers, or doctors and always shopped in the borough of her birth.) Our piano was a Brooklyn "Brambach," a brand I'd never heard of before or since.

10

Mom played a happy sounding stride piano, a kind of jazzman's old-fashioned, bouncing swing (think Fats Waller)—octave (or arpeggiated tenth) in the left hand, then, quickly, with the same hand, chord, octave, chord, octave, chord. There was great joy emanating from my mother's fingers, if not from the rest of her. Later on, I learned that in the early twentieth century black musicians who played in whorehouses (the only places they could work at that time) created stride piano, but as a child, I thought my mother had invented it.

Every week Mom and I would go to buy the latest sheet music at Woolworth's. The colorful covers had pictures of Alice Faye or Bing Crosby, Margaret Whiting or Bob Hope adorning them, and the music was demonstrated at the piano by a salesperson—usually an elderly woman or an effete young man. After making our choice and maybe having an egg cream soda, we couldn't wait to get home and try out the songs ourselves. Those were the happy memories: the whole family standing around the piano singing a new song while my mother played.

It was this memory that was responsible, many years later, for a suggestion I made to producer Norman Lear when he was filming the opening credits for the television show *All in the Family*. Lee Adams and I had written a song called "Those Were the Days" that everyone loved, and with only a few hundred dollars left in the budget, the vocal chorus and full orchestra Norman wanted were out of the question. Thinking back to my youth, I suggested that Archie and Edith Bunker sing the song, while Edith accompanied on the piano (it's actually me playing on the soundtrack, by the way). Norman took my advice, and now all over the world, you can hear the wonderful screeching sound of Jean Stapleton's voice. It always makes me think of my mother.

𝄢

My sister, Lila, was almost four years older than I, and yet I can remember the day I met her.

"This is your sister," a nurse said with a thick German accent, as my brother and I sat on a bench on what is now the edge of Riverside Park. Lila was beautiful and brown-eyed (my brother and I had blue eyes), and in time, she would come to be the object of one of my first sexual fantasies. But now, at the tender age of five or six, I didn't question how I could have an older sister I had never met. We rarely spoke of it, and those few mentions of it were always in a whisper that children weren't supposed to hear. As the years went on, the story started to take shape. Sometimes late at night, when I should have been asleep, but was kept awake by my chronic headaches, my grandmother would visit and I would hear fragments of conversation coming from the kitchen.

". . . Poor Lila. To have been left like that."

"My Marjorie was only thirty-three."

"Six years she spent in foster homes!"

Their voices would be even softer and more reverent when the "word" was mentioned: "suicide."

Ironic how hushed that word was now, when my mother would toss it around all the time.

Years later, I found out that it was my grandmother (my mother's mother) who found her daughter, my aunt Marjorie, dead in a kitchen filled with gas fumes. It must have been devastating for her. Marjorie was her favorite. Next to the body was a suicide note that Grandma concealed from the police so that the death could be ruled "natural" or "accidental." Anything but suicide. When Aunt Marjorie's husband, Lila's father, realized he was ill-equipped to raise a four-year-old, "poor Lila" was sent from foster home to foster home until that fateful day six years later when the German nurse introduced her to me as my new sister. Adding to the drama was my mother's never-to-be-spoken-of knowledge that my father had been engaged to her sister before marrying her.

Were I Italian, I would surely have written operas.

𝄢

One Christmas, I was given a shiny, new drum set. (Yes, we were Jewish and, yes, I grudgingly went to Sunday Hebrew school, but mostly, I think, we were sent just to get us out of the house. In fact, at my father's insistence, I was never formally Bar Mitzvahed. We were not what you would call religious, and this has stuck with me to this day.) The drum set had a small light bulb inside that, when turned on, showed a forest scene. I hit those drums so convincingly that it was decided by the family that I possessed "good rhythm."

Mom soon decided I had all kinds of musical talent. In my tenth summer, I was shipped off for a few weeks to Camp Wigwam, a camp for boys in Harrison, Maine (famous alumni campers include Frank Loesser, Richard Rodgers, and later on Stephen Sondheim), where I was taught piano. Although, at the time, I had very little interest in this kind of "serious" music (no one in my family had ever even been to a concert, and we seldom went to the theater), I persevered with my Hanon finger exercises and excruciatingly slow two-hand piano pieces, laboriously counting each note aloud. For an adolescent with the mental concentration of a flea, this was torture.

My feelings changed when, upon my return home from camp, my mother hired a piano teacher to come to our house once a week. Abraham Sokoloff was very cheerful, and instead of doing exercises, he taught me popular songs; I didn't read actual notes but played from chord symbols. What was best was that he didn't make me practice as much. He simply let me "chord" well-known songs. As I'd already heard most of these songs, I was actually playing by ear, and consequently, I never learned to read the bass or treble clefs. But I was happy and Sokoloff was happy and even Mom was happy because Sokoloff came from Brooklyn, so he must have been good.

Sokoloff may have been good, but my next piano teacher was more memorable, if not as musically qualified. Every Thursday afternoon, she arrived at our apartment on the Upper West Side, and sat next to me on the piano bench, her skirt riding up, revealing her thighs. I can still see those thighs with an edge of garter peeking out, reminding me that while tonal music has been with us a relatively short time, thighs are forever.

𝄢

If grade school came easily to me, I practically raced through high school, skipping grades here and there and graduating at fifteen years old in 1943. Smack in the middle of World War II.

We had all been aware of the war "over in Europe" since it began in 1939, when I was eleven. Like every other good Jewish boy, I had hatred and fear of the Nazis but had no thought of how Japan would figure in the war picture. Still, I can remember that "day that would live in infamy" as if it were yesterday.

It was Sunday, December 7, 1941, when, typically, we were at home listening to our deluxe, expensive Philco radio (it had short wave and everything!), when the news came over the airwaves. The whole family was filled with fear and apprehension. When my grandmother (my mother's mother, Salina) arrived, we told her that Pearl Harbor had been bombed by the Japanese.

"That reminds me," she said, "I dropped one of my favorite pieces of china, and it smashed in pieces! I'm so upset!"

"Nana," I told her, "it's Japan that did the bombing, not China!"

She just didn't get it.

But my brother David got it. He knew that, at sixteen years old, if this war went on, he might be drafted and sent off to fight it. To avoid the draft at seventeen, David applied for a government program that would pay for a pre-med college education. If he stayed with it, he would go on to medical school. His dream.

After a very short time, David quit the program and joined the fleet marines as a medical corpsman. I didn't understand why he'd want to change tracks from pursuing a medical degree to having one of the most dangerous jobs in the armed forces. He told us it was because he wanted to fight the Japanese and the Nazis. It wasn't until years later that I learned that he had flunked out of the government-sponsored program and was too scared and ashamed to tell us. My heart still breaks for him, but then again who could blame him for not telling us? Mother, after all, contemplated suicide over a common cold and Pop's health hung by a thread. David must have felt that any admission of failure would have set our already precarious family over the edge.

At about the same time, in 1943, at the age of fifteen, I graduated from the academically prestigious Townsend Harris Hall (my father had gone there before me). Alumni included songwriters Richard Rodgers, Frank Loesser, Ira Gershwin, E. Y. Harburg, and actors Clifton Webb and Edward G. Robinson. At the time, entrance to this high school (located in a building on Twenty-third Street and Lexington Avenue which now houses CUNY's Baruch College) was based on a competitive examination, so I was proud to have been accepted. Now I was faced with finding a college and, convinced that my father was going broke (Mom's pennypinching ways were very convincing and contagious), only one thing was important: It had to be cheap.

Because I was lousy in math and not interested in anything except girls wearing form-fitting, striped T-shirts (and removing them at my command—which appeared improbable at that point), my choices were limited. As I scanned the circulars for schools, I found one that had a low tuition and taught music. I had been dabbling in music for several years now. I'd even written a song with my friend, Skippy Ungar, when I was fourteen and in love with a girl named Janet who lived on West Eighty-third Street. Naturally, the song was called "Moon over 83rd Street." I didn't think much of it, but Skippy thought it would be a big hit.

So, despite having never attended a concert or played classical music during the first fifteen years of my life (I had only seen one Broadway show: the 1941 Cole Porter show *Let's Face It!*), I found myself sitting next to my mother in the admissions office of the Eastman School of Music across from a man who told my praise-hungry mother that her baby had an "aptitude" for music.

"How about majoring in composition?"

Later on, I heard that those who chose to major in composition were never, ever heard from again.

When I looked at my newly minted student I.D., it told me in bold letters that Charles Strouse was going off to college, but when I looked in the mirror and saw the fat, pasty-faced little boy of fifteen with dark circles under his eyes, I knew that Buddy was going along for the ride.

CHAPTER THREE

The Hard-Knock Life

THE EASTMAN SCHOOL OF MUSIC was an ornate and gloomy building located in downtown Rochester, New York. It was connected by a fourth-floor pedestrian bridge to a newer (but somehow even gloomier) building that housed fifty underground cubicles, each with a small, double-glazed window in the center of a two-inch-thick wooden door. These cubicles contained students hunched like slaves in the hold of a Roman galley, their trombones and fiddles rhythmically swaying like oars. Looming above was a beige-brick building holding six floors of dark, fluorescent-lit rooms with blackboards and double-thick wooden doors intended to shut out the sounds emanating from the cubicles below so as not to disrupt the music theory and singing classes on all floors. Still, the never-ending writhing and grinding of clarinets, trumpets, and fiddles underground perpetually conflicted with those trying to sing or construct fugues above.

If you closed your eyes as you walked down these halls, it sounded like musical hell.

And after all this, if and when the galley masters gave a thumbs-up after four years of rowing (and should there be no homosexual activity or left-wing politics among the rowers), the student would arrive at a solemn graduation ceremony in June.

For the typical wind player or fiddler, that diploma could lead to a position teaching music in a local high school. For the more ambitious, it could result in an assignment playing with the Rochester Philharmonic Orchestra, which was at the time conducted by Dimitri Mitropoulos, with a young Leonard Bernstein as associate conductor.

In 1944, I arrived in Rochester—which in my memory is painted grayish brown, like a cheap hamburger, fried medium—a confused fifteen year old. It was disconcerting to say the least. I knew no one, and being younger than the average freshman, I was extremely lonely. As they had for years, girls occupied my thoughts, and I was thrilled to notice that the girls on campus didn't seem to wear those stiff corsets favored by my mother. Instead there was an incredible softness behind their skirts. Being fifteen, over-weight, and insecure didn't get me very far with the co-eds though. To alleviate my sense of alienation, I started drinking bottles of Genesee beer with a new circle of male friends who seemed to understand my feelings. They were all homosexual in a 1940s world that considered their lifestyle to be illicit, immoral, and unpatriotic. I was just glad to be part of a group that liked me.

Among the group, and clearly a leader of it, was a tall, cynical, sallow (he always drank), Irish-Catholic, *brilliant* composition major from Detroit named William Flanagan. Bill was five years older than I, and, although he was gay and I was straight, I mimicked his attitudes, picked his brain, and generally idolized him. Slowly, we became good friends, although, deep down, I always felt he merely tolerated me (or was that just Mama's little Buddy talking?).

I made other friends at Eastman, some who drifted away as we grew older, and others who remained close for years. There was Larry Rosenthal, who was able go to a movie with me and later play the whole Max Steiner score by ear. I always thought he was the best musician in our group. He went on to write the Broadway musical *Sherry!* and to become very successful as a film and TV composer, at which point his first name was transformed into Laurence.

There was also Noel Ferrand. Friends with Bill as well, Noel was funny, kind, and always overweight. In hindsight, as another overweight outsider, I see that he was a version of me, but Noel coped with great humor and a sense of the ridiculous. Together, we created our own personal language keeping us separate and apart from others. Noel was outrageous and smart and really took me seriously.

Whether I knew it or not at the time, these friendships (I had never had really good friends before college) nurtured me and allowed me to begin to grow up.

But it was from another friend, Sam Krachmalnick, a fine conductor (he conducted the original Broadway version of Leonard Bernstein's *Candide*), pianist, and French horn player that I discovered the secret joy of masturbation. Thinking that Sam knew a lot about life (he was a whole two years older than I), I asked him what people meant by the term "jerking off." At first, he laughed and then, realizing I was seriously undereducated, explained the process to me. Afterward, I went back to my room and spent the next hour putting his lesson into practice.

All of my life I had suffered from what would later be termed "compulsive thinking." But I didn't have a word for it then. I just knew that the gears in my head turned at warp speed.

When I was young, it was hard to turn off the compulsively spinning, repeating, and demanding thoughts: "Girls, career, money... girls, career, money." I could never make it stop.

Until now.

I discovered that by creating and manipulating my own sexual excitement, I was able to control, or at least briefly hide, these compulsive thoughts. Wow!

To paraphrase Ira Gershwin, "How long had *this* been going on?"

𝄢

As a composition major, I worked diligently at honing my sense of pitch (via endless exercises of copying down notes and harmonies played on the piano by someone else), as well as four-part writing in the style of Bach. We did endless analyses of the Beethoven Quartets, and of the piano music of Mendelssohn and Brahms. It was incredibly challenging. Learning had come easily to me when I was younger, but this was something completely new, and I was feeling my way in the dark, not knowing what was at the end of the tunnel. I couldn't even see the light.

I dutifully spent my days buried in musical theory and practice, but patriotism (plus the fact that I lost the expensive fountain pen my brother and sister gave me as a going-to-college gift and wanted to replace it) prompted me to take a job at a war plant helping to make shells for navy rockets. Each shell weighed fifty-seven pounds, and was very hot. I had to lift each one from a passing rack (wearing thick gloves and protective shoes in case I dropped one), then measure the shell's width with a caliper, and weigh it. I did this each evening from six p.m. until midnight. Then, the next morning, it was back to Bach and Palestrina.

Besides being exhausted, I was homesick. There were no dormitories for me, so I lived in a dark run-down Rochester hovel lorded over by a landlady who probably would have been more comfortable running a prison. She spent most of her time blaming Roosevelt for the war, complaining about the profusion of blacks in Rochester, and loudly lamenting the shortage of sugar and stockings.

In an act of desperation, one night I phoned home collect and begged my father to let me end the pain by leaving school and coming home. He was having none of it.

"A man's got to finish what he starts," he proclaimed.

So I persevered. Lacking the imagination yet to have, or even seek, my own voice, I would go to classes and to concerts, not knowing if I liked or didn't like the music. I just listened, absorbed, and later tried to write music in similar styles.

In 1945, the first George Gershwin Memorial Award (Gershwin had died in 1937) for a new symphonic work was presented to Peter Mennin, a graduate student at Eastman, who later went on to become the president of Julliard. As I listened to the workmanlike and energetic piece, I thought (as lyricist Edward Kleban in *A Chorus Line* put it), "I can do that!" Suddenly, I knew that I could be 1946's George Gershwin Memorial Award winner. This could be the answer to all my problems. Everyone would notice: friends, family, teachers . . . the whole world. Charles would be triumphant, and Buddy could be banished forever.

The piece I wrote was called *Narrative for Orchestra*, a cunning title, I thought. The orchestration was sonorous, and the composing itself was sober, yet not without charm—filled with humor and craftily put together. I became more and more convinced that this was my time. I would have my moment in the sun.

After waiting for what seemed an eternity, the letter from the judging committee finally arrived. It read, "Thank you for your submission. This year, out of the many submissions we received, we didn't find any worthy of the prize."

I reddened as I read it.

I'd studied and worked so hard. But no one cared. No one, that is, except my friend Bill Flanagan, to whose dorm room I ran for solace. Bill was just reassuring me that I was a really good composer when, to my surprise, Buddy poked his head into the room. "What does it matter if you were a good composer, anyway?" Buddy said. "Nobody's listening."

"Does it matter?" Bill replied, as he took another puff on his cigarette.

For me, it was as if a light bulb had just been turned on. What was that slogan MGM used after the lion roars at the beginning of every movie?

Ars gratia artis. "Art for art's sake."

That same year, in 1946, I wrote a short opera that was never performed and never shown to anyone. In it, two musicians—a violinist and a cellist—in a trio that plays dinner music in a restaurant are waiting in the kitchen for the third player, the pianist, to arrive.

When the tardy player finally gets there, he is sloppily dressed and full of attitude. The violinist, the eldest of the group, tells him his demeanor must improve.

The young pianist says, "Who cares? We're just background music for eating. Nobody's listening."

The cellist says, "We're listening. That's somebody listening."

I was beginning to learn what that MGM slogan really meant.

By the time I was a senior in 1946 and '47, the war had been over for a couple of years, and little by little, I felt that my peers were finally noticing my music. I had written a kind of pop piece called "Ditto" to please my parents, and everyone in school seemed to like it. After a while, even I thought it wasn't bad. And, even although Buddy would say he never felt like he fit in, amazingly, Charles was elected class president against one of the most popular and respected guys in school, my friend Larry Rosenthal. I was even starting to date and get somewhere with girls. Confidence at eighteen! It can do wonders. Maybe the little, fat kid was on his way out.

In 1947, I was finally set to graduating with a Bachelor of Music (or as my father liked to joke, a B.U.M). With all my newfound confidence and comparative popularity, I decided not to invite my parents to graduation. I had become a snob and was just too embarrassed to have my sophisticated new friends and members of the faculty meet my corny, sickly Dad and my self-deprecating, overweight mother.

Besides, I would be seeing them soon enough. Following graduation, I went back to New York to live in their big, seven-room apartment on West Seventy-eighth Street. My sister Lila had married and my brother David was living on his own, but, at twenty years old, I was back in my old room, this time complete with my own upright piano and a maid who served fresh-squeezed orange juice at breakfast, laundered my clothes, and made my bed.

Things hadn't changed much since I left home. Dad was still sickly and gambling (although, in retrospect, the family finances had obviously gotten better) and Mom's dismal outlook and talk of suicide hadn't abated at all. But, always, I took it with a grain of salt and figured she was kidding.

Then one day in 1948, soon after I got home from college, Dad told me that Mom would have to be committed to a psychiatric hospital.

It was the saddest day of my life.

CHAPTER FOUR

Those Were the Days

DESPITE MOM'S CONSTANT threats of suicide, that wasn't why she was committed. For years, she had been taking a liquid medication for an intestinal problem. Looking back, I can remember that whenever there was a tense situation, Mom would excuse herself and take a swig of the medicine. It always seemed to calm her. What none of us knew was that the medication had small amounts of opium in it. (Even today, Imodium and other medications used for colitis and intestinal disorders contain opiates that are highly addictive when taken in large quantities.) As with her anxieties about food and money, Mom overdid it with her opium-based medication and wound up institutionalized in the Yale Institute of Human Relations for two-and-a-half years.

I have never been sure whose decision it was to put Mom away, but I suspect that she had a say in the matter as she was smart enough to want to try to break the chains of unhappiness.

My father and I brought my mother to New Haven and signed her in for treatment. After the paperwork was done, we walked down the dark corridors with their rows of identical cubicle-like cells, and I couldn't help but be reminded of the antiseptic practice rooms in the basement of Eastman School of Music where one could practice and practice and still not be allowed to leave.

Dad and I watched helplessly as Mom was locked into a room with steel wires molded inside the glass windows, and a thick door with just a small window to peer through. When the steel door closed between us, my mind closed off as well. I felt a darkness beyond sadness that's hard to describe, and for the next two-and-a-half years, I was to relive it each weekend with every visit I made.

Mom's treatment and convalescence was slow, but small rays of sun peered through the clouds every once in a while— like when she made me a ceramic ashtray decorated with eighth notes and the title of one of my piano pieces painted on it. That made me feel better—the idea that at least my music gave my mother pleasure. I played piano for her in the common room, and one day, I played something I'd written for her that moved her to tears. She really liked it, she said, and she wasn't just saying so. Not like the string quartet I wrote that I knew she didn't like but said she did. This time she meant it. Of course, a part of her needed it to be good to help her see her through her sadness.

During this time in the winter of 1948, Dad and I lived alone in the big apartment on the Upper West Side, and I continued to compose and study privately with Arthur Berger, an influential composer whose works straddled neoclassicism and serialism. Exceedingly serious and intellectual, Arthur composed works for orchestra, solo voice, and choir, but his most durable and varied compositions were for chamber ensembles and piano. His first major work, *Quartet for Winds*, was a neoclassical piece dedicated to Aaron Copland. It is still performed regularly. A series of duos, for violin and piano, cello and piano, and oboe and clarinet were also popular at the time.

Arthur was big proponent of Stravinsky, and together, we would analyze the master's pieces. I confess I hadn't even realized modern music *could* be analyzed. Arthur also told me I had been composing notes incorrectly all of my life, saying that I needed justification for writing an E-flat or a C-sharp, other than the fact that "it occurred to me." Throughout the course of our studies, I learned a lot about other composers' music but somehow managed to compose very little myself.

It took another noted American composer to begin to unlock my potential as a composer.

David Diamond was a fellow Eastman alumni who was considered by some to be one of the preeminent American composers of his generation. He was charming and flamboyant and irresistible. He knew everyone and everyone seemed to know him. He seemed enchanted. I longed to be in his circle but was happy to stand even on the periphery. I was thrilled to be his student.

Each week I would join my friend Bill Flanagan, and together we would trudge up the stairs to David's "studio" over a garage on Hudson Street in Greenwich Village. Against the unglamorous setting, David Diamond was glamorous indeed. After a while, it began to seem commonplace when the phone would ring and David would pick it up to say hello to "Lenny" or "Aaron" or "Betty and Adolph." These people didn't need last names. We all knew who they were.

To a large extent, David Diamond succeeded in changing me as a composer. Instead of trying to justify each note as Arthur Berger had instructed, David encouraged me to "let go" and to simply let the music "come." Could I really start to feel that free? I began to try.

Bill and I spread the word among our friends and made David's classes, given for a fee of ten dollars a week, even more popular. Soon Noel Ferrand was attending. He had introduced Bill to his childhood friend Edward, and they became very close; and when it became clear to me that they were more than "just friends," I found myself jealous and lonely. It seemed that everyone had someone.

With the summer of 1948 approaching, I knew I didn't want to spend hot summer in New York City, alone with my father, so I applied to Tanglewood.

Located in the Berkshire Hills of Western Massachusetts, the Tanglewood Music Center had been founded in 1940 by Boston Symphony conductor Sergei Koussevitzky. By this time, it had not only become the summer home of the Boston Symphony, but also had provided a unique and an in-depth musical experience for emerging artists. But for me, there was only one reason I applied: Aaron Copland.

Copland was my musical hero. At the time, in fact, he was almost every other musician's hero as well. Copland's music (*Fanfare for the Common Man*, *Appalachian Spring*, and *Rodeo* among other masterworks) achieved a difficult balance between modern and American folk styles, and the open, slowly changing harmonies of many of his works seem to evoke the vast American landscape. That summer, Aaron was teaching at Tanglewood, and I allowed myself to dream that I might become his student.

On May 14, 1948, a neatly typed letter on Boston Symphony Orchestra stationery arrived saying that I was being given a two hundred dollar scholarship for the composition department. (Two hundred dollars would not only cover my lessons with Copland, but also my accommodations as well. Times have sure changed.)

I can still remember that first day when I knocked on Copland's studio door in July of 1948. A wooden plaque hung outside the door with his name on it. It was a name that was such a firm part of my musical life that my feeling was of actually touching greatness, of belonging—just by touching that plaque. Maybe some of his genius would rub off on me.

Aaron was very much a regular guy, or at least he was with me. I never knew him to be mean or foolish or stubborn in his opinions. I suppose that's what made him a fine teacher: He let the student find his own way. He could also convey a feel for colors possible in the orchestra that no one had ever made me feel before. I blossomed under Aaron's tutelage (even though, most of the time, I couldn't believe I was sitting in the same room with him) and several of my works—*Duet for Oboe and Bassoon*, *Scherzo for Violin and Piano*, and *Music for Woodwind Quintet*—were performed that summer in the Chamber Music Hall.

I can still see Aaron listening to stretches of music I'd written. He wouldn't speak much but would kind of let his head bounce side to side the way rabbis do. As I sneaked a peak at him doing this, I hoped it indicated approval. Was our musical thinking so in sync that he felt he didn't have to say much? Or was he just being reserved?

My uncertainty stemmed from the fact that I've noticed that Jewish people have a way of saying yes and no with the same nod of the head, lift of the eyebrow, and tilt of a shoulder. There's a kind of resignation built into the movement as though one were saying, "What's the difference? Life goes on."

(Later on, in 1955, during the rehearsals for *Shoestring Revue,* I would teach Chita Rivera this same "shoulder-eyebrow" move because for some reason she wanted to learn to become Jewish. She still makes those "old world" moves better than any Hispanic—or Jew—I know.)

I felt privileged to be close to Aaron Copland. Jazz and hymns and square dances, the common man, the crazy mountains and prairies—that's where we all first loved him. No other composer could pull off the same use of folk music; Aaron was the master. As the years went on, though, his music started to become less fashionable among this new wave of composers. I saw his frustration about age and about not being hired to compose film scores anymore. The only way he earned enough money in his later years, he confided to me, was through conducting. This, from our most revered and performed American composer.

Even after studying with him for three years, I must say that I never saw the *inner* Copland. I'm sure he never meant me to—but on some level, I felt I really understood him.

During those summers at Tanglewood, I also got to know Leonard Bernstein.

At this time in the late 1940s, Bernstein was a god. He was the lionized hero to one and all. Ever since his meteoric rise on November 14, 1943, when he substituted on a few hours' notice for the ailing Bruno Walter at a Carnegie Hall concert, Leonard Bernstein had been in demand as conductor, composer, and teacher.

In 1940, when he was only twenty-two, Bernstein was among the first students to study under Sergei Koussevitzky the summer that Tanglewood was founded. He soon became

Koussevitzky's conducting assistant and protégé, and returned to Tanglewood summer after summer. When Sergei Koussevitzky died in 1951, Bernstein became head of the orchestral and conducting departments at Tanglewood and held the position for many years.

But the summer of 1948 was not my first encounter with Bernstein. Just the year before at Eastman, I had escorted him to my senior prom.

In June of the previous year, Leonard Bernstein visited Eastman after conducting a Rochester Philharmonic concert. It just happened to be the day of our senior prom. As class president, I was assigned to escort him and show him around, which I am sure was more exciting for the students than for the glamorous Lenny.

He put in a perfunctory appearance at the prom and then left. Standing around watching a bunch of dancing bassoonists and music-ed majors couldn't have been very stimulating for him.

After he left, I started to feel sick. I thought it was the flu, but, in retrospect, it was probably the toxic combination of the stress of being the class president, my fear about having no one to love me (my real date for the prom had little feeling for me), and the thrill of being Leonard Bernstein's escort.

I threw up all over the men's room.

I tried cleaning up my mess as best I could, but the next day, the school sent me a bill for "damages."

It was with this memory of our "first date" that I reacquainted myself with Lenny. I am sure that he took notice of me mainly because I was studying with Copland. Everyone admired and respected Aaron then.

But I had also admired and respected Bernstein, in part, for his bravery. It may seem of little consequence now, but back then, when every celebrity changed his name in order to sound "American," Lenny didn't. From the beginning, it was *Bernstein* conducting at Tanglewood, *Bernstein* with the Philharmonic, *Bernstein* with the Vienna. I was impressed, and I believe many other Jews were, too. It's hard nowadays to comprehend the shock it was for me, as a youth, to associate such a Jewish name with celebrity, back when anti-Semitism was commonplace and only half hidden. In a world of Robbinses, Kings, Laurentses, and Diamonds (all changed from Jewish-sounding names), Jews like my mother made sure to distinguish between Slavic and German Jews. Even when I grew up and continued my musical education, I was instructed to pronounce the last syllable of Lenny's name "stine" instead of "steen."

Our acquaintance was always very cordial over the years, as he called me Buddy and I called him Lenny (which I thought a big honor, only to discover that everyone did). But when I played auditions in late 1952 for his Broadway show *Wonderful Town*, I couldn't get him to give me a job as rehearsal pianist. Meanwhile, my friend and fellow Eastman alumnus Sam Krachmalnick rose to the heights of conducting Lenny's magnificent score of *Candide* in 1956. It wasn't until 1960, when *Bye Bye Birdie* flew high over the Broadway sky, that Lenny took real notice of my talents and became my friend.

Back in 1948, it was hard to imagine I could ever be on any kind of equal footing with the likes of Leonard Bernstein.

♪:

Sometimes you get a Christmas gift that you really didn't expect and don't even know if you have use for and, although you don't know it at the time, it turns out to be something that you cherish the rest of your life.

At a Christmas party in 1949, I was given Lee Adams.

I was at the home of my friend George Kaufman (not the playwright), who, over a glass of eggnog, casually introduced us: "You write music, he writes lyrics. You guys should get together!"

Bad dialogue perhaps, but significant, as it was the beginning of a friendship that has lasted a lifetime.

Lee hailed from Mansfield, Ohio, and both he and George had attended Ohio State University together. After graduation, George got into real estate, and Lee was now studying to get his master's degree at the Columbia University Graduate School of Journalism, even though writing lyrics had always been his real ambition. Back at Ohio State, Lee assured me, he'd had several triumphs writing musicals.

I had little experience in that regard. In fact, it was just recently that I started to become more interested in musical theater. My friend Bill fell in love with Cole Porter's *Kiss Me Kate* and, under his influence, I wore out a few needles playing the original cast album.

I made sure not to tell him that, though, and so Lee and I decided to meet and try to write some songs together. I didn't expect much to come out of it.

𝄢

After I studied with Aaron Copland for a few years, he must have seen something special in me, because he got me a scholarship to study with Nadia Boulanger in Paris.

Paris!

My father gave me one thousand dollars (an astronomical sum at that time and enough to live on in postwar France—where the dollar bought many francs—for a year), so off to Paris I went in 1950 to work under this famous French teacher of composition. Copland, Virgil Thomson, George Gershwin, Elliott Carter, Walter Piston, and even Bernard Rogers (a former teacher of mine at Eastman) had studied with her.

Not to mention Lenny.

Arriving at Nadia's studio, I was impatient to show Madame (as she liked to be called) a large, symphonic work I'd recently written, but she insisted on hearing my entire musical output—student attempts, childish scribbles, *everything*. I even played her the song I had written with Skippy Unger back when I was fourteen. That Boulanger received these offerings in a serous manner made me even more embarrassed.

Later, when I had worked with her for some months, she proclaimed that I had a talent for light music.

I was crushed. What did she mean?

"To make someone forget illness and suffering," she said, "is also a calling."

How did she know my parents?

But in Paris, it wasn't all study. One Saturday afternoon, Ned Rorem invited Bill and me to meet Paul Bowles. Bowles, the composer and novelist who had come over from North Africa, brought some hashish packed in a Chesterfield tin.

Bowles explained to me, "This is what well-to-do Arabs traditionally do in the late afternoon: sip strong tea, and then on an empty stomach, let the hashish melt in their mouths"—

the melting part, as opposed to chewing, was of paramount importance—"then wait, and only then surrender to it."

I thought immediately of my mother, back on West Seventy-eighth Street in Manhattan who I couldn't imagine would want me to do anything Arab.

Paul's hashish had the texture of chopped liver mixed with dates. I put a bit more of it in my mouth than your average Arab might. And, of course, I promptly chewed and swallowed it since, of my many bad traits, impatience ranks high.

Nothing happened.

I stole a look at Bill. He shrugged. He wasn't feeling anything either, so we waited for what we thought would be a decent amount of time in Middle Eastern circles, and then made our departure.

"It was wonderful. I've never experienced anything like it," I lied as I said my good-byes.

Bill went off to see one of his tricks, while I headed back to my hotel, L'hotel du Prince. It was what was called a "B joint"—that is, an establishment that permitted legally licensed prostitutes to use the rooms for free, in exchange for drinking at the bar with their tricks. I now actually lived with one of these young girls. Her name was Coco, which I thought a very unusual name until I found out that many girls were named that.

To say I "lived" with her is a bit of an exaggeration. It was the beginning of my Paris experience, she was "away" a lot, and I spoke minimal French. (I might stop a man on the street to ask for a light for my cigarette, and discover as he looks strangely at me that I'd asked him for a lightbulb.) The five English words Coco knew were *I love you darling* and *chocolate*.

Nevertheless, it wasn't such a bad arrangement. Almost every evening when I came home after a hard day sitting at the piano, she brought a basin of warm water and soap, and washed and massaged my feet. I tried to explain that American girls never do that and that I didn't really use the piano pedal that much, but, after a while, I accepted her loving gift. It's quite nice to have a pretty young French girl rub your feet and I didn't want to hurt her feelings.

It was after such a massage, the same night that Paul Bowles smuggled the Chesterfield tin that I was sitting there and, all of a sudden, couldn't help but think about how the foot bone was connected to the knee bone, which was connected to the . . . well, Paul's hashish had started to kick in.

The experience that night with Coco was the longest and most sexually pleasurable of my life. But after she left to go to work, my heart began beating so violently that I was convinced I would die. My bed took off as if on a cloud, through my twin French windows, floating over the Sorbonne (which was on my street) and the city. I saw brilliantly lit colors and changing shapes as in Disney's *Fantasia*

Then suddenly, I felt short of breath, alone and home-sick, convinced I would die on that foreign street. What had I done? I was up all night, rattled and panic stricken from the experience.

Oddly enough, I was told years later by jazz musicians, that I had, in fact, had a *good* trip: the flying, the gorgeous colors. But I didn't feel cool or hip. I felt scared. If there ever was a moment I might have joined the Beat generation, or gone on to be a hippie, it was gone. If there ever had been a chance, I knew at that point I'd never be a rock-and-roller.

This would turn out to have a lifelong effect on my career, as I'd go on to co-opt this lifestyle that scared me, making my rock-and-roll in the safe space of a Broadway stage.

Two weeks before I was to sail back to New York on the SS *Rotterdam*, the money my father had given me for the year ran out. They were two of the worst weeks of my life. My composition lessons were over (and I couldn't call Madame Boulanger, as she was off lecturing somewhere), and Bill and my other friends were in Italy. I was crashing at a friend's apartment while he was in Italy, so I had a place to stay, but still, I was all alone in Paris. I'd never been starving, but now starving was conceivable. I was convinced I'd almost destroyed my heart and mind on dope, which would surely push my mother over the top.

I managed to grub off some distant acquaintances, and made it through. Finally the day of my ship's departure arrived. I rushed aboard, and consumed every last spoonful of the chocolate ice cream I found in a kitchen in a deserted corner of the ship. First-class guests would have no chocolate ice cream this crossing.

During the voyage, I took stock. Diamond, Copland, Boulanger each had their distinctive effect on me, and slowly, I was beginning to learn some truths.

To write music—extended melodies, complex harmonies, cross rhythms, etc.—one must have knowledge of ear training, counterpoint, and analysis. But to really *make* music, these tools must be forgotten, just as a practiced writer can't think too much about the alphabet, or a talented orator can't be running to the dictionary for every other word.

Over the years, I'd begun to think that what most people

love is music that was dreamed, not music that was cogitated or too thought out.

I think the ability to write this "dreamed" music has to do with something that, for lack of another word, I'll call genius. It's different from inspiration. Many good composers sketch a great deal before organizing notes into a final shape. And the best of these (to my mind, the very best was Beethoven) have been able to hold onto that original dream through all the revisions. How do you "hold onto" a dream? Who the heck knows? Relaxation, perhaps; maybe meditation. Can one have a dream, forget it, and trust it will come again? It takes a lot of quiet confidence. Few have that.

Some composers desire to impress rather than to move their audience. They allow themselves to be influenced by music critics and esthetes whose purpose, above all else, is to demonstrate erudition.

But then here I was in the early 1950s, the guy with the shameful love of Shirley Temple. It wasn't suave; it was out of place, outré.

Suddenly I didn't care. The direction of a melodic line, the stringency and resolution of a harmony—they were riddles to me that I wanted to spend my whole life solving. Maybe someone would pay attention, admiring a song's technical excellence or a particular turn of phrase, or perhaps unexpectedly hum a refrain. Or the music might call up a long-forgotten memory or stir up patriotic fervor. As my ship approached New York Harbor, I knew that was what I truly wanted.

That, and a chocolate ice cream soda.

CHAPTER FIVE

Nice to See Ya

BACK IN NEW YORK, Paris faded into the mist, and life quickly went back to the way it had been before I left.

My choral work "Captain Kidd" was featured on the radio (on the same bill as works by Peter Mennin—the Gershwin Award winner—and my teacher David Diamond) on WNYC's tenth annual American Music Festival. One critic called the piece "short and crisp and the texture is light," and it was awarded second place in the National Federation of Music Club Student Composition Contest Class III. The prize was twenty-five dollars.

Obviously, I needed a day job, even if it was at night.

So, besides playing piano for rehearsals, auditions, and dance classes, I started to play in various nightclubs around the city. Ever since the 1930s, jazz clubs had proliferated along Fifty-second Street. The clubs I played, though, were frequented not by jazz lovers with a trench coat casually tossed over their shoulder but by the kind of men who liked to keep their trench coats on their laps. In other words, strip joints. They were places like "The Pin-Up Room," where I was featured nightly at the Pin-Up Piano.

I can still see one sign in a window: "Continuous Stripping Plus Buddy Strouse and His Band." I am really sure that those guys came just to hear me!

As the strippers stripped, I played Duke Ellington's "Harlem Nocturne," David Rose's "The Stripper," or sometimes "Blues in B-Flat." No matter what I played, one of the working women would complain to me (usually with bare breasts) that I had played "her" music for somebody else, and we'd become embroiled in an argument. These were the kind of music lovers I was getting used to.

During the day, I coached aspiring singers and actors and sometimes accompanied at auditions. The money was steady, and my modestly sophisticated skills from Eastman meant I was able to write piano arrangements for them to bring to their auditions. I was also able to transpose songs into different keys, able to play "Young and Foolish," "Oh, What a Beautiful Mornin'," and "I'm Not at All in Love" in any key, tempo, mood, or national dance step known to man. Because I was also white, inexpensive, and could read music and play passable jazz, I became musical director for a number of black performers including that diminutive, squeaky-voiced veteran of *Gone with the Wind*, Butterfly McQueen.

Butterfly (her real name was Thelma, but she took the name Butterfly when she appeared as one in *A Midsummer Night's Dream*) McQueen had been discovered by veteran writer-director George Abbott. At the age of twenty-eight, she made her screen debut as Prissy, Scarlett O'Hara's silly, incompetent slave, uttering the immortal words: "I don't know nothin' 'bout birthin' babies!" Butterfly continued her acting career playing maids, both credited and uncredited, on screen and in radio. When I met her in 1950, she was appearing as yet another maid on Ethel Waters's popular television show *Beulah,* and to capitalize on her success, she took her "act" to high schools and churches in small black towns in Alabama, the Carolinas, and Georgia.

Lena Horne she was not, but Butterfly had a fairly good business with her touring show. There were no advertisements or handbills announcing her, but somehow everyone knew when Butterfly was in town. The rural black audiences would come in droves as Butterfly would sing in that same funny, high-pitched voice in which she spoke (her repertoire included songs like "Waiting for the Robert E. Lee"), dance (she had been trained as a dancer, she told me, but one would never know it from the way she moved her body), recite (Rudyard Kipling's "If"), and tell anecdotes about appearing in *Gone with the Wind* eleven years earlier. Before the show, she would stand at the door and collect the one dollar admission from each audience member (and she actually did very well), punctuating every transaction with her familiar, high, girlish laugh. At the end of the week, Butterfly would take out the crumpled dollar bills she had collected, and count out my salary.

Working with Butterfly exposed me to the Deep South for the first time. I also got a good whiff of racial hatred and prejudice, the likes of which I hadn't experienced since I was thirteen and my father had sent my brother David (then sixteen) and me to work on a tobacco farm in Connecticut to toughen me up and make me a man and to teach David the value of a dollar.

Back then, it was anti-semitism that reared its ugly head. Knowing that we might be exposed to it, my brother and I decided to pretend that summer to be Greek Orthodox! How one acted Greek Orthodox, we had no idea, but we knew the game was up when, during lunch the first week, somebody yelled, "Hey, Jew boys!" Then, they grabbed us, beat up my brother as they held me, and then tied me to a tree and lit a fire under my feet. I still recall my fear and the sting of the smoke as it curled up my nostrils.

Thankfully we were rescued by what the workers called the "Jew boss" as he rode by in his pickup truck. He put out the fire, untied me, and scolded the offending parties: "This is not the way you're supposed to spend your lunch hour."

Despite that unsettling but enlightening experience, I was unprepared for the racial hatred that was hurled my way almost a decade later.

Since we had to get from one hot, sweaty town to another even hotter, sweatier town in an un-air-conditioned car, Butterfly and I drove mostly at night. One moonless, airless night, we stopped at an all-night diner for some food. I didn't think anything of it when Butterfly said she would just stay in the car and I could bring her something "to go." A man in a greasy apron holding a spatula greeted me at the door.

"You with that nigger out there?" he asked almost pleasantly.

My blood ran cold, but before I could answer, he said, "We won't serve y'all in here. Y'all have to go 'round the back."

Despite the feeling that I should get in the car and drive as fast as I could, I was starving, so I went around the back where I was met by a huge, beefy truck driver (or was he a wrestler with insomnia?).

"You the one with that nigger out there?" he asked, not quite as pleasantly as the first man.

"Yes, I'd like to get a couple of hamburgers," I answered. "You see, we've been driving all night and—"

Then something happened that I'd never seen before except in movies. The man took a deep breath and spat at me.

It was a very large spittle, and it landed on my chest, where part of it sank into my sweater while the other part slid slowly down my pants. Even today, I can remember my astonishment, the wetness, and the humiliation.

I wiped myself off, walked back to the car, and drove off. Suddenly, neither Butterfly nor I was very hungry.

Years later, in 1965, I would remember this moment when I decided to joined Sammy Davis Jr. and 523 other people to march on Selma, Alabama, for civil rights.

$$\mathbf{9}\mathord{:}$$

One morning, my father read an advertisement in the *New York Times* that said the New School for Social Research (today it's just "the New School") was giving a course in composing for films. Although, I usually didn't take my father's advice, something about this course intrigued me, and I signed up for it.

A gruff, unpretentious, and totally pragmatic musician named Jack Shaindlin taught the course. Jack knew what he was talking about because he was also head of the 20th Century-Fox music department in New York. Most of the other students—non-musicians who simply aspired to be in the movies—were completely out of their element. Because I'd actually studied theory, composition, and orchestration, I quickly became Jack's star pupil. He took me under his wing, and after hearing what I could do, offered me a job writing music for *Fox Movietone News*.

It seemed a godsend. Maybe Pop wasn't as out of it as I'd thought!

In the days before television, people went to the movies to get the news that now is delivered to our TV screens and computers ad infinitum. To that end, *Fox Movietone News* produced sound newsreels from 1928 until 1963, when daily news shows obliviated the newsreel format.

The first two assignments Jack Shaindlin gave me were to compose music for the segments "Australian Aqua Belles" and "Koreans on Parade." These were not regular titles, but simply file names used for catalogues to be searched and used whenever such opportunities arose. Because the music didn't have to be synched to scenes or dialogue (normally, narration would be spoken over the music and picture and then the volume of the music raised or lowered accordingly, but we didn't have to worry about any of that), I figured it would be a snap. The secret to these orchestrations was that all the instruments had to be doubled in their melodies and harmonies, and that drum rolls and harp glissandi had to abound so that cuts could be easily made to suit the quick changes of subject within the newsreels.

I was simply told to include a lot of sustained trills and/or long glissandi so that the audiotape could be easily cut and spliced. That way, when the Aqua Belles were ending their playful swimming routines, their music would simply cut off, and ominous music would be immediately played for the Koreans.

At Eastman, our assignments had been to write sonatinas in the style of Mozart, and fugues in the manner of Bach. That had been difficult. Setting music to swimming Australians or threatening Asian armies seemed like it would be a piece of cake. I was to learn otherwise. The music didn't just come to me. I had to work for it.

Hard.

On a typical day, I would appear at the 20th Century-Fox building on Eleventh Avenue at ten in the morning. Jack would give me assignments, and I would compose up to five minutes on the themes he designated. This "canned" music I created was referred to as "product," which was dispiriting because all my teachers before this had conveyed the idea that music was sacred.

The orchestra that recorded these tracks was made up of the very best musicians in New York, so the salary scale was high. They didn't rehearse but simply read the music as it was put on their stands. Jack had a conductor's beat that I thought undecipherable, but the orchestra was able to record about forty minutes of music in about forty-two minutes, so clearly, they knew what he wanted.

It was harder than I'd imagined composing "bad," or rather "unoriginal" music. No matter how unoriginal, the music, of course, had to be well orchestrated with cohesive parts for all of the instruments. Somehow my experience writing Bach chorales didn't cover all the *Movietone News* needs, and my "Australian Aqua Belles" wound up sounding a little bit Bartók, while my ominous Koreans marched to Roy Harris. Rules I thought I'd mastered in school were now were being put to the test, and I found I was wanting. Having my work played by the top musicians in New York made my weaknesses seem all the more transparent.

But the more I wrote, the more I learned, and I began to master a new craft within my art. It was one that would serve me well in the future.

(In fact, it's just occurred to me that "It's a Hard-Knock Life" sounds vaguely Korean.)

When my job at Fox ended and the strip club at which I played was raided by the police, it was back to playing dance classes.

It was an unusually hot spring day in 1952, and I was sweating out each minute of my $1.50 per hour rate, playing a silly gigue to which the incipient ballet dancers were twirling. Right in time to the music, a dancer named Ray Harrison jetéd breathlessly to the piano.

"Buddy," he breathed. "I've been hired to stage some shows at a most *wonnerful*"—Ray hadn't time to pronounce his D's—summer resort. You'll love it: the birds, the trees . . . you know." He painted a bucolic picture and then, after taking a big breath, asked if I'd be interested in being a "choreographic composer" up there.

The "wonnerful" summer resort "up there" in the Adirondacks (Chesterton, New York, to be exact) was called Green Mansions, and it proved to be a turning point in my songwriting career.

But not this first summer.

Green Mansions, which took its name from the popular 1904 novel, was one of several "adult camps" (including Tamiment, which today is known because the musical *Once Upon a Mattress* emerged from there) that were immortalized in the play and film *Having a Wonderful Time,* and its subsequent musical version, *Wish You Were Here.* In fact, that musical had just opened on Broadway that spring of 1952, with music and lyrics by Harold Rome, who had gotten his start at Green Mansions in the 1930s. (Back then, it was the summer home of the Group Theatre, where Clifford Odets was a member. The 1930s Green Mansions also happened to be the inspiration for the setting of Herman Wouk's *Marjorie Morningstar*.) Rome, a skilled songwriter who first made his name in revues, started the tradition of doing an original revue every Saturday night. Such future theatrical luminaries as Danny Kaye, Bea Arthur, Imogene Coca, Barbara Cook, Dorothy Loudon, Carol Burnett, Max Liebman, Herb Ross, Joe Layton, Jerome Robbins, Sheldon Harnick, Jerry Bock, Mary Rodgers, Sylvia Fine, Jonathan Tunick, Woody Allen, and Neil Simon all got their start at either Tamiment or Green Mansions.

And now I was going up there to be a "choreographic composer."

I didn't know it at the time, but that was a position coveted by composers about as much as a summer in Baghdad would be today.

My only other alternative for the summer was four weeks at the MacDowell Colony, an artists' retreat in New Hampshire, where I'd been offered a fellowship to complete the magnum opus I'd been working on for the last three years: my *Woodwind Quintet*. Suddenly, that seemed less inviting than the idyll that was forming in my mind of what Ray offered: beautiful young dancers, smiling yearningly at me as they leaned over the piano.

So, twenty-four and lonesome, I accepted. My *Woodwind Quintet* would wait.

Of course, the beautiful young dancers I had in mind for the summer turned out to be like untouchables in India. After rehearsals, they washed their leotards, chattering among themselves, and went straight to bed too tired to do anything but go to sleep.

Sans moi.

Arriving at the resort, the first thing I noticed were the fourteen nondescript brown wooden cabins, four brown tennis courts, a brown dining hall, and a not-too-solid, two-hundred-seat brown wooden theater. All unaccountably called *Green Mansions.*

That first summer, I was a pianist, a musical director, and an occasional actor (I played the role of a plainclothes man in *Light Up the Sky*). My dance music (pieces "Barbados Bandit" and "Flamenco Flame") would regularly appear in the Saturday night revue, danced by the likes of Rod Alexander and Bambi Linn (for whom I would later write special material).

On July 11, 1952, Lee Adams and I had one song, "Let Me Walk Under Your Umbrella," featured in a revue called *Enjoy Yourself.* The next week our song "Bound in Blue" was performed in *It's a Good Feeling*. Both shows were repeated in August when a new crop of campers arrived, and suddenly people were walking out of the theater humming my tunes.

Maybe at the end of the summer I would be going back to New York with no more luster to my career than I'd left with two months ago. But having spent the time since my graduation from Eastman imprisoned by my self-doubts, I felt, for the first time, if not free at Green Mansions, at least paroled. You see, I'd

had a taste of
the sound that says love:
Applause! Applause!

and for music I had written! It turned out to be a magic tonic.

Our songs had made such a hit that Lee and I were invited back the next summer to write a new revue every week. So, heading back to the city on the train after that first summer, I felt that I would at least have something to look forward to while accompanying those dance classes and singers at their auditions.

One of those singers was a young comedienne, Fay DeWitt, whom I'd met that fateful summer at Green Mansions. She was pretty and funny and a wonderful singer, and I played for her regularly. One day in the winter of 1953, I accompanied her while she auditioned for a new "book" musical (one with a continuous story uniting the whole piece) that was to be presented at an East Side nightclub called the Versailles. This would be a first for a nightclub that generally ran revues and cabaret acts on its tiny stage.

After Fay's audition (they liked her a lot), someone asked, "Who wrote that material you just sang?"

"He did," she said, and pointed to me. "My pianist. Buddy Strouse."

There was a moment of subdued conversation in the darkened club, and then someone said to Fay, "We want you in the show," before turning to me and saying, "Kid, could you write music for some new material we're going to put into this show?"

It was appropriate they called me "kid"— "they" being, collectively, 225 years old. (And, as it would turn out, "kid" was one of the nicer things I was called during the ensuing weeks.)

But—a composer! Paid money to write music!

Okay, Green Mansions had given me room and board and seventy-five dollars for the summer. But, except for the few songs we placed, that was for twelve weeks of basically thumping someone else's music and occasionally adding a few thumps of my own so the dancers would have extra thumps to get them from here to there.

Ten years before, my mother and father had paid the Eastman School of Music more money than I could ever have imagined so I could be a composer. And now, thrust into this time capsule piloted by these three 225-year-old men, I actually would be!

To sweeten the deal, the three men were famous: Irving Caesar (he'd written the words for "Swanee" with Gershwin and "Tea for Two" with Vincent Youmans, and he wore ultra-thick glasses, so I was never quite sure he knew who I was); Jack Yellen (lyricist of "Ain't She Sweet" and "Happy Days Are Here Again," among other hit songs); and George White (*the* George White, who had produced *Scandals* on Broadway with many of the century's greatest theater composers, and who had risen from the dead for this occasion, his comeback).

I was definitely not in Kansas anymore.

The show was called *Nice to See You,* and that was about all I knew. Still, I was ready to work whenever Irving or Jack (who both tried to be nice to me) handed me lyrics to set. Like a good composer, I asked questions like, "Who is supposed to sing this song?"

"Don't worry about it," they'd say.

It seemed Mr. White had promised the song to every girl in the show.

Okay, I'd deal with that if I had to.

"Where does this come in the script?" I'd then naively ask.

"There isn't any script yet," they'd respond.

"But it's a book musical!" I'd reply. "What's the story about?"

"Not sure," they'd say nonchalantly. "There's one song about a soldier; maybe it'll be about a returning GI. We'll figure it out later."

In fact, the plot (if you could call it that) eventually turned out to be about a GI returning home to his girl only to discover that she was engaged to a banker's son. Not exactly *My Fair Lady.*

When I played my settings for Irving and Jack's lyrics, I got either completely blank reactions or the suggestion of another tune entirely. Maybe I could just change some of my notes, they'd say, singing back their version of what it should be. I'd feel as if I had no choice but to use their suggestions. Who was I, after all? They'd worked with Gershwin! Yet I couldn't help but wonder: Was this a first step slipping down the ladder of integrity, or was I simply an obedient young man willing to learn?

But anything—*anything*—was better than playing a new song for George White himself. A former tap dancer, whenever I'd play for him, he'd sway a little, half-moving his shoulders and arms this way and that (as though he was trying a dance step), then say, "Don't give me that fag shit, I don't want fag shit!"

That made it hard to engage in conversation.

What was the appropriate response? Should I have said, "I'm not homosexual, Mr. White"? Or perhaps, "They're as good as you or me, sir"? Neither sounded right.

What I should have done was walk away. But it was my first job as a theater composer. I wanted my parents to see my name on a poster. Longing to be Leonard Bernstein or Cole Porter, I was feeling more and more unsure that I would ever become either. What I had become was a coward. I just went along.

The night before the first preview, we still had no book for the show. Even the club owners were getting nervous.

Irving, Jack, and George, all completely calm, gathered in Irving's suite at what was then called the Park Central Hotel (a suite, by the way, that both Gershwin and Youmans had worked in) to write it.

And they did.

It was lousy, it was cheap, and it was held together by spit and song cues. It was written like a child's coloring book that turns into "art" when you draw lines connecting numbered points that eventually become a clown or a sunset. Even when the book started to become credible, it would stop for an acrobatic tap number for no apparent reason, and the whole show finished with an overly loud reprise of an ensemble number that had nothing to say in the first place. To add insult to injury, they had two of the cast members, Barbara Stewart and Carol Ohmart, sit at the side of the miniscule stage and explain the plot to the audience.

I'd had it!

I took Irving aside and asked him to take my name off the program. I was out! I wanted no royalty (I'd been promised thirty dollars a week; the whole budget was a walloping thirty-five hundred dollars), no credits on the poster, and no connection to this trash.

"You're young, kid," he said, and smiled at me. "I'm not going to take your name off."

"You're not going to . . . Don't you have to if I ask?" I was shocked. Who knew from lawyers then?

He took off his thick glasses for the first time since I'd known him. He looked almost affectionate.

"Figure it out later, kid, when you write your memoirs."

I didn't go to opening night. I felt lost, angry, sad, hurt, and disillusioned. I was still living at home with my parents, and felt like I had no future in music. What was I even doing?

The next morning, I woke up to the best reviews I'd ever seen:

"George White, the old master, in remarkable comeback."

"Sprightly tunes . . ."

"Hit of the season!"

The critics even praised the "fragmentary plot" because it never got in the way.

My success was a cure to everything that ailed my family. My father's cough disappeared for the day, and his blood sugar dipped to a normal level. My mother, who was back home after two-and-a-half years of being institutionalized, spent the whole day cheerfully answering the phone, which was ringing off the hook with congratulatory calls.

I may have still not been sure who I was, but to my friends and folks, I was definitely *somebody!*

Was it the worst thing that could have happened to me or the best? There's no moral, and even if there were, it wouldn't be "to thine own self be true," for there was no "thine own self."

Perhaps the life lesson could have been something more along the lines of "relax and shut up! You don't know everything."

The show ran on and off for the next two years, but luckily, I didn't have to see it. The summer of 1953 soon arrived, and I was off once again to the brown cabins of Green Mansions.

CHAPTER SIX

Coming Attractions

THE AD FOR THE 1953 summer season at Green Mansions promised dramas such as *The Country Girl* by Clifford Odets (a man Lee and I would collaborate with one day) and opera sung by Patricia Neway (who would condescend to sing in an opera of mine that season, called *Triad*), dance concerts by Ray Harrison, and revues starring Bernie West, Joan Coburn, and Charlotte Rae written by yours truly and librettist Lee Adams.

Writing a new revue every week was exhausting and exhilarating. Collaborating with Lee in close quarters under severe deadlines turned out to be much more stimulating than I had expected. I'd never shared creative kinship with anyone before. A new kind of friendship, this: collaboration! That summer, I also met and began collaborating with a very funny sketch writer-lyricist named Michael Stewart, who would be instrumental in my first Broadway success.

Many of the songs Lee and I wrote that summer of 1953 (for shows with titles of *What's the Rush? It Takes Two, Follow Me*, and *Near and Far*), we reused in other revues later in the fifties. Even a fragment of what was to become "Put On a Happy Face" was used in a sketch about comedy and tragedy. It made little impression at the time, but we filed the snippet away. One other song received a tepid response there, but then, nine years later, surfaced in a Mabel Mercer performance (where had she heard it?), before being recorded by Frank Sinatra in that mysterious way songs become popular. That was "Once Upon a Time," which went on to be a great hit for us after it was put into *All American* in 1962. Still, at Green Mansions, I couldn't figure it out: Was I good, or was I just lucky?

With no glimpse of the light at the end of the tunnel that would be *Bye Bye Birdie*, I just plodded on. Girlfriends came and went until I fell in love for the first time with a girl named Georgia. I had met her on the same night I met Lee Adams. She was beautiful and a composer too, and I felt like I knew her from the moment I met her. It was all so exciting!

Not to her, however. She was in love with someone else: Andre Previn, who was (a) an incredible musician, (b) famous and successful as a composer and orchestrator at MGM Studios, and (c) a great jazz player. One year after that first meeting, though, she and Previn broke up, and Georgia and I began our three-year on-again, off-again relationship. I was deeply in love and wanted to marry her, but the closer I would get, the more she would pull away. Then I would woo her back but she would feel pressured and pull away again.

My mother called that Jewish hockey.

We never married. I was too unsure of my emotions and always broke; things were starting to take their toll on me.

One day in 1954, I began sobbing uncontrollably at the breakfast table. Not only couldn't I stop, but I had no idea what I was crying about. Was this what they call a "breakdown"? My mother, who perceptively saw much of her own darkness in me, insisted that I "see someone."

"No son of mine is mine is going to one of *them*!" bellowed my father. "He's not crazy!"

My mother, who knew a thing or two about crazy, insisted.

The psychiatrist I went to was a type I didn't like: a "know-it-all" with a hand-woven African cloth on the back of her sofa. She probably sang a lot of folk songs in college, and now went to every event at the Brooklyn Academy of Music. I was falling asleep, but aware that it was costing $150 for fifty minutes (my mother would just die!), I decided to speak.

"The tunes that fall from my fingers, as opposed to those I sweat out, shame me," I said. "*Anyone* could have written them."

"Yes. Go on," Dr. K (not her real name) prodded.

"I told that to Ned Rorem in Paris, and he said—obviously trying to lift my spirits— 'Remember, Buddy—nobody hears music the same as you.'"

"What do you think he meant?" she asked.

"I think what Ned meant was that uniqueness is reason enough to exist. But everyone's unique," I whined. "Snowflakes are unique. Trees and leaves and porcupines are unique. I don't *feel* unique. That's not true, is it? That nobody hears music the same as I do?"

She was silent, and I imagined seeing 150 bucks flying out the window.

"We're out of time," she finally said. "I'll see you at ten o'clock on Tuesday?" I could have sworn she stifled a yawn.

I decided not to see her again.

Despite having heard my songs performed every Saturday night that past summer, 1954 found me pounding the keyboard in a rehearsal studio on West Forty-fifth Street, trying to find the right key for Ginger Rogers. She was about to make her television debut after over twenty years on the silver screen, including ten classic films with Fred Astaire and one Oscar.

Ginger was to play three different roles in a TV "spectacular" of three of the plays Noel Coward wrote under the title *Tonight at 8:30*. Two of them were musicals.

This huge undertaking was also to be the television debut of film director Otto Preminger. With his Teutonic accent, Preminger was also well known for playing sadistic Nazis in World War II movies. That day as I futilely searched for a good key for Ginger (I found out later there was no right key for Ginger Rogers to sing in), Otto stood on the side, waited impatiently and glared. "Vell, vee begin now."

It sounded reasonable enough. But which key? And what arpeggio should I play to start Miss Rogers off? My hands were jelly.

I'd never seen or heard this music before, but my fingers made a split-second decision, and a very curious one: to play an arpeggio in two different keys at the same time. "Vat iss this?" and what sounded like "Who are jew?" Preminger hissed, apparently noticing me for the first time. "Vere iss Buster?"

Buster was Buster Davis, a very popular musician and choral arranger who had another, more lucrative gig and left me with a quick kiss on the cheek and a flurry of endearments as he exited the room. "Darling, this is Ginger. Say hello. She's a dear! Now, the music's in A-flat, but I think she does it in E natural, and I've got to fly now!"

Now, here I was faced with Ginger and the Nazi. And we weren't off to a very good start.

At subsequent rehearsals, I made sure that I knew the music, but I had the distinct feeling that my very presence bugged Preminger. Even before he got to know me, there was a chemistry that I can only describe as flammable.

Herr Preminger could bear no noise during rehearsals. Not a peep, not a sound. So if a sheet of music, say, fell off the piano (and music falls off pianos; ask anyone), he would stop the entire rehearsal.

There would be a deep silence in which the cast, grateful it wasn't them, would stare into space or look at their nails, waiting for the Preminger tirade. Otto never disappointed. I'd never known anyone to be driven into such fury so quickly. He stamped, pounded on tables, and threw chairs. Ginger just opened her compact and fixed her face.

On the day of the broadcast (remember, TV was live back then, and this was to be the color premiere of a series called *Producers' Showcase*), we were to have a final dry run with just piano (the orchestra would come in later for another run-through, and, of course, play for the broadcast) on the huge NBC soundstage in Brooklyn.

I was ready.

I'd been through the show many times, but, even so, I'd practiced my part the night before at home. The music was all in order, my cues were memorized, my earphones were double-checked, and my hands were poised like thoroughbreds at the starting gate. Preminger had not screamed at me for almost three days. I had a right to be almost relaxed, even confident.

Not many of the cast had experienced color television before, so during long breaks between cues, some of the actors wandered into the commissary—a few short steps from the main soundstage—to view it on a monitor. Not me. I sat through every scene and held for a commercial, so I'd be sure to be ready.

At last, there was a fifteen-minute break announced, and I went to the bathroom. On my way back, I stopped at the commissary to watch a little of this exciting new technology, then sauntered back to the piano. The whole journey left me with ample time before my next cue.

I didn't have my earphones on, but it didn't matter, because, from the commissary, I could see and hear the actors. Even that didn't matter, though, as I'd just about memorized the entire script and the actors' blocking (where and how they were directed to move and stand on the stage) by this point. I knew exactly where they were, and more important, I knew exactly where I was in the script, in the huge studio, and in my emotional life—you get the idea.

However, when I reached the place in the studio where my piano was . . . it unaccountably wasn't.

Where *was* the piano?

Almost immediately, I felt a bit of moisture in my hair, and then a trickle of water down my face. That drip multiplied, until sweat started to seep through my clothing and into my socks and shoes. Even so, full-fledged panic hadn't quite gripped me yet. After all, my cue wasn't for another three minutes or so.

I calmly stopped a stagehand. "Have you seen my piano?"

"Your piano?"

"Yeah," I said with less composure, "my piano!"

He looked at me as if to say he had important things to do.

Still (relatively) calm, I glanced toward the glass control booth. In there, it was like a silent movie. People scurried about as Preminger sat there and smiled, occasionally pointing or soundlessly nodding in satisfaction at something. Every once in a while, someone would leave a mike open and a burst of short, businesslike bits of phrases would pop through:

"Okay, on mike number two . . ."

"—Stage manager on the count of . . ."

The three minutes before my music cue dwindled to one minute, then to mere seconds. I looked once more at the glass booth with its smiling Preminger and the smoothly moving technicians.

Then came my cue.

Then came no music.

I watched as the silent Preminger turned an odd color, his face growing purple as his chest heaved and his mouth moved wordlessly. I saw the technicians parting as if a tsunami had struck. Then someone touched a microphone switch, and I heard a short blast of sound.

"—fucking piano, vere's the—"

It took three men in the booth to physically restrain Preminger as the mike cut out.

Then, a more reasonable voice came over the speaker. "Mr. Preminger would like to know where the music is."

"I've lost the piano," I replied meekly as I watched Preminger struggle to free himself from his keepers so that he might kill me.

Glancing around frantically, I finally spotted the piano behind a piece of scenery someone had put in front of it. I quickly jumped to it and started playing the music. My last glimpse of Preminger was of a lunatic, mouth working, but no sound coming out being restrained by assistants as they escorted him back into the asylum.

A new show business lesson was learned that day. One that Irving Berlin's famous anthem didn't mention: There is a very thin line to cross that will change a director from kitten to rhinoceros. Do not cross it—ever!

And keep your eyes on the piano.

Soon after *Tonight at 8:30* aired to good reviews, Lee Adams and I teamed up again to recycle some material from the shows we'd done at Green Mansions. We auditioned it for a new, low-budget project called, appropriately, *Shoestring Revue,* which was being produced by a man named Ben Bagley.

Some men live to cross an ocean or cure an epidemic. Ben Bagley lived to produce revues written by people no one had ever heard of, dealing with subjects no one cared about. If he is remembered at all today, it is not as a producer of revues but as the producer and creator of a series of over forty recordings that "revisited" the obscure songs from famous Broadway songwriters beginning with Rodgers and Hart and continuing on through Cole Porter, Harold Arlen, Irving Berlin, and almost every other well-known songwriter from the first part of the twentieth century. His record company, Painted Smiles, would also go on to release several original cast albums.

When I met Ben, he was just twenty-one years old. He had a scarecrow's frame and looked a bit like a bird. He had a giggle that frequently turned into paroxysms of coughing, particularly when he found something amusing. This was disconcerting because he found almost *everything* amusing.

When a writer would demonstrate even mildly funny material, Ben would start giggling. Then laughing. Then coughing. And the hapless writer playing or singing had to attend to Ben on the sofa or in a nearby bathroom, where Ben would still be laughing and coughing and spitting into his handkerchief. As a result, Ben simply chose almost any material anyone played him to go into the show, and the first preview of *Shoestring Revue* lasted well over four hours.

Ben had the double theater curse: He had no money *and* he lived in New Jersey. Yet he could no more quench his desire to produce *Shoestring Revue* than he could suppress his cough. He worked for a solid year gathering material and backing.

I became the musical director and arranger for the show simply in part because Ben laughed and coughed and spit at more of my songs than at anyone else's, but also because no one else would work for Ben based on the curious barter system he employed: future pay for present services.

In an attempt to induce Charlotte Rae (a wonderful comedienne whom I'd first known at Green Mansions, Charlotte is known to millions of TV fans as Mrs. Garrett in *The Facts of Life*) to join the cast, Ben and I went to her apartment, where I played and sang some of the songs from the show. I thought things went well, so I was surprised when Charlotte turned the show down.

I learned why later: After I left, Ben had asked Charlotte to lend him a quarter so he could get a train back to New Jersey.

"Lending you a quarter doesn't necessarily shore up her confidence in you as producer," I explained to him.

(Fortunately, after *Shoestring Revue* opened, Ben managed to woo her to do his next revue, titled *The Littlest Revue*. Lee and I contributed material to that show as well as to *Shoestring '57*. Exposure was exposure.)

At our first run-through of the original *Shoestring* production on the stage of the 350-seat President Theatre (later the site of Mamma Leone's restaurant and now a hotel), I walked down the aisle and saw Dania Krupska, our choreographer, weeping. When I asked what was wrong, she pointed, still in tears, to a haphazard pile of lumber on the stage.

"That's our set," she sobbed.

"Don't worry," I said wisely, having had months of experience at Green Mansions. "When they put it all together, it'll be terrific."

"It *is!*" she managed to choke out in the midst of a renewed round of hysterical crying. "It's all put together!"

At least we had a great cast. Our leading ladies were Bea Arthur, Dorothy Greener, and Dody Goodman, and in my twenty-six years on Earth, I had never heard women curse like that. Mike Stewart, with whom I wrote the opening number ("Man's Inhumanity to Man") and several others, and I would stand outside their dressing room and listen in awe. The C word, the F word—we'd heard vocabulary like this before, but never from women.

Chita Rivera, fresh from the chorus of *Can-Can*, had been hired to dance in the show, but when I heard her sing, I kept throwing songs her way. Her energy was boundless, and her vocal range was as long as her legs. During this time, she wondered if she should change her name to seem less ethnic. Chita O'Hara was one idea she came up with, but saner heads prevailed.

Everything about *Shoestring* was strange. We played three previews (with twenty or thirty people in the audience each time), and no one even cracked a smile. Despite the stoic response from the audience, Ben Bagley would invariably be off by himself, laughing hysterically. However, the audiences just didn't seem to get it. Questioning the cast, I learned most of them didn't know what the sketches were all about, either.

The tunes weren't very good (which I could see, despite the fact I'd written many of them), and I had nothing substantial to play as an overture, so at one preview I simply played two songs from *Oklahoma!* Three people laughed, so it stayed in the show. (This was copied for *Shoestring '57*, in which the overture from *My Fair Lady* got huge laughs.)

The night *Shoestring Revue* opened, it was raining quite hard, and people were all arriving late. Walter Kerr (then the critic for the *New York Herald Tribune*, who would later break my heart at the birth of *Annie*) sat in the first row right in front of my piano. He was soaking wet and clearly irritable. He never once cracked a smile. And as for those sketches that no one had laughed at during previews? No one in the opening night's audience laughed at them either, save one: Ben Bagley. I could hear his cackle cutting through the silence during the entire performance.

I was embarrassed, the cast was despondent, and there was no opening night party, for there was little hope and no money.

But then the reviews came out.

"Novel!"

"Different!"

"Splendid cast of unknowns!"

By the next morning, *Shoestring* was a huge success!

What was it that Irving Caesar had said to me? "Figure it out later, kid, when you write your memoirs."

Ben felt the cast deserved a party to celebrate our triumph and, in keeping with the style of the show, invited us to the restaurant next door for "a sandwich and beer." (The invitation was very specific about the menu.) The cast and I were regulars there, as it was just around the corner, on Eighth Avenue and, though modest, was a decent place. So we had a nice party, and each of us had a sandwich and a beer.

The day after the party, we went back for an early pre-show dinner. We couldn't help but notice that our waitress, normally the best humored of people, was acting rather sullen.

"What's wrong?" someone asked her finally.

She was hesitant to say but finally told us that the bill for the party had come to forty-five dollars, and Ben had left a forty-five-cent tip, which I suppose, he figured out was 10 percent.

We straightened things out.

𝄢

By 1956, life felt like it was moving at warp speed. Lee and I had several songs featured in a revue on London's West End called *Fresh Airs*. In New York, Charlotte Rae brought down the house nightly at *The Littlest Revue* with a satire by Lee and me about a Wagnerian soprano making her Las Vegas debut. Performers such as Kaye Ballard, Dick Shawn, and Jane Morgan performed our material in their nightclub acts to enthusiastic applause. "Six Finger Tune," a remnant from an ill-fated Broadway play called *Sixth Finger in a Five Finger Glove*, was featured as the theme for a new TV game show called *The Price Is Right* (and continued on until replaced in 1961). *What's the Rush?* a revue by Strouse and Adams, played at the Pittsburgh Playhouse and then toured summer theaters starring TV celebrity Robert Q. Lewis and Bea Arthur. Lee and I were at work on a musical based on a novel by Bernard Wolfe. We had even had several of our songs recorded by the artists such as Annette Warren and the Four Esquires.

And then my father died.

After a lifetime of witnessing my mother's worries about my father's health, it had finally happened. I was alone with

Pop in a starkly antiseptic hospital room in St. Vincent's Hospital on Staten Island when it happened. My mother, coincidentally, was having "minor" surgery at Mount Sinai Hospital in Manhattan (which turned out to be not quite so minor), so I was alone, and I was terrified.

I ran out of the room before he took his last breath.

I left him lying in a bed in a Catholic hospital, coughing and staring through a plastic tent at a white wall where all he would have seen was Jesus on the cross—not the most comforting sight for a middle-aged (he was fifty-nine), terrified Jewish man.

I never said good-bye. Never took his hand. Never said, "I love you, Pop."

He didn't live long enough to see *Bye Bye Birdie*.

Earlier that year, though, he did fly to Pittsburgh to see *What's the Rush?* During intermission, I went to the men's room and, there at a urinal, was my father. But he wasn't doing what one usually does there. Instead, he had taken the speaker of his hearing aid from his pocket and was dangling it from the wire in his ear, twisting it this way and that, trying to pick up any comments.

As soon as my father spied me (he didn't think I'd seen him), he slyly put the speaker back into his pocket as though he'd just taken it out to examine it or clean it.

Perhaps because my father was away so often or perhaps because my mother sometimes took delight in putting him down in front of me, I never felt that he paid me much attention. Yet, he listened to my music when I played it and always said he liked it, even if he didn't. Looking back in my files, I find a yellowing cutting from a newspaper about the party he threw for me in 1944 at the Glass Hat, a nightclub at the Hotel Belmont Plaza before I went off to college.

The article goes on to tell how the bandleader, Mickey Alpert, played one of my songs, "Wanted for Stealing My Heart," four times that night.

It turns out that Pop had paid him to play it.

After my father died, Lee and I continued our collaboration, resulting in *Off the Top*, a follow-up review at the Pittsburgh Playhouse, which reused our future hit song (originally debuted at Green Mansions) "Once Upon a Time." I collaborated once with pop lyricist Fred Tobias, and with Fred Ebb, whom I met through a girlfriend who lived at the Whitby apartments where Fred lived. (Years later, listening to some old tapes of the songs Ebb and I did together, I realized they were some of the worst songs I'd ever heard.) Later on, Fred would team up with John Kander and write some great musicals.

To get through my grief, I also relied, as always, on Bill Flanagan. By now, Bill was writing music reviews for the *Herald Tribune* and not drinking as much, although he still had that Irish thing for booze. He was still dating Ed, the telegraph delivery boy Bill had brought to David Diamond's counterpoint classes. Ed insisted on calling me "Barney," a variation of my nickname that barely concealed his Bronxville hauteur toward us ethnics of West Side Manhattan. And though I was jealous of his having "stolen" my best friend, we all hung out together drinking beer at the Carnegie Tavern. Ed eventually seemed to have adjusted to me, and I got used to his *chutzpah*.

I noticed that Ed had more than *chutzpah* when he showed me a few of his poems (I still have them—something to do with a royal court and a jester), plus a play he'd written. I thought the play was wonderful, though it was written "all wrong." He'd written it out on yellow legal paper with the characters' names placed in front of, rather than above, their speeches. That was not how professionals did it.

Nevertheless, I volunteered to show it to some of my show business contacts because Ed hadn't any at the time. I took it to a director and an agent—friends who both liked it very much but couldn't figure out what to do with it as it was only an hour long.

However, David Diamond had a friend (who may or may not have been his lover) who was a theater director from Germany who did figure out what to do with it: He translated it into German and staged it in Berlin—to rave reviews.

Now why hadn't I thought of that?

It was called *The Zoo Story*, and virtually overnight, Ed, the telegram delivery boy was transformed into "Edward Albee, playwright."

In fact, years later, when I first saw *Who's Afraid of Virginia Woolf?* I couldn't help but notice that the dialogue sounded very much like the way all of us had talked back in the days when we all hung out and drank in Bill's apartment on Christopher Street.

9:

Ed Padula had been around Broadway for a while. He started out by directing the book portion of Lerner and Loewe's first "success d'estime" (or as playwright George S. Kaufman would say, a success that ran out of steam) *The Day Before Spring* on Broadway, but in the 1950s, Ed settled into a career as a stage manager of such shows as *No Time for Sergeants* and *Seventh Heaven.* Secretly, Ed wanted to be a producer.

In 1958, Ed was stage-managing *Saratoga*, a musical starring Howard Keel and Carol Lawrence, for which I was playing dance rehearsals, waiting for the choreographer to count off his "5-6-7-8" so that I could play the same music I'd played 486 times in the last hour.

Finally, lunch was called, but before I could leave, I heard Ed's voice.

"Hey, Buddy!"

"Hi, Ed," I responded and turned to leave.

"Listen," he went on, "I heard some of Lee Adams's and your material in *Shoestring Revue*, and I liked what I heard. I have an idea for a musical." I stopped and turned around to listen.

"It's about teenagers," he continued.

That day I didn't have lunch.

CHAPTER SEVEN

We Love You, Conrad

THE SHOW ED PADULA told me about was then called *Let's Go Steady*, and it was indeed about teenagers. Ed wanted it to be a "happy teenage musical with a difference"—the difference being our teenagers would be nothing like the ones portrayed in 1957's *West Side Story*. Ed had contracted two book writers named Warren Miller and Raphael Millian, and Lee and I quickly wrote seven songs (three of which would survive to see the stage) to fit their libretto.

To flesh out the rest of the creative team, we turned to Marge and Gower Champion, who, in the 1950s, were a famous dance team who had appeared on stage, screen, and television. I had seen them in the MGM film *Show Boat*, and I was aware that Gower had staged *Lend an Ear* (a 1948 revue starring Carol Channing), choreographed *Make a Wish* and directed, choreographed, and starred with Marge in a piece called *Three for Tonight*. In the summer of 1958 (after both Fred Astaire and *The Music Man* director Morton DaCosta had already turned Ed down), Ed, Lee, and I trooped out to New Jersey to check Marge and Gower out at a nightclub called the Riviera. Their act was brilliantly staged, and we all agreed that Gower should direct the show.

But Gower didn't like the book at all. So Ed fired the book writers and subsequently hired and fired a succession of five librettists, including Mike Nichols and Elaine May (Elaine simply didn't show up after our very first meeting). Still, no one's take on the material had given us what we wanted.

Finally, Ed agreed to try the writer Lee and I had suggested in the first place: Michael Stewart. Our experience at Green Mansions working with him had convinced us Mike was an inventive and witty writer, and so, in December of 1958, with our endorsement, Ed gave him a try.

Mike, trying to accommodate our songs, wrote a draft called *Love and Kisses*, keeping the plot device of a couple on the brink of divorce whose children persuade them to reconcile, but cutting the idea of a teenage girl trying to lose her virginity. Gower liked family shows, so there wasn't to be any of that.

But Champion hesitated to demand more rewrites, as he still wasn't fully committed to the show. He wouldn't commit quite yet, as he wanted something more out of the plot.

The "something more" had been right there in the newspaper. On September 22, 1958, rock-and-roll idol Elvis Presley, having been drafted, boarded a ship for eighteen months in Germany, unleashing torrents of teen anguish. There was a media circus including Elvis giving a specially selected WAC "one last kiss."

After much brainstorming, Mike and Lee came up with the idea of a rock-and-roll singer going off to the army and its effect on a group of teenagers in a small town in Ohio. Elvis Presley became Elsworth (which was changed to Conway Twitty before we discovered there already was a Conway Twitty who was threatening to sue us, and then, finally, Conrad Birdie) and we were off and running with the then-revolutionary idea of a rock-and-roll musical, first called *The Day They Took Birdie*

Away, later *Going Steady*, and still later *Goodbye, Birdie, Goodbye*, before finally being christened *Bye Bye Birdie*.

A rock-and-roll musical?

In 1958, rock and roll was virgin territory for Broadway. Most adults thought it was a fad that would run its course. With very little knowledge of the form, I spent weeks researching the recordings of Fats Domino, Elvis Presley, Buddy Holly, and Annette Funicello trying to cross the borders of teenage land. It was not something that had been stressed at Eastman or recognized by the likes of Arthur Berger.

My rock-and-roll research must have seeped into my subconscious, because it gave me my first hit song.

One night in early 1958, a pal, lyricist Fred Tobias, was the only one who showed up on time for a poker game. We felt we shouldn't let the time or the cold cuts go to waste, so we wrote a song in fifteen minutes. We called it "Born Too Late."

I took it to a publisher whom I knew at the time; he really didn't want to see me, but his secretary had become an ally of mine and told me to wait until five p.m.—just before he left the office. I played him the song, and he thought it was okay, but he put it on the bottom of a pile of other songs, and I forgot all about it.

A few months later, a new girl group, the Poni-Tails, chose the song as the B-side of a recording (the side no one ever plays) that they were about to make. It was released and, a week later in Cleveland, a disc jockey flipped the record (which was rarely done) and played the song on the radio. Groups of teenagers screamed whenever the Poni-Tails performed it, and "Born Too Late" sold millions of copies.

Even before *Birdie* reached its final version, we had to get backers, and so we played the show for everyone who would listen: friends, friends of friends, agents, friends of agents (there are some). The usual suspects attending these backer's auditions included people with money, their lawyers who advised them not to invest their money, theater owners who didn't feel quite comfortable with their taste unless George Abbott was directing, and a smattering of others who had no intention of investing from the start but who wanted to see what was going on so they could be the first to gossip.

We thought we were in clover when Hilly Elkins, who managed both Mike and me, was offered a vice presidency at a leading theatrical and music agency. As part of the deal, he was to bring along his clients (we were all of them) to sign on with the agency. We were more than willing.

As the agency was already poised to sign us, we auditioned in front of every agent on the staff in one room at the same time. After the five-minute intermission following Act I, not one of the agents returned to the room, instead sending their secretaries and assistants. It was a measure of our lack of pride that we nevertheless blustered through Act II. Still, the humiliation was so thick you could feel it.

Still, the backer's auditions played on. I've always felt humiliated by this ritual, though, once in a while, someone listens who cares. And even if the show doesn't raise its money, sometimes something good can come out of it all. That's what happened the day we sang the score for Frank Loesser.

In addition to being a genius songwriter who, after writing movie songs for years, had three big Broadway hits in a row (*Where's Charley?*, *Guys & Dolls*, and *The Most Happy Fella*),

Frank was also a music publisher (he published the scores of *The Pajama Game, Damn Yankees,* and *Kismet,* along with his own shows) and producer. Under the banner of "Frank Productions," he lent his name to his own *Most Happy Fella* and the 1957 smash hit *The Music Man.*

When Lee and I played him our score, he seemed to like it, but Frank was tough with a buck. He wouldn't actually invest any money; he would simply lend his name. And, for that, he wanted 50 percent of the producer's share, which Padula couldn't afford.

But Frank liked the way a musical phrase was turned in the song "One Boy," with the melody landing on the leading tone of the scale. It didn't seem particularly novel to me, but Frank liked it, and he offered me a job to assist him, which I grabbed. What a thrill to get to know one of the great composer-lyricists of the American theater! While *Birdie* was still aimlessly flying around, I worked alongside him for almost two years.

He didn't play piano well, so I became his "other" hands. He enjoyed referring to me as his "little colored boy," as uncouth as the nickname was. (There had been an apocryphal tale going around for years that Irving Berlin kept a "little colored boy" in the backroom who wrote all his hits.) Once in a while, as I got to know him, I would suggest a different voicing for a chord or a connective phrase of some sort.

Most of the time, he said no to those suggestions.

Frank knew what he wanted, though sometimes, when we would work deep into the night, Frank would admit his insecurities to me. Long after midnight, drink in hand (scotch in a Baccarat glass over crystal-clear ice—not the kind of crinkly ice our refrigerator made at home), Frank would tell me how he felt his mother favored his brother Arthur, a classical pianist. He'd say how he felt he was a no one—a "dese, dem, and dose" guy. A "mug." Actually, I thought it his most endearing quality. I tried to reassure Frank, telling him how great he was, but I couldn't help but appreciate the irony: There I was, an insecure thirty-year-old music-school graduate (big deal), trying to help Frank Loesser appreciate his own genius.

My job with Frank lasted for almost two years—until *Birdie* went into rehearsal. When I did leave, I left a guy who smoked too much, and drove himself crazy thinking he was no good. I also left behind a mentor who taught me consideration of others in collaboration and whose genius for popular music was unmatched.

Most importantly, I left behind a friend.

𝄢

One day, while Lee and I were writing the umpteenth new song for the latest draft of whatever the show was then being called, the phone rang. It was Ed Padula.

"I have a 'pigeon' flying up from Texas," he said. "Can you play the score for him at your publisher's office?"

Ed, the producer, had no office himself, because Ed, the producer, had no money. Also, of course, Ed had never produced . . . anything.

"Of course," we said, without missing a beat.

The Texas "pigeon" turned out to be a guy named L. Slade Brown. He looked to be about forty, and had a thick southern drawl. He sat on a straight-backed chair alongside another man who looked like his keeper but who said he was in "banking." I had little time to wonder about his real occupation, because we launched right into our presentation. We knew it was bound to be the usual waste of time, but we were now accustomed to performing each time the bell rang—like Pavlov's dogs. *Sit up, beg.* Or, in our case, *sit up, perform*—whenever an investor entered the room.

"It's about this rock-and-roll singer who gets drafted," we began. "And there's this couple"—a blank stare from Mr. Brown—"Oh, she's Polish, but he's not . . . well, what we mean is . . ." He wasn't getting it. So we shut up and sang our songs, finishing with a big flourish.

The banker was unimpressed, his mind plainly somewhere else. But Slade Brown, the pigeon, unexpectedly cooed. "Ah laak those songs. Vurry nice."

The banker associate just smiled blandly.

Walking over to the piano, Brown asked, "How did that song go again, the ballad?" He sat himself at the keyboard and picked out the melody of "One Boy," showing off his down-home music larnin'. I forced an appreciative smile.

"How much do you fellas need?" he asked.

We paused, never having anticipated the question.

He continued, "Ah mean, to put on the show. How much?"

Still, no one spoke. It was like we were all stuck in a freeze-frame. Was this some sort of cruel joke?

Then Slade took out his checkbook. I peeked over his shoulder to see the heading on the check. "Brown National Bank, Orange, Texas." He wasn't a loony, then!

Or maybe he was a very *rich* loony. With his own bank!

After five different book writers, months and months of pitching the show, and total rejection from every knowledge-able theater professional in town, we'd take what we could get.

Still, no one had spoken a word, until Ed, very coolly, said, "To start casting, rehearsals, designing costumes: Seventy-five thousand dollars."

I was convinced it was the largest amount Ed could think of. With L. Slade Brown on board and Mike Stewart's latest draft in Gower's hand, on August 8, 1959, the press reported that Gower Champion would direct and choreograph our show. After years of black and white, the scene suddenly turned Technicolor: *Birdie* was about to take flight.

Now that we had a director, we had to find our stars. Originally Ed thought that Marge and Gower would play the leads, but Gower had no intention of directing and performing in the same show, and Marge would be his assistant in any case.

We needed a strong leading lady for the character of Rosie, originally written as a woman of Polish descent. Dancer Carol Haney, who had made a big splash in both the stage and film versions of *The Pajama Game,* immediately wanted to do it. We all thought that, with her comedic dancing skills, she would be perfect. After I spent two weeks coaching her in the songs, I was ready to have Gower, Mike, and Lee hear her sing.

The moment she opened the door, though, it was clear that Carol Haney was *not* ready. She had totally lost her voice. The woman who had been belting it out for two weeks could now barely speak. We spent an uncomfortable half hour of chitchat while we waited to see if her voice would return. Finally, Carol rasped, "I don't know what happened!" (It wouldn't have taken Freud long to figure out.) And we all said our sad good-byes.

We then asked singer Eydie Gorme (married to Steve Lawrence) to do the role. Dancing could take a back seat to her wonderful voice. "You see, it's about this Polish girl, and her mother-in-law can't stand her, and—" Our pitch was cut short when we found out Eydie had just gotten pregnant.

The next name on our list was Shirley MacLaine. She had been Carol Haney's understudy in *The Pajama Game*, and had been discovered by a Hollywood producer the night she went on for her. So now, of course, her agent never called anyone back.

Well, then, what about Jane Powell? She sang, she danced. But, Polish? We didn't think so.

What about Helen Gallagher? Besides winning the Tony for the revival of *Pal Joey*, she had recently appeared down in Florida in *A Pound in Your Pocket*, the first book musical Lee and I had written. She was a brilliant singer, dancer, and actress. Unfortunately for us, she was also Irish.

We were running out of ideas.

Finally, someone said, "What about Chita Rivera?"

After working with me in *Shoestring Revue*, Chita had climbed the Broadway ladder going from featured roles in *Seventh Heaven* (staged managed by Ed Padula) and *Mr. Wonderful* (starring my future *Golden Boy*, Sammy Davis Jr.) to the very prominent role of Anita in *West Side Story*, both on Broadway and in London.

Brilliant! Chita Rivera was wonderful! But Polish?

We played the show for Chita and she loved it, so suddenly Rosie Grant became Rosie Alvarez. Every Polish joke quickly became a Spanish joke, and Albert's mother's diatribes against Poles were rerouted against the fastest-growing minority in New York.

Curiously, many years later, a well-meaning critic in Los Angeles criticized us for poking fun at Hispanics, not being able to see that we were poking fun at certain biased Americans who poke fun at Hispanics. I couldn't help but think of years earlier, in the South, when I was spit at for being too close to an African-American woman.

The role of Birdie was originally written for comedian Dick Shawn, who did a mean Elvis impersonation in his act and for whom Lee and I had written special material while we were at Green Mansions. Dick departed early on when the role was so small it was two lines and a belch. Our search continued.

In 1959, while still waiting for the show to get on, I took a job as vocal arranger and rehearsal pianist for a short-lived Broadway revue starring Bert Lahr and Nancy Walker called *The Girls Against the Boys*. A tall, gangly, Stan Hardy-esque newcomer named Dick Van Dyke was also in the show, and he and I struck up a friendship. (Understudying Dick was Martin Charnin, with whom, later, I was to write a musical about a redheaded orphan.)

While the revue was having its out-of-town tryout, I'd often have coffee with Dick, whom I grew to like a lot. He was very unusual in that his prime motivation in life—at least as he expressed it to me—was taking care of his family and pulling in steady bucks. He didn't seem to crave the limelight at all, and we got along really well. I was shocked when I read years later that he said he was battling alcoholism during that time.

I only knew him as this shy, considerate guy who was of the absolute conviction that he couldn't sing. I thought differently and often talked to him about "this show I'm going to do one day, and it would be great if you could be in it."

Of course, by the time Padula had gotten the money together to actually do the show, my memory had grown shorter while my head had gotten larger. This was *Brrroadway!* (Imagine that with background singers.) I didn't actually forget about Dick, but I knew that, when it came down to casting, we had hit the big-time with this, and we needed "a name." Dick was unknown. What we needed to find was a great "Dick Van Dyke type"!

I wanted Jack Lemmon. But I didn't know Jack Lemmon. Also, I didn't know anyone who knew Jack Lemmon. (And I still don't think I know anyone who knew Jack Lemmon.)

However, Dick had a persistent agent, Richard Seff, who kept calling to suggest Dick for the lead. But would audiences flock to see an unknown?

Dick came in and auditioned the part for us. Surprisingly enough, he was a very good "Dick Van Dyke type," and we decided to take a gamble, despite the ridiculous image in my mind of this implausible poster: "Chita Rivera and Dick Van Dyke in BYE BYE BIRDIE"—ten words that sounded *mishugena* to me.

With our two leads signed, a director, a script and score, and the money in place, I found myself at a casting call in a rehearsal studio on Eighth Avenue in New York City with a stage manager, a rehearsal pianist, and a fantasy that was poised to become reality.

I arrived, wearing my best sweater, and waved a cheery hello to Gower. He gave me a subtle nod in response as he explored the space, Marge following in his wake. She was very pretty and totally in his thrall. I'd played enough dance classes at that point to know there's an obedience thing between dancers and their choreographic masters. Gower was ready to work and completely in control—as he normally was.

No one had ever seen Gower Champion sweat. If hair could look choreographed, his did: one small strand tumbling nonchalantly toward his right eyebrow. Pastel baby blue sweater loosely tied over his shoulders; semi-starched pink dress shirt, two buttons opened at the neck; his pants a soft, silky material (cashmere?) enclosing the smallest ass I'd ever seen; and dance shoes that looked more expensive than the advance I'd been paid to write the music for this show. I couldn't believe this gorgeous person would be directing a show I'd written the music for.

The large number of dancers and singers who appeared before us apparently had not really understood the title of the show when they'd read the official announcement in the *New York Times*. Most of them auditioned by singing "Bye Bye Blackbird," an Al Jolson song having nothing whatsoever to do with our show.

The title had taken us a long time to come up with, and it still didn't seem quite right to me. But Alan Jay Lerner later told me that they had also struggled with the title for his musical version of *Pygmalion* and had settled for the least "rotten" one: *My Fair Lady*. Positioning myself behind the audition table (a place I'd never been during auditions before, my place generally being behind the piano), I began feeling that my best sweater was shabby. I tried to push little fat Buddy out of the room. I was one of the big boys now, passing grades on others.

Brroadway! (*sung Gene Kelly style*)

The very first person that walked through the door to audition knocked me out. Her name was Nancy Dussault, a clever actor and comedienne. She was gorgeous—and she sang and she danced, wow!

Brroadway! (*up a minor third*)

She was great! This was wonderful! Were they all going to be like she was?

I turned to Gower and whispered, "She's marvelous." He said nothing to Nancy but a pleasant thank you before turning to the stage manager. "Next!"

Damn. I had been too enthusiastic, uncool even. Maybe I just didn't have the feel for it. Here I was, picking from a lineup of actors who were nervous and insecure themselves, and so full of doubt myself.

I glanced down again at what I was convinced was my worn-out and threadbare sweater. I then looked over at Gower. He was smart, thin, and cool, and acted as though I wasn't there.

$9:$

Somehow the show got cast with wonderful people such as Dick Gautier to play Birdie, Kay Medford to play Albert's overbearing mother, nineteen-year-old Susan Watson as fifteen-year-old Kim MacAfee, and Paul Lynde, who had been such a hit in *New Faces* of 1952, to play her father, Harry.

When Paul was offered the role, there really wasn't much to it. But Gower had an instinct that this show, with all the real teenagers he had cast, needed a strong and funny performer to give the parents' point of view to an audience that would be made up of adults. As rehearsals progressed, Paul's role grew, and it was marvelous to watch him bring his patented, satirical edge that was impossible to define. Looking back, I wonder if it was his "gay sensibility" that made him able to satirize fathers in general or his unconscious aggression toward the typical American family. Whatever it was, his comic take on impatience and the fever of his frustrations as head of a household in which he was given no respect gave the show much of its identity, and permitted adult audiences to identify and poke fun at the so-called ideals of marriage and family.

Mike Stewart wrote one of his best comic speeches specifically for Paul Lynde, and every once in a while in rehearsals, Paul would ad-lib something hilarious, and we would all say, "Keep it in!"

For example, at the end of the song about Ed Sullivan, "Hymn for a Sunday Evening," Paul stepped out from his onstage family and ad-libbed, "Ed, I love you!" Lee and I thought it was hysterical, and told him to keep it in.

At a run-through that day, Paul said the line, and everyone broke up. Gower, who had no taste for surprises, yelled at Lee, Mike, and me. There had been no time to tell him about the new line, and we all apologized profusely. But the line stayed in.

Rehearsals began on February 1, 1960, at an old Second Avenue theater (which was actually on Third Avenue) that used to house Yiddish plays. Although rehearsals went smoothly, I still felt like the little fat kid who wasn't really wanted in the room. None of the cute teenage girls in the company cast a glance my way, and Gower, never the warmest of men, looked as though he was forcing himself to smile when we crossed paths.

On Friday afternoon, March 11, 1960, right before we went out of town, we did our gypsy run through. Traditionally, this was an invited rehearsal at which only close friends, Broadway insiders, and casts and crews of shows currently running come to see a raw performance with only piano and with no sets or costumes. A gypsy run is the first indicator of what the audience reaction might actually be. That day in March, the reaction was ecstatic, and we traveled to Philadelphia with our heads held high.

We arrived at the Shubert Theater in Philadelphia, and there it was: our red, white, and black poster announcing "Chita Rivera and Dick Van Dyke." Every time I saw these names in bold above the silliest of titles, I couldn't help but think, tequila and milk—what kind of a restaurant is this?

To say the theatergoing public was apathetic would be putting it kindly. Our ticket advance was nonexistent—a record, in Philadelphia, I was told. After all, we had no stars, Lee, Mike, and I were newcomers, and Gower had never directed and choreographed a big show. I quickly learned one of the sadder experiences of the theater: to walk from an intense rehearsal inside the cozy, spot lit, energy-infused darkness of a theater into a day-bright and very empty lobby overseen by bored box-office personnel with deep stacks of unsold tickets behind them. To me, it was yet more proof of the non-love and disinterest of the real world.

On March 16, just as the curtain was about to go up for our first tryout performance, there was much drama backstage. It seemed that Ed Padula was still short seventy-five thousand dollars for the Equity bond. Ed frantically and futilely phoned everyone he knew until he reached Goddard Lieberson, the president of Columbia Records.

Very early on, Lee and I had auditioned the score for Goddard (also present at our audition were Clive Davis, who later went on to do okay in the record business, and Schuyler Chapin, who would go on to become the general manager of the Metropolitan Opera as well as the Commissioner of Cultural Affairs for New York City). We all knew that

Columbia Records had put up all the money for *My Fair Lady* in exchange for the cast album rights, but although Goddard liked our songs, at the time, he only gave us some seed money to keep us going. Now Ed was asking for more. Perhaps the great word of mouth had gotten out after our gypsy run-though, because Goddard agreed to put up the bond in exchange for the cast album rights in the show.

And the curtain went up.

On the opening night of *Birdie*, Mike Stewart, Lee Adams, and I paced past one another a hundred times with blank stares, like we'd had the life sucked out of us by vampires.

Lee was nervous, but a good-natured nervous— Midwestern nervous: laughing and cracking jokes. He was from Ohio, where, I imagined, if things got tense, he would just walk it off in the cornfields.

I was New York nervous—a cab-can-hit-you-anytime nervous. People-jostle-you, subways-pull-out-of-stations-without-you, elevators-are-crowded, lawyers-overcharge-you nervous. New York nervous.

Compared to Mike Stewart, though, I was serene as a Buddhist monk on Valium.

For those of you who remember the Shubert Theater in Philadelphia, you might recall there was a marble staircase descending into the center of the elegant lobby. Few of you, however, would know that underneath that staircase was a broom closet. Fewer still could know that the closet was dank and dark and contained mops, old playbills, paper towels, and the strong smell of disinfectant. How could one know?

When the opening night curtain fell (to the sound of what I considered minimal applause), I ducked into that broom closet under the marble staircase. I was desperate to avoid the phony congratulations of friends, and I couldn't bear to share the disappointment with my collaborators.

As I pulled the closet door closed behind me, I sensed another presence in the darkness—a breath that wasn't mine. As the sound of the muffled voices of the departing audience members passed outside, I froze.

"Get out of here," hissed a voice in my ear. "It's my broom closet!"

Of course, it was Mike Stewart. Together we waited in that broom closet, tense and silent, until the theater emptied.

Years later, Alan Lerner told me that on the night *Brigadoon* opened on Broadway, only half of the audience returned from intermission. He went back to his hotel, turned off the phone, and considered suicide. Alan usually exaggerated things, but that night, I would have believed him.

The next morning, the reviews were ecstatic and there were lines of people curling throughout the lobby and into the street.

I had never seen anything like this. I had never even imagined anything like this. And I had myself never experienced such a mood swing. Ever. I had, in the past, changed from sad to somewhat less sad or from jittery to a short-lived calm. But from the depths of despair to this?

I stood watching the crowds until I thought I must have looked like an idiot to anyone observing me. But still, greedy for more, I ran inside, and then exited again to the lobby, now carrying a toolbox and posing as an electrician. Then, I borrowed a briefcase and some glasses and did another pass as a lawyer. Parading back and forth, I subtly stole looks at the crowds. I repeated this two or three times: as a plumber, a blasé jazz musician, a crippled person (I do a good limp). Method acting—thank you, Mr. Strasberg.

Funny thing is—I never thought to "play" a composer.

Going out of town meant having the opportunity to make the show better and tighter, and under Gower's guidance, that is what we did. We added an eleven o'clock number (that's a song that comes toward the end of the evening designed to stop the show and send the audience out with the best possible impression) for Chita called "Spanish Rose," which she learned overnight and put into the show, dance and all, in one day. We pruned and shuffled, but nothing too extreme. Things were working.

Except for a number in Act II called "Put on a Happy Face."

We all thought that this was going to be the great Gower Champion second-act showstopper. It took place at the *Ed Sullivan Show* rehearsal while Dick Van Dyke as Albert was setting up microphones and asking technicians for different colored spotlights. Then, as they were shined on his face, Dick, with that rubbery smile of his, would sing our song, and the "stagehands," "cameramen," and chorus would join him for a big dance number.

What happened during the first performance in Philadelphia was something other than we expected. The audience applauded anemically at the conclusion of what we thought was our show-stopping number, and during bows at the end of the show, Dick received the weakest applause of any of the principals.

I immediately said that the song had to go. Dick had to shine.

But Marge Champion had an idea: What if the song was moved to earlier in the show? Dick could sing the song to cheer up two little girls who were unhappy that Conrad Birdie was leaving for the army. Dick was a good tap dancer, and this would show him off in a better light.

I was mortified at this suggestion. I was not long enough out of the Eastman School of Music to be unembarrassed at this: Dick, two kids, and a cheap song and tap number as my virtual introduction to the theater world! I wanted the song cut.

I lost the argument, and the song stayed in, done Marge's way. And, of course, it was an instant hit, Dick became a star, and the song itself became famous.

Things that you think you know—in the theater—you don't always know, but audiences do. As Alan Jay Lerner once said to me, "Audiences have idiot genius!"

Bye Bye Birdie opened on Broadway at the Martin Beck (now the Al Hirschfeld) Theatre on April 14, 1960.

In those days, there were seven major New York City newspapers, and all the critics came to the opening night unlike today when only the *New York Times* matters and the critics are invited to different preview performances. In 1960, they all saw the same show (even if sometimes it didn't seem that way). Opening night parties can be festive or funereal depending on those reviews. I have seen rooms cleared faster than a speeding bullet when the notices are bad.

The first review to come out for *Birdie* was in the *New York Times*. Brooks Atkinson, then coming to the end of his reign as leading drama critic, wrote (and this is indelibly imprinted on my brain), "'Bye Bye Birdie' is neither fish nor fowl nor good musical comedy."

When I heard the review being read, I excused myself and went into the men's room, where I passed out. I remained there until a worried Lee Adams (always there for me) came and found me on the tile floor.

I spent the next week in a darkened room in my ground-floor apartment on West End Avenue, never venturing outside. I felt I'd been found out as a failure—and what made it even worse was that a lovely young girl with whom I had a date on the opening night of the show took pity and stayed with me. But there was nothing in me to give back to that beautiful Florence Nightingale and I felt even wormier than usual. Will she ever forgive me if she should happen to read this?

Not until almost two weeks later did I find out we had gotten rave reviews from all the other papers!

Soon, *Birdie* was selling out. I quickly became used to the stagehands greeting me with a "Hey, Charlie" (was Buddy actually receding into the past now that thousands of playbills read: "Music by Charles Strouse"?) when I went backstage, to the noisy crowds in the cramped lobby of the Martin Beck Theatre, and to the flow of money into my savings account.

Was this it? Was this the answer to it all? Could I finally "put on a happy face"?

CHAPTER EIGHT

Everything's Easy
When You Know How

BYE BYE BIRDIE changed my life.

Because I didn't know much about investing money, every week I simply deposited my royalty check into a neighborhood savings bank that had just opened. I was actually its second customer, and my passbook number was "2." The checks I deposited were very large, yet my lifestyle hadn't changed very much. I still spent every day sitting at the piano, wearing the same old clothes.

I gave some money to Tanglewood to repay them for my scholarships. I also moved into a slightly larger apartment and hired my mother's old maid, Beatrice. Now, in the mornings, when I returned to my bedroom from the bathroom, I'd find my new king-size bed already made, my T-shirts starched, and my socks and handkerchiefs pressed. One morning I awoke to find that Beatrice had ironed my new shower curtain; that's how desperate she was for something to do. I smoked at the time, but my ashtrays were always wiped clean, and telephone receivers put back into their cradles. Still, because I was always working at the piano and I ate most of my meals out, Beatrice wasn't all that busy with housework. She spent most of her time extremely bored and lecturing me about how I should get married, like Lee had.

Lee's marriage had felt like a death knell to me. My work was my life—who had time for a girlfriend? I guessed this wasn't the way I should be, completely centered on myself, yet no one interested me romantically, and I seemed to have a similar effect on them. I kept working to fight off the twin fears of poverty and depression—my familiar childhood companions—and was saddened every day when, after working together, Lee would say, "If I leave now, I can catch the 4:03 to Westport," leaving me alone in my surgically clean five rooms. How I wished I were like Cy Coleman, who always seemed to be out with beautiful girls and who always had his name in gossip columns. He seemed so suave and confident. A fine songwriter, he would confidently play his new songs at parties. I was too embarrassed to do that.

And besides, no one asked me to play.

With the money rolling in, I sent my mother on the around-the-world cruise she had always wanted. When she got back, she reported that she'd met Stephen Sondheim's aunt and the two had argued from South America to Greece about who was the better composer, Steve or me. I felt sorry for Sondheim's aunt, for my mother could be very needy.

After Mom returned, she bleached her hair blond and moved into a small apartment on Manhattan's East Side. She was lonely, so my sister Lila and I persuaded her to take a job. She enrolled in a training program that landed her a position selling neckties at Lord & Taylor. Many of the men who worked in the men's department were gay, and they welcomed her into their group. For the first time in her life, she felt loved and wanted, and I am convinced these men saved her life in a sense.

I would walk into the Lord & Taylor men's department, and all at once, the various clerks would circle about me. "He needs a new shirt!" one would say, while another said, "Here, darling, these shoes are on sale." They'd all fight over who could tend to me, "the one who wrote that new show with Chita Rivera."

My mother—accustomed to being depressed, overweight, and lonesome—understood them, too, and they watched over her, just as I had been watched over when I first went to Eastman. Funny thing about gay men, how they recognize sadness in others.

Mom went on a few dates, and some of the men tried to kiss her. This only mortified her, but she still insisted on telling me about it, in turn mortifying me. And suddenly she seemed impatient for me to marry. I remember thinking, "Could she be ill?"

𝄢

ONE DAY, IN 1961, after *Bye Bye Birdie* had been running about nine months, I received in the mail a beautiful invitation printed on gorgeous stationery with embossed letters. It said that *Bye Bye Birdie* was nominated for ten Antoinette Perry Awards, including Best Musical. The invitation—dinner for me plus a guest at the Waldorf-Astoria—was hard to refuse (today, of course, there's a huge show at Radio City that's broadcast coast to coast, but back then these events had no entertainment, and so the Tonys were only televised on local television), but new to the business, I didn't really understand the significance of the evening. My mind was occupied with a string quartet, and Lee, despite the royalty checks rolling in, still had his job working at NBC Radio writing traffic and weather reports.

(In fact, for years, all of the lyrics for *Birdie* had come to me on NBC stationery, making me wonder how many cars were stuck in traffic and how many people got caught in rainstorms without umbrellas because Lee was busy writing "gray skies are gonna clear up" instead of checking with the U.S. Weather Bureau.)

Because we had opened after the Tony award cut-off date back in 1960, we were eligible for the 1961 awards. My date for the evening was Barbara Siman, a smart, cute, young dancer who was in *My Fair Lady*. We had met at a Christmas party. Barbara wanted to leave early, but it was snowing so badly that she had to stay, and we got acquainted. Lucky me. I asked her out for New Year's Eve, but she was already busy. She was a very popular girl. But I was persistent. We had been dating a while, when the time for Antoinette Perry's dinner at the Waldorf came around.

That night, we ate our dinner and drank our wine, as we watched our friends and colleagues accept award after award: Dick Van Dyke (who, despite having the lead, won in the supporting actor category because it was all governed by billing, and both Dick and Chita were below the title, thus not stars . . . yet!) Michael Stewart, Ed Padula, and Gower Champion (who won twice—for both direction and choreography). By the time they reached the Best Musical category, I had had a lot of wine. Perhaps a bit too much. I was gazing at my beautiful date when she said sternly, "Go up to the stage. They've just announced your name."

We had won Best Musical, and I had heard nothing.

Lee, getting up, said, "Follow me—this way!"

"That way is blocked," I said, picking another route.

Lee pulled on my arm. "You can't go around your way. There's a tray full of dishes."

And still, Barbara was urging us, "Will you two just get up there!"

Then the voice from the podium said, "Apparently, Mr. Strouse and Mr. Adams are not here, so Mr Padula will accept the award."

I looked at Lee, and he looked at me. I looked at Barbara's raised eyes—a look of "Oh my god, how did I ever get into this?"

How had Lee and I ever managed to write a song when we couldn't even manage to sidestep a waiter!

In a time before shows ran on Broadway for twenty years, *Bye Bye Birdie* had a great run of 607 performances and spawned a national touring company, a 1961 London production (once again starring Chita), and countless stock and amateur productions. And best of all, in 1962, it was sold to Columbia Pictures.

Hollywood here we come!

Although they tested everyone, ultimately only two original cast members got to re-create their roles: Dick Van Dyke and Paul Lynde. Lee and I were not really consulted, although the suits at Columbia Pictures made a point to adamantly tell us that there were no Hispanics in America (or South America or Spain, I suppose) who could sing and dance.

"What about Chita Rivera?" we offered, only to be told, "She's not suitable for films." (Amazingly no one even thought of Rita Moreno, who had nabbed Chita's *West Side Story* role and gotten an Oscar for it just before.) Instead, casting went with Janet Leigh in a black wig and dark makeup. Blond Janet Leigh, as Caucasian as you can get, could neither sing, dance, nor speak with a Latina accent. So, of course, she'd been cast in the role of Rosie Alvarez, a singing, dancing, Hispanic spitfire because . . . well, because.

And, of course, Susan Watson wasn't even remotely considered to play Kim. There was only one girl who was ever considered: Ann-Margret.

I was dead set against the casting of Ann-Margret. I thought her wrong for the part—she, who turned the film into a hit; she, who was beautiful, lithe, and sweetly idealistic; she, who became a sexpot when she performed, and who gave the film much of its impact. That's how stupid I was.

Mike Stewart had written the character of Kim as a less-sexy and less-aware young woman. But Mike Stewart was not the writer of the movie. As I found out, when a writer writes a play and the studio pays a million dollars to use it, one of the first things they do is hire someone else to write the screenplay. (It was one of the many unwritten rules of Hollywood I learned very quickly.) But clearly George Sidney, *Birdie*'s director, and Fred Kohlmar, the producer, had their minds made up: Ann-Margret it was. And she sure was something else.

I guess Lee and I were lucky that they were using as many of our songs as they were.

After all, they had changed the plot. We were also unlucky because they wanted another song—a title song. And although this meant a trip to Hollywood and lots of money, I had always loathed our show's title, and although Lee and I had even once, in a desperate moment, tried to write a title song, we had found the experience as pleasant as eating cardboard.

We arrived in Hollywood on a sunny Thursday, relaxed by the pool, had a meeting on Friday with Abe Schneider, the president of Columbia Pictures, and our lawyer Bella Linden that ended at four p.m., which was apparently the end of the working day in L.A. on a Friday. Lee and I had been flown, driven, fed, per diem'ed, and we'd written nothing—just eaten. So, naturally, the head of the studio suggested we take the weekend off and relax.

After a relaxing weekend doing not much of anything, I breakfasted Monday morning in the Beverly Hills Hotel coffee shop. (Lee always liked to stay in his room, have room service, and read a newspaper.) Like my room upstairs, here, everything was pink and green. I picked up a starched pink napkin, and then ate a pink grapefruit served by a waitress dressed in pink. I expected my bagel and cream cheese to be colored that way, too, but no—although the cream cheese was served on a green leaf.

I heard my name called by a bellboy, who said, "Your car's upstairs, Mr. Strouse." As a mark of my new position, I left part of the bagel on my plate.

Lee was already in the limousine with his *New York Times*. (If he were in Antarctica, he'd still find the *New York Times*.) The weekend, having taken its California time about it, had surrendered to the Monday morning smog. We settled back into the soft leather upholstery. There were chilled sodas in an ice bucket, and half a dozen 3 Musketeers bars (my favorite) on the seat facing us. Palm trees nodded, and the hum of tires wapped the pavement in rhythm as we drove down La Brea to meet with the president of Columbia Pictures and hear Ann-Margret sing.

The limousine deposited us on grounds where kneeling Mexican gardeners were manicuring and watering exotic flowers that framed the front entrance to the studio. It was ninety-six degrees outside our car.

Lee and I entered and walked down a cool hallway, passing a dozen gorgeous women waiting to audition or to be interviewed. They all smiled at us, and that was the first time I noticed what I would later call the "Hollywood-Look-of-Supplication," the look that pleads, "Please like me," "I can see how nice you are," and, "Even if you don't hire me for your film, I'll understand, for that's the kind of simple, loving person I am." Nowhere else in the world do people look at you like that with such reverence. I've seen big-time directors cast that look at studio heads; I've seen film editors, orchestrators, reed players, and even stars throw that look at personal trainers, gardeners, or shop owners on Rodeo Drive.

It is, I think, special to California, where fame is short and love even shorter.

As I caught a young woman's eye, I tried to appear sincere, powerful, and humble—all at the same time (a look made famous much later by Bill Clinton). I became convinced she would like to sleep with me but was worried that I was too famous for her. (It was my first movie, and it was clearly getting to me already.)

The day's meeting was in Columbia Pictures' president Abe Schneider's carpeted office. Down the hall, phones were ringing quietly as secretaries took messages, for there was nothing and no one important enough to disturb this royal sanctum.

As a composer, I couldn't help but notice the lawyers were performing a kind of duet: the gross, the net, the mechanical rights; with all due respect, whichever is less. Air-conditioning hummed efficiently as the lawyers continued in muted counterpoint: ". . . royalty from the subsidiaries, subsidiaries from the royalties. . . ."

Abe Schneider spoke, cutting off my thoughts of the beautiful supplicants in the hallway. To his assistant, he said, "The boys can have the large corner office on the second floor," and then, to us, "We want you to be comfortable. You'll have your private bathroom in your office in the writers' building." (Presumably, all non-musical writers had to urinate beside another lowly writer of mere words down some dark hallway.) Then, to someone else, Abe said, "Show them where it is, will you?" before turning to us and saying, "And if there's time, in the afternoon we'll drop by and say hello to Ann-Margret." Then, back to his secretary, "Am I free in the afternoon?" and then back to us, "And after that, if there's time, you guys can start on the title song."

Uh-oh, I'd almost forgotten about that damn title song.

It was only eleven a.m., but I felt exhausted.

Schneider continued: "Someone from the music department will take you over to the soundstage, where we keep the pianos. We have more than fifty different kinds there: Steinways, whatever—you can choose anything."

I told him that any "in tune" piano would do. He stared at me. (Years later, I have learned that saying "any piano will do" is the sign of a loser.)

Lee just wanted to know Ann-Margret's last name.

♪:

In spite of my modest request that "any piano will do," I found myself accompanying he-whose-job-it-is-to-show-pianos in order to select one from a great mass of them on a soundstage. I did, and it was quickly brought over to our office by smiling workmen.

Sure enough, the piano was in tune.

Lee had gone out to get some pencils and pads (he's used to doing these sorts of things on his own, whereas I can never even find a pencil), and so I let my fingers wander idly over the smooth keys.

That damn title song. We had to write a title song, using that title I had always hated.

Looking out from our new office window, I watched dinosaur-like machines slowly sucking at the rusty brown hills. I was starting to feel dizzy, like when I was playing piano in a sky bar in Ohio that slowly turned so that everyone would be sure to get a 360-degree glimpse of beautiful downtown Akron and after the gig was over, my head continued to spin, and I staggered like a drunk through the empty streets.

Only we were not in Akron anymore.

I told myself it was jet lag and got to work.

Lee and I been paid a lot of extra money to write a song called "Bye Bye Birdie." This was to be our second attempt. We'd originally tried to write a title song for the Broadway show, but it turned out that there was no sensible reason to write it, and the end result was so stupid and painful that anyone who heard it writhed in agony and died on the spot. You want to know how bad that song was? If we'd been at war, our government could have used that song to destroy the will of enemy troops to fight.

Oh, yes, the powers that be also wanted the title song to be in the teenage rock-and-roll vein. Lee and I were stumped. We'd farmed the land to exhaustion in "The Telephone Hour," "Honestly Sincere," and "We Love You, Conrad!" There wasn't another "yah yah" or "woo woo" in us. Well, here we were now: dry, dry, dry. Damn the dollars, damn Ann-Margret, damn the limited vocabulary of teenage girls!

But we'd taken the money, and it was time to pay up. I closed my eyes.

Suddenly, a man flew in the room, with red tights, a cape, and a big "S" on his chest. It was the big "S" himself: Satan!

"It's time, suckers," he said. "I got you the hit on Broadway, and now you've got to come up with a song called"—he paused, and laughed a mad laugh—'Bye Bye Birdie.' Your other songs? Oh, I hear them once on a while on the radio—though, really, not that often— but they don't have the classic quality or longevity of Oklahoma!"

That hurt. "Did Rodgers and Hammerstein make a pact with you too?" I asked.

He curled his lips. "Listen, Buddy—"

"It's Charles," I corrected him.

"Charles," he snarled, "there's no way out. A contract's a contract, and besides, your lawyer isn't as big as my lawyer."

That was hitting pretty low, given Bella Linden's height.

Lee returned with his pads and pencils and I snapped out of it. I improvised to him, feeling goofy, but he was used to me:

We gotta write something,

Not too wordy,

Should be purdy,

Rhyme with Birdie (glissando)

Help me, help me, (big flourish!)

I love ya, Lee!

Lee paid no attention to me. As usual, he was calm. Thank God for Lee. He'd taken out his new pencil and pad, so I knew something good would happen. Lee was always there for me.

I paused, and waited for inspiration to strike him. My mind wandered to food, of course. Why did I eat that 3 Musketeers bar? (All right, two of them.) I pushed my thoughts back to the title song.

Desperately I sang (well, half sang, half spoke), "Bye, bye, Birdie" with just one finger plunking whatever keys it landed on, a dopey kind of tune.

"'I hate to see you go,'" Lee said. "I like that."

Lee's my best friend. I'll love him forever.

"'Bye, bye, Birdie,'" I continued singing. "That tune? You like that? You're mad; that's no good."

But Lee just snapped back with, "Gee, I'll miss you so!"

Improvising, I repeated the inane musical phrase, and Lee said without a pause, "No more sunshine," and then, as if by magic, we said together, "They've taken you away!"

We finished. I suppose this is what we paid the devil for. But, really, was it composing?

Ann-Margret sang that title song with a wind machine blowing through her flowing hair. It is still the film's most vivid image, and the song became a hit.

Years later, I was lecturing to theater students at the University of Miami when a young man came up to me afterward and said, "When I heard Ann-Margret sing 'Bye, Bye, Birdie' in the film, I knew then that I wanted to be in the theater."

Humbled, I responded, "You knew then you wanted to be a composer?"

"No," he replied. "I wanted to be Ann-Margret."

𝄢

Having fulfilled our assignment, Lee and I got to go on the set, where we met the stars. Janet Leigh had just broken up with Tony Curtis, so she just kind of moped around. She was gorgeous and sweet as chocolate pie, and I found myself giving her that Hollywood-Look-of-Supplication that I'd hated so in others. I never thought that little ol' me could make her forget Tony Curtis, but still, I tried, acting in turns with a tough-guy routine and then playing up the "serious composer" angle. In any case, she never noticed.

But other people sure did. On the set one day, I casually asked if someone had a nail clipper (I still had that nerves-induced bad habit of biting the skin around my nails), and immediately a lovely young girl wheeled over a tray filled with scissors, clippers, nail files, and knives—enough to do prostate surgery. She was eager and thrilled that she was able to help me, and she had such beautiful legs.

Ah, Hollywood!

𝄢

When the film wrapped, the parties began. First, there was a party given by the studio at a swimming pool, where Maureen Stapleton, who had played Albert's mother, was overheard saying, "I'm the only one here who doesn't want to fuck Ann-Margret!" There was also a fabulous buffet.

Next, Lee and I were invited to the home of the wonderful and wise Ira Gershwin, where he showed us memorabilia and paintings by his brother, George. Ira was warmhearted and loving but offered us no buffet.

Then, I was invited to a party at a famous ex-Hungarian director's house, where there were lots of photographers (I'd never even heard of photographers at a private party), and where, happily, I met Esther Williams for the first and last time in my life. And it was a great buffet.

I'm the top, a melody by Strouse, I'm Mickey Mouse!

Lee accused me of having hubris.

Little did he know, it was just the opposite.

I still had an emptiness inside of me that even the most sumptuous buffet wouldn't fill.

𝄢

In March of 1963, Columbia Pictures had its sneak preview of the film version of *Bye Bye Birdie* in New York. I'd been told to contact Mr. So-and-So when I arrived at the theater. I was supposed to meet Barbara, but I got there first, so I went right to the box office to ask where I could find this Mr. So-and-So. The man in the box office said, "Please wait on line." And so I did.

When Barbara arrived, she asked me why I was on line. I told her it was because the man in the box office had asked me to wait there. Barbara said, "Are you crazy?" and walked right through the glass doors of the outer lobby, where I saw her speaking—with some emphasis—to two men in tuxedos. They immediately came out, saying, "Please come right in, Mr. Strouse."

I loved Barbara for doing that.

CHAPTER NINE

Fight Song

BY ALL RIGHTS, *All American* should have been our second big hit.

It had all the ingredients for success: (1) the same producers as *Bye Bye Birdie* (Padula, in association once again with L. Slade Brown's money); (2) the same composer and lyricist (Lee and yours truly); a very funny book writer (the book being not only everything that is not sung, but also the structure of the show) who, although he'd never written a hit musical, had worked with Sid Caesar on his famous TV outings, including *Your Show of Shows* (Mel Brooks); (3) a great star who had been a showstopper since the late 1920s and was known the world over as the Scarecrow in *The Wizard of Oz* (Ray Bolger); and (4) a film and stage director who had guided hit after hit, including *Annie Get Your Gun, South Pacific, Fanny,* and *Mister Roberts* on the stage and *Picnic, Bus Stop,* and *Sayonara* on the screen (Joshua Logan).

How could it miss?

Even while *Birdie* was running, I had become interested in musicalizing a novel of Vladimir Nabokov's called *Pnin*, about a Russian professor and the seductive effect America has on him when he immigrates to this country. Nabokov, however, wasn't interested in a musical of his book (the only Nabokov book to become a musical, much later, would be

Lolita, written by my future collaborator Alan Jay Lerner). Then Ed Padula discovered a 1950 novel called *Professor Fodorski* by Robert Lewis Taylor, which had a similar theme to *Pnin* if not Navokov's literary polish, so he optioned it and hired Lee and me to write the score. We, in turn, suggested Mel Brooks to write the book. This time, after our suggestion of Mike Stewart to write *Birdie* proved so fruitful, Padula took our advice at once. (This, despite the fact that, in terms of musical comedy experience, Mel had only written some sketches for *New Faces of 1952* and the book for the 1957 flop *Shinbone Alley*.)

Mel and I were friendly acquaintances ever since I had written dance music for *Your Show of Shows*, when Mike Stewart was also on the writing staff. In fact, in early 1961, I introduced Mel to his future wife.

At the time, he was separated from his first wife, Florence, who oddly enough resembled Anne Bancroft. "You know who I'd like to meet?" Mel said to me one day, seemingly out of the blue, "Anne Bancroft." Anne was a reigning star of stage and screen, having starred in *The Miracle Worker* and *Two for the Seesaw*, winning a Tony for each and an Oscar for the screen version of *The Miracle Worker*.

Mel was asking the right composer, as I knew Anne from my Actors Studio days. In the late fifties, before *Birdie*, when I was still supporting myself behind the piano, I had a job accompanying musical theater lectures at the Actors Studio. This was the time when serious method actors were beginning to become interested in performing in musicals, which, at the time, were likely to bestow fame and money. (Rod Steiger had sung in the film version of *Oklahoma!* and even Paul Newman,

Joanne Woodward, and James Dean had tested for roles in the movie.) So there I was at the keyboard again, at the Actors Studio (directed by Lee Strasberg), in order to help teach these actors musical techniques.

At each lecture, an audience of actors (some of them quite well known) would form a semicircle, some upstairs on a rickety balcony, others on chairs below. It was always a full house, and it was fascinating to get this intimate glimpse of celebrity without all the lights, costumes, and makeup. Many of the stars dotting the crowd had their hair down or were fatter than they looked in the movies or wore sunglasses, even inside.

In the center, lit by a spotlight, was Strasberg. The piano was nearby, in shadow. Typically, I would have accompanied Kevin McCarthy and Marilyn Monroe in a scene from *Oklahoma!* or John Forsythe and Anne Bancroft in *My Fair Lady* (years later, Anne still remembered us rehearsing "Just you wait, 'enry 'iggins") while Strasberg dissected the performances stressing that, in the pursuit of "truth," the actor's instincts about dynamics or tempi could—and should—prevail. The orchestra would follow along, he said, as the actors bent and yielded to the flow of his words like wheat in the wind.

I thought he was full of it.

But—hey—it was a job. And, through it, I got to know Anne, Mel Brooks's dream girl.

Once he asked about her, Mel wouldn't let up and so, on February 5, 1961, I decided to end his constant pestering. As Lee, Mel, and I were walking along, trying to keep warm, I decided that we should stop by the Ziegfeld theater where *The Perry Como Show* was rehearsing. I knew that his guest this week was Anne Bancroft.

We watched as Anne, in a gorgeous white dress, rehearsed her number, "Married I Can Always Get." When the applause died down, before I could even make the introduction, Mel marched up onto the stage and walked right over to her. "Hey, Anne Bancroft," he said boldly. "I'm Mel Brooks!"

Now, reigning stars traditionally take up with reigning actors, important directors, or the occasional Wall Street banker, but Anne and Mel took to each other immediately. Who would have guessed that a certified Italian (her given name was Anna Maria Louisa Italiano) would go for the "Jew of Jews" from the *Your Show of Shows*?

But she did, and together, they've leapt into the pages of this memoir—a tiny grace note to their great marriage. (Mel went on to titanic success with *The Producers*, of course. And though in 2005 Anne died, a very brave Mel continued with the musical *Young Frankenstein*.)

𝄢

Josh Logan, then on top of the world as a stage and screen director, had come to see *Bye Bye Birdie*. At intermission, Logan ran into Ed Padula and told him that he was "entranced" with the show.

"Please find a show like that for me someday," Logan was reported to have said.

Ed took the opportunity to tell Logan about our idea, and Josh was intrigued enough to bring the creative team up to his home in Stamford, Connecticut.

The Logans' country home was beautifully landscaped, with a Japanese garden, stunted Japanese trees poking through polished Japanese rocks that bordered a glass-clear brook with smiling Japanese fish gliding by. We met in a renovated barn transformed into a comfortably leather sofaed-and-chaired library that overlooked that idyllically peaceful Japanese garden.

And then, into this scene, as if in a Kabuki drama, leapt the screaming samurai, Mel Brooks!

(Green tea and *gribnetz*—is it any crazier than Dick Van Dyke and Chita Rivera?)

We spent the day going over the story and Mel, who was oddly shy at first, made some good contributions. When we left, Logan still hadn't decided if he would direct the show, but we had more of a sense of what the show could be.

Over the course of several months, Mel wrote draft after draft (well, Mel didn't actually write, he just talked. He had a secretary who would transcribe what he said. Mike Stewart told me that on *Your Shows of Shows*, none of the writers actually wrote, they simply copied down what Mel said), and we began constructing the score. While this was going on, Logan was off in Marseilles filming *Fanny* and when he returned, he committed to our show, which was then called *Fodorski*.

At first, we were thrilled, and began work with Josh in both the country and at his New York apartment.

Josh's home in Manhattan was in a well-guarded, exclusive building called River House. His wife, Nedda (daughter of the famous song-and-dance man Ned Harrigan, of Harrigan and Hart), was elegant, warm, and friendly. She spoke in what used to be called a mid-Atlantic accent and the cultivated voice of a trained actress, which she had been, and all her clothes, whether she was at a party or in the kitchen, were impeccable and designer-made.

Josh told us how, when he and Nedda bought their apartment in this very exclusive building, they thought of all the show business friends they had who might visit, and so asked the broker if there were any "other types" living there besides Wall Street bankers and CEOs. The broker, worried about breaking some discrimination law—and wanting very much to make this sale—got all rattled, turned to the apartment manager, and hissed, "Find me a Jew!" The manager ran out and returned with a puzzled Jascha Heifetz.

As we were writing what became *All American*, Mel would tell Lee and me about another idea he had. It was going to be a movie or a play. Mel called it *Springtime for Hitler*, and it stemmed from an old joke that was often told about a producer who oversubscribed investments in his show, which would only turn a profit if the show failed. Mel would outline it for us scene by scene, regaling us with some of the dialogue, and if we laughed (which we always did), he would take particular note. We were amazed when in 1968 Mel's film *The Producers* was released, and we recognized so much of the story and dialogue from those sessions.

Under Josh's supervision and in between the laughs, we revised our show while a butler served lunch on impeccable china, accompanied by beautiful silverware and starched napkins, all supervised by Nedda. It was delightful. So enjoyable was all this that we hardly noticed when a student from Northwestern University, writing his doctoral thesis on the American musical theater, joined the merry group, quietly taking notes. It was all just a bigger audience for Mel.

As the collaboration went on, it grew more and more apparent that Josh was not seeing eye to eye with our vision of the show. Josh was from a different generation and saw our satirical musical in a more flesh-and-blood way. While Mel treated America and her immigrants in his wacky comic way, Josh was attempting to make the characters more life-like.

Once we started casting for our lead, still other disagreements arose.

Victor Borge, the Danish-American humorist and pianist who was very popular in concert and even had his own one-man Broadway show, was our first choice to play the leading role of Professor Fordorski. Borge was interested, but after we flew to Los Angeles to play the score for him, he revealed that his schedule made it impossible to commit to the project. Next, Ron Moody, the superb British actor (and star of *Oliver!*) agreed to do it but then angered Josh when the news of his casting was leaked to the British press. Mel, Lee, and I couldn't quite see what difference this made, because few people on Broadway read the *Evening Standard*, but Josh was pissed, and that finished Moody.

My suggestion of Zero Mostel, then not the great musical theater star he would later become, went unheeded because Josh could not visualize him as a romantic lead. The same went for Barbra Streisand, whom I brought in to audition. (I had played piano for her.) Josh threw up his hands: "Where am I going to hide her?" (Attitudes toward women were different then, and for Josh, his female leads had to be girl-next-door-beautiful and his men butch-handsome.)

Mel wanted opera star Jan Peerce, but Josh wasn't interested.

One day, Josh announced that he had found the perfect lead: Ray Bolger.

Ray Bolger?

Mel was confused. We all were. Ray Bolger as our little Jewish immigrant? The scarecrow? The guy from *The Wizard of Oz*?

"You think he's the right guy?" Mel asked.

"Oh," replied Josh, "he's perfect for Professor Fodorski."

Well, what did we know? He was Josh Logan. Didn't he cast Mary Martin and Ezio Pinza in *South Pacific*? But deep down, I felt we were on a slippery slope with our miscast star who hadn't starred on Broadway in more than ten years.

And yet, for the first time, the auditions for our backers (the curse of the modern musical) were fun. People cracked up at Mel even before we began, and Lee and I had our new brand of celebrity preceding us. "That's Adams and Strouse. They wrote that cute rock-and-roll show. Smash hit in London, too," we'd hear as we entered the room.

And so we performed *All American* in a string of sumptuous apartments overlooking the East River—Lee and me on piano, Josh and Mel on book, and Nedda on the hors d'oeuvres—and in rolled the moolah.

The rest of the casting fell into place. Ron Husmann and Anita Gillette both gave great auditions, and they were cast as our juveniles. We knew we would be fine there. The stream of bodybuilding types who came in to audition seemed at odds with the general tone, but it was, after all, a football story, and when you think about it, all Josh Logan shows seemed to have one scene with men stripped to the waist. And eventually we had a showstopper called "Physical Fitness."

Eileen Herlie was cast opposite Ray as the American dean of the college who falls in love with him. She was an English actress whose brilliant talents unfortunately didn't include the vocal arts, and with this, I felt the slope become steeper.

Rehearsals began in November 1961 and were held at the Fraternal Clubhouse rehearsal hall on the West Side of Manhattan. Everything appeared to be going smoothly, but in some way, I felt let down after the exuberance of our writing sessions.

Despite my misgivings, *All American* had all the trappings of a hit show: Jo Mielziner (he had designed *South Pacific* among other huge hits) was designing the sets, Danny Daniels was doing the choreography, Robert "Red" Ginzler, who did *Birdie*'s orchestrations, was once again on board, and John Morris, an old and valued friend of mine in addition to being a fine musician, was the musical director and dance arranger.

Lee, in fact, was so pleased that he put the final touches on the first outline of his Tony Award acceptance speech. (Mel wasn't the only crazy one in our group.)

The first inkling I had of *real* trouble was when Ray Bolger debuted his version of a Slavic accent, and Mel turned to me and whispered, "Why is Ray speaking Japanese?"

To say it was downhill from there would be an exaggeration, yet in hindsight, ominous signals had begun to sound.

Josh and I had gotten closer, and I felt that I was beginning to understand him a bit. Josh had been one of the first celebrities to tell the world he was a manic-depressive, which he chose to do on the *Ed Sullivan Show*. One had to admire that about him. But Josh was also immature and needed constant attention. Fortunately, being a very talented artist, that immaturity was part of what made everyone love him. Yet, I saw other sides of him as well, as he was, in turns, forceful, angry, and thoughtful. Josh was smart enough to know how childlike he was and sought someone to restrain him. I loved Josh, but I was too much in awe of him, and too full of self-doubt, to be that person.

With Mel courting Anne and Lee happily married, romance was in the air. Josh strongly advised me to marry Barbara Siman, whom he'd met on several occasions. He not only liked her, but he had also become quite fatherly toward me and sensed I was without an anchor.

I was.

By the time we were in previews in Philadelphia, Barbara and I were seeing each other more seriously. She came to Philly from New York, still in her stage makeup from performing in *My Fair Lady*, having barely caught the train from Penn Station and looking cute and hot and "chorus girl-y." Sometimes she'd say to me, "I know how much you think of Mr. Logan, but I think he's wrong on this or that in the first act." Or something like that.

Ha-ha, I'd think. What the heck could she know, dancing in ballet and a few musicals? I admired her intelligence and her spirit, but I thought I knew a little better, having written the music for a successful Broadway show.

I mean, really. Ha-ha.

Our reviews in Philadelphia were mixed: some good, some very bad. This wasn't a good sign, because only "hit" musicals make money, given the expense of theater rentals, travel, costumes, sets, etc. Broadway shows are usually only profitable when all the reviews are good or when the score takes off on the radio.

The day after the reviews, Josh called for a full-company rehearsal in the theater with the entire orchestra. This was odd, because of the tremendous expense incurred by having an orchestra sitting in the pit with no new music to rehearse. The copyists and the orchestrator were still in their hotels on per diems. Lee and I were not writing new songs (Josh liked all of them, even though I didn't), and Mel was not writing new scenes. And yet, the rehearsal had been called for one p.m.

We were all there at the prescribed hour. The orchestra was in the pit, the cast was on the stage, and the lights were all fully lit by a well-paid union stagehand. Everyone was there.

Everyone, that is, except for Josh.

We all chatted in that forced way—theater-veterans humor, gallows humor—yet sensing the ship might go down. Then it was one thirty, and still no Josh. Someone called his hotel. Twice. Finally, at two p.m., a full hour into all these well-paid people waiting for him, he arrived.

He complimented everyone on the previous night's performance, mentioned that a few changes would be made, and generally cheered up the cast and crew. Then he came into the darkened audience, sat next to me, put his arm around the back of my seat, and said, "What do you think we should do first, Charles?"

It was a little like being on a stormy sea, with the ship taking aboard water and having the captain turn to the busboy for advice.

It would still be years before this busboy felt like a first mate.

𝄢

When I think of our tryout in Philadelphia, I think first of the sea of half-eaten sandwiches, wilted lettuce, cigarette butts, and cups of cold coffee that littered Josh and Nedda's suite at the Ritz-Carlton. We used their room as our headquarters for re-writing, an incredibly stressful process, as the tension and indigestion simultaneously mounted. From the mess, though, emerged a great idea.

There was a dialogue scene of Mel's in which Ray explained to Eileen Herlie where he was from and what his impressions of America were. The scene just wasn't working. Eileen, as the dean, acted like she cared, but the audience certainly didn't. Lee and I remembered the ballad we wrote at Green Mansions, dusted it off, and put it into that scene. Suddenly the scene became interesting and "Once Upon a Time" became one of our most popular songs.

Writing a song for a character that the audience is beginning to know and like—but perhaps not yet love—is probably a songwriter's greatest luxury and opportunity. Three times, I've been given that luxury and wound up with a hit. Here, "Once Upon a Time" fixed a scene that was too long and uninteresting. In *Birdie*, it happened when a songwriter-publisher needed to suddenly be loveable and grown-up after having been a Mama's boy; that was "Rosie." It also happened when a little orphan girl simply needed time to move from one scene to another, so we gave her a dog and a song called "Tomorrow."

Soon after we put "Once Upon a Time" into the show, Tony Bennett agreed to record it. When I played it for him, he loved it, but he wondered aloud what he could put on the B-side of the recording. He told me about a song he did in his act that he didn't think would work on a recording because it had a verse with just a piano accompaniment. He asked my advice, and I said I thought it would be fine. It was a pretty song—something about San Francisco—but who cared? "Once Upon a Time" was going to be the A-side.

Well, "I Left My Heart in San Francisco" took off like a rocket, so there was little airplay of our song to help our show. The one upside of the whole deal was that, being on the other side of the hit recording, we sold many copies. Still, it was never listed anywhere, and few singers sang it at the time. It wasn't until much later, when Mabel Mercer, a great supper club and cabaret performer, started singing it that Sinatra and others paid attention, and "Once Upon a Time" became a well-known standard.

Duke Ellington's orchestra recorded the whole score—a great compliment—including a gorgeous sax rendition of one of Lee's and my most overlooked songs, "I've Just Seen Her."

But our advance in Philadelphia (money already paid into the box office) was slack, and new business was slacker. Despite the new second act showstopper we wrote for Ray, called "I'm Fascinating," audiences weren't buying it.

So the long nights of revising continued.

Certain traits emerge in hotel rooms when rewriting a musical. They're similar to those exhibited by laboratory mice when they're forced to overpopulate a too-small cage: hyperactivity, squealing, fighting, biting, etc. Our late nights at the Ritz-Carlton were not terribly unusual in that respect, and the Northwestern student continued to take notes on each discussion and argument. He was there when Mel and I almost had a fistfight. I don't even remember the specifics, but Mel grabbed me by the shirt collar, raised his fist, and said, "If you don't take that fucking song out of the show, I'm going to kill you." Not wishing to descend to his level, I recall I replied coolly, "Yeah—you and who else?"

On another gloomy January night after a rather dispiriting and sparsely attended performance, we all (including the Northwestern student, who was still writing his thesis) reconvened in Josh and Nedda's suite, grimly trying to figure out what to do next. Suddenly, the door flew open to reveal a woman in a flimsy nightgown. It was Thelma Padula, Ed's wife.

"You have no talent!" she screamed at Mel. "You can't write a line! You can't tell a joke! You can't smell what an audience listens to! You stink!"

For once, Mel didn't have a funny comeback line.

Thelma's husband, Ed, was as white as a sheet and paralyzed with fear. No one in the room but Ed and I knew that Thelma had some mental problems.

I tried to calm her down, but that only fanned her anger as she wheeled on me.

"And you can't write a tune! No one can whistle anything you write!" she continued with her diatribe. "You're going to end up in the poorhouse, and you're going to drag us all down with you! You stink, you have stunk, and you will go on stinking!"

When Lee tried to defend me, she told him that he couldn't rhyme and that he was "an ass without a hole."

Josh tried to hold and comfort her, but she pushed him away and went to an open window. Thinking she might jump, I screamed, "Don't Thelma! Don't!"

The student from Northwestern kept writing.

We tried to get to her and steer her to the hall, but she grabbed a pillow to fight us back. During the melee, one of her breasts fell out of her nightgown. Just at that moment, a very composed, very elegant Nedda Logan came in from the other room dressed in a lovely brocaded hostess robe.

"I thought you all might all like some tea," she said in that even tone of hers as she calmly took in the figure at the center of our scene: Thelma, with her breast hanging out of her night-gown while she brandished a pillow as a weapon. "Why, Thelma, how lovely to see you."

In a flash, Thelma jumped on Nedda's back and began pummeling her with the pillow.

Security, who had been called, finally showed up, pulled Thelma off of Nedda, jostled her out of the room as the house doctor tried in vain to give her a shot. Through it all, the Northwestern student never stopped taking notes.

As Thelma was taken back to her room, I explained to Mel and Lee about her mental condition. Of course, they both sym-pathized, but Lee—ever the writer—also immediately started improvising a scene in which he imagined the head of the drama department at Northwestern reading the young man's doctoral thesis, "Traditions of the American Musical": *Screaming, the producer's wife—breasts exposed—leaped onto Josh Logan as Charles Strouse tried to pull her off. . . .*

Mel joined in, too, and by the time they got through the sketch, it was funny as hell.

Real life wasn't so riotous as we recovered from Thelma's outburst and got back to work.

My memories of those six weeks in Philadelphia are not so much of rewriting but of overeating. Josh was more than a willing partner. An obsessive eater like me, we waltzed nightly through the sumptuous buffets at the Ritz-Carlton, at least when Barbara wasn't around.

I recognized that I was piling in food to cover depression and to fill the emptiness, but, like all obsessive people, I couldn't slow it down. My brother, David, called to tell me Mom was having a small operation at Mount Sinai and not to worry. (Of course, I did.) I also wasn't a particularly good boyfriend to Barbara, as I was moody and depressed after each show, convinced that the two thousand people at the Erlanger Theater didn't really like me.

In time, David informed me that Mom's "small operation" was for stomach cancer. It was now at an advanced stage, but he and Lila had been afraid to tell me because they knew of my fragile feelings.

Barbara continued to be there for me, but I was sad and distracted and unfit company for her: a lousy boyfriend. It was as though the more Barbara tried to understand me, the more I pulled away, reluctant to let anyone enter the black box of my depression with me.

It made me think back to when I was about five or six years old, and my brother and sister had locked me in a trunk. It's a joke, I told myself, and laughed for about two seconds. Then, as the dust fell into my nose and eyes, and I felt the walls closing in on me (this may have been the root of my claustrophobia), I began screaming and hitting the sides. They still didn't open the trunk, and I felt so alone and certain that I'd always be alone. How could there ever be anyone I could really trust?

How could I ever learn to lean on this lovely Barbara? As a dancer, she had mastered the ability to fall backward into a partner's arms. Could I ever be that partner or indeed trust myself to lean on her?

I developed ugly bumps on my back and chest. They were a clear symptom of stress, but I could barely look at them, they were so disgusting. Also, my back went out, and I was forced to wear a brace. Which didn't stop me from overeating.

I went to a therapist, who told me that the hives were a way of sharing my mother's cancer and the back pain was because I was carrying too heavy a load.

My mother was dying, and I felt like my show was failing. I was thirty-four. Schubert hadn't lived much longer. But, what had I done with my life? A couple of lighthearted shows that would soon be forgotten?

Depression, black depression. I was a carbon copy of my mother. Buddy was never going to leave.

♪:

All American opened at the Winter Garden Theatre on Broadway to fairly good reviews.

"Fairly good" in New York does not a hit make.

Ray Bolger, in an attempt to make himself look good and to remind the audience that he was a star who had been in hits, shamed Lee and me by insisting upon singing his *Where's Charley?* showstopper "Once in Love with Amy" as an encore after the curtain calls.

Of course, it got sensational applause.

Two days after we opened, I found myself in Mother's East Seventy-ninth Street apartment—the one she had rented after becoming first a widow and then a blonde. Her cancer had returned. Her physician, Dr. Gabrilove, told me she hadn't long to live, and he recommended giving her an extra-large shot of morphine. "So she goes out on a high," he told me. Grateful, I said yes, and then left the room.

It was a repeat performance of my father's death. I was just unable to bring myself to listen to my mother's coughing and moans. Barbara, now much more than a girlfriend, comforted me, and I began to lean on her in more ways than one.

The only review my mother heard before she died was on the radio. It was Arlene Francis, raving about our songs, the show—everything. I'll always be grateful that my mother died knowing her son did well.

𝄢

It was the worst of times, the best of times. My mother was gone, and I was still weighed down by her depressions, her compulsion for food, and her overwhelming feelings of inferiority, despite having already had a hit show with *Bye Bye Birdie*, and some decent things written about me by the critics. I was lonesome and spent time guiltily with many different girls trying to shake Mom's feelings of worthlessness from my soul. Still, she maintained quite a grip.

I knew Barbara to be a smart, sympathetic young woman, and beautiful, but I'd never stayed long with one woman. I was sure I was destined to be alone, convinced that I'd never succeed in changing the feelings of worthlessness my mother had nailed into me.

I underestimated Barbara.

We talked very long and often about commitment, about her life (which was complex yet becoming more and more centered around me), and her need to move on.

This was "Jewish hockey" at its most intense, but I couldn't just close the door and throw away the key to my bachelor life.

"Then," she coolly told me one night, "it's over."

"What?!" I sputtered, completely shocked. But she stood firm.

"Okay," I said. "We'll get married, but let's not tell anyone for a while."

And she said, "Fine, we'll wait."

And we did.

For about fifteen minutes—until I felt I *had* to call Lee and tell him the news. I mean, after all, it was Lee.

We stumbled toward a wedding date. Invitations were sent, a dress was bought, and then finally, in September 1962, it was the day. A rabbi showed up, and Barbara walked down the aisle as someone played Mendelssohn's "Wedding March." And I fainted.

I woke up in the arms of the headwaiter, completely drenched with perspiration. "Don't worry, sir," he said to me. "Men do this all the time. Women? Never." He helped me stand up, and I stumbled toward Barbara, who had a quizzical look on her face. That's all I remember because flashbulbs were popping all around us and Barbara's father was calling me "son."

In my haze, I looked over at the invited guests and shouldn't have been surprised at what I saw: There among them was the little, fat boy with dark circles under his eyes. He was shoveling a piece of cake into his mouth.

If I was getting married, I sure wasn't about to leave Buddy behind.

CHAPTER TEN

Before the Parade Passes By

IT WAS NEARING Christmas 1963 when Gower Champion phoned me from Detroit. *Hello Dolly!*—his latest show—was in need of a new number at the end of the first act that he said Jerry Herman, the composer, couldn't seem to write. Gower wanted to know if Lee and I would come to Detroit to try to come up with something.

Hello, Dolly! was the brainchild of producer David Merrick, who brought Michael Stewart in to write the book after Michael had done a brilliant job on Merrick's production of *Carnival!* the show he wrote after *Birdie.* After hearing five songs that Jerry Herman (he had already had *Milk and Honey* on Broadway) wrote on spec (that is, without pay in the hopes of getting the job), Merrick famously told him, "Kid, the show is yours!"

Now the show was trying out, and it was in trouble. The Detroit reviews were not good, and more than the usual rewriting and restaging was happening. There was no real reason in the world why Jerry Herman, the most gifted of songwriters, couldn't come up with a new song, other than the fact that we all dry up once in a while, but I called Lee to see how he felt about stepping in as Champion asked. Lee said he would be flattered to try, but only if Jerry wished it. Of course, I concurred.

Assured by Gower that Jerry did, I called the producer, David Merrick, to make travel arrangements. He, too, promised me that the request to write a new song came with Jerry's approval. *Should I have called Jerry myself?*

So it was off to Detroit, where first thing, we bumped into Jerry Herman in the theater lobby. He immediately turned white. (Actually he *is* white, so I should say he turned pasty.)

"What are you guys doing here?" he stammered.

We told him.

He'd never heard of the entire idea.

We swore up and down that what we were telling him was exactly how everything had happened, and we begged him to have dinner with us so that we could lay out the entire sequence of events. We assured him that we would never have come otherwise and guaranteed we'd be on the next morning's flight back to New York.

At dinner, sufficiently calmed, he suggested that we might as well take in the show that evening and that we could meet in the morning. His reaction was everything we could have hoped for under the circumstances. It looked like this tangled situation would unravel just fine.

Of course, what we didn't know was that Merrick had already done this to Jerry, bringing in Bob Merrill (whom he wanted in the first place) to help Jerry with a couple of other songs.

This out-of-town experience was a minefield.

Walking down the hallway of our hotel that evening after the show, a door opened and a hand pulled Lee into a room. Fearing the worst, but being the good collaborator that I am, I followed him inside.

There, breathing hard, was a thin-lipped Michael Stewart. His look was not unfamiliar—I knew it well from our Green Mansions days.

"Whatever you do," he hissed, "don't listen to *anything* Gower says. He'll want to change dialogue, shift a scene, something—I know him. Whatever he says, don't do it, and report back to me!"

I'd never seen Mike like this. Dramatic? Yes, always. But now he seemed almost demented.

"Is something going on?" Lee asked. "We saw the show and enjoyed it—"

Mike cut him off. "Nothing, do you hear? Not a word, not a syllable, nothing—the bastard!" With that, we left the room.

Obviously there was tension in the air, for as soon as we were out in the hallway again, we met Peter Howard, who had been doing the dance arrangements for *Hello, Dolly!* Peter had also been with us back at Green Mansions.

"Have you heard?" he began in a voice I knew he used only when he was about to impart a scandalous bit of news—nothing malicious, but rather delicious, with the ripe aroma of something juicy having *just* happened, and *he* was the only one in the world who knew it.

"Have you heard?" he started again in that same voice. And then he told us that the principal female lead in *Hello, Dolly!* was hemorrhaging. "It's the abortion, of course. It's terrible— the ambulance came, and of course, *he* couldn't go to the hospital with her, and she's still in love with him. Everyone knows about the affair. It's awful! You're not to say a word."

We assured him we wouldn't, but sure enough the word would be out shortly that there was an opera seria going on backstage. I was thankful that Lee and I would not be spear-carriers in this production.

The very next moment, as we passed the open door of a suite, a voice called out to me. "Lee! Buddy!"—I was still Buddy at the time—"I heard you saw the show. Is it too late to talk?" It was a haggard Gower Champion. Granted, it was now about two in the morning, but I'd never seen him looking so poorly—Gower, who was always impeccably fitted out, and whom I imagined would not wrinkle his clothes while having sex.

Figuring that no one was talking to anyone in the Feydeau farce of a hotel (that is, Gower obviously wasn't speaking to Jerry, Mike wasn't speaking to Gower, and David Merrick, of course, speaks only with the big guy up there), and knowing that we'd be on a flight back to LaGuardia first thing the next morning, we figured no major harm would be done if we stepped into Gower's suite for a moment.

Our main thought was just not to step on anyone's toes, so we exchanged pleasantries and chatted for a few minutes. Then, Gower asked us if we thought we could write the song ending the first act. "It should have the verve and complications of 'The Telephone Hour,'" he added.

Though flattered, we said immediately that Jerry had not been informed of our being here, and that under the circumstances, we couldn't do anything.

"That goddamn Merrick," Gower spat. "Divide and conquer. Son of a bitch. I should have known." He said he would talk to Jerry, straighten all of that out, and if he could, would we then stay a few days?

We both gave affirmative shrugs. Gower was coproducer as well as director and choreographer, so the request had an official ring to it.

Also, he didn't look good.

Also, it was flattering being asked.

He phoned us the next morning, said it was okay with Jerry, and would we see the show again that evening?

We would, we did, and we came to an unexpected conclusion after seeing it again: Jerry's song wasn't the problem (as a matter of fact, that was a wonderful song, which would end up in another part of the show) but something in the structure of the scenes that was undermining the moment in question.

We asked if we should follow this line of reasoning; it might turn out to be a new song, or it might turn out to be a dead end. Gower said go to it and gave us his copy of *The Matchmaker*, the published play on which the musical was based, and the stage manager's latest version of the most up-to-date musical book.

Lee and I hid out, reread Wilder's original play, and read and reread Mike's adaptation. Then, with Gower's encouragement, we cut some sections from the Wilder play, pasted them right into Mike's version of *Hello Dolly*, and revised some parts of what Mike had already written. By inventing a few sequences, rewriting others, and connecting one scene with another, we restructured the end of the first act. Our key discovery was a line from the original play about having to grab life "before the parade passes by." We said, "That should be the song title," and Gower agreed and instructed us to go back to New York to write a song titled, in fact, "Before the Parade Passes By."

Before we left Detroit, Gower confided to us, "You've saved the show." (Theater people are known to be passionate, excessive, and generous.) "I knew all along that it was this structural aspect of the play we had overlooked," he said. (Theater people also like to take credit for every idea.)

We left for New York feeling satisfied we had done friends a favor and, more importantly, acted like professionals. We were neither offered, nor did we ask for, any remuneration.

As Gower requested, we did write a song called "Before the Parade Passes By." We sent it to Gower (and Peter Howard), but nobody ever called, so we were surprised when we heard that Jerry was adding a song called "Before the Parade Passes By" to the show.

Our surprise was accompanied by complicated feelings. It was our complex reconstruction and our song title, though it was based on a phrase of Wilder's. But we were the ones who had found that phrase, and the reconstruction of the first act of Mike's book was ours as well. If they were going to use it, I half expected Merrick to—at the very least   send us an ashtray (we didn't smoke any more, but you know what I mean) or a note.

Right before *Hello, Dolly!* opened in Washington, D.C., I called Lee, and he confessed he felt a little low, too, but he said, "Forget it. You know how people are."

I swallowed my pride, called Washington, and asked for Mike at rehearsal. The stage manager called him to the phone, and I said, "Hi, Mike. It's Charles."—I was slipping in "Charles" now, a result of my wife's sense of how a successful composer should speak and dress—"What's happening?"

Quickly he said, "I can't talk now. Here's Gower." And handed the phone over.

Gower spoke right away. (Was he standing right next to Mike at the phone?) "Buddy, how are ya'?"

"Fine," I said. "I'm just calling because—well, we never heard from you. Was our work of any help? Oh, by the way, happy holidays."

The rest of the conversation went like this:

GOWER: Didn't Merrick tell you?

ME: No. What do you mean? About what?

GOWER: Oh—we're putting in Lee's and your changes tomorrow night.

ME: Oh, no kidding . . . swell. I wish someone had—I mean, it would have been nice to . . . y'know—it was a lot of—you're using *all* those scenes and the restructuring? The song, too?

GOWER: No—Jerry loved the idea, but he wanted to write his own "Before the Parade Passes By." You'll have to work this all out with Merrick.

ME: Work *what* out? I didn't call to work anything out. I just wanted to . . .

GOWER (*a little waspishly*): I can't talk now, I have to get back.

It was Christmastime. Chestnuts were roasting all over Manhattan, but why was I starting to feel like I was the one over the open fire?

Maybe Gower was worried that I was asking for something, but I wasn't aware of asking for anything but appreciation. Maybe Gower and Mike and Jerry had given that to us, and it had slipped by us somehow. But hey, man, maybe the people who need it most (and I certainly was one of those who do) are the ones who don't seem to get it. There's something wormy about having to ask for appreciation, anyway.

I called Lee again, and he simply reechoed his low opinion of people in general: "Nobody loves you but your mother."

But it wasn't love I wanted, it was something more concrete: maybe a little respect, a little recognition for what we had done. We had rewritten and structured parts of the first act and written a song called "Before the Parade Passes By." Jerry had used the song title we'd given him. Had he used my music, too?

This should have been the point at which our lawyer would have entered the picture, except that our lawyer Bella Linden also represented Mike Stewart and, as such, was not allowed to be involved. Bella further warned us (whose side was she on, anyway?) that it would cost a fortune to proceed because Merrick had a battery of lawyers who would surely tatter our attempts to receive proper restitution.

I responded, "We'll inform them of legal action we'll take as though we *were* lawyers. Hell, we've written musicals—surely we can compose telegrams as though we were trained lawyers."

Bella said we couldn't because that was against the law, and we began to feel more and more that she was not on our side.

Nevertheless, that's exactly what we did. Using an address and name of a friend, we sent a letter written in our impression of legal language, the secret being to repeat every word with another, more formal sounding version of the same word: "You shall cease and desist performing, using, or in any manner exposing to an audience any and all material claimed to be written, rewritten, suggested, or composed by Lee Adams and Charles Strouse. We shall expect a written or telegraphed response to the undersigned by twelve noon (p.m. EST) or we will be compelled to consider further action." It was all bullshit, except for the truth of what Lee and I actually *did* write.

Hello, Dolly! became the hit it was in part because of written, rewritten, and newly structured material of Lee's and mine. As a result of our legal letters, we ultimately did wind up participating in a monetary way in *Hello, Dolly!* but, more importantly, were given half ownership of the ASCAP performing rights in "Before the Parade Passes By."

Real lawyers told me years later that, if we had actually enlisted a lawyer, we would have received much more money. But, for us, the emotional satisfaction was by far the more valuable currency. And, plus, we had fun collaborating on our "lawyer's letters."

𝄢

After *Hello, Dolly!* Gower and Mike didn't talk with Lee or me for years. My silence with Mike finally ended when his partner died; I sent him a note of condolence, and we made up.

Then, when *Applause* was in Baltimore and Gower came to see it, we found ourselves in the same bar, not speaking to each other. Gower's agent, Lester Shurr, came over to me and said, "Why don't you two say hello?"

"I don't think Gower wants to speak to me," I answered.

"Try it," Lester said.

I did, and we embraced, and Gower said, "Why have we been fighting all these years?" and I said, "I don't know," and he said, "The whole thing was David Merrick's fault in the first place."

𝄢

For truth's sake, and because sharing one's memories, like sixteenth notes in midflight, is a peculiar pleasure of mine,

because some hurt remains in my heart, and because antago-
nisms, in time, are known to turn into love, I want to clear up
a belief among musical comedy buffs that Lee and I wrote
Hello, Dolly!'s "Before the Parade Passes By."

We did not.

We did, however, write a song called "Before the Parade
Passes By" based on material we unearthed in Thornton
Wilder's play, and we restructured Act I of the musical *Hello,
Dolly!* so that the song fit. We gave all that work to Gower dur
ing and immediately after that hellish week in Detroit. And so,
of course, we did have an important hand in *Hello, Dolly!*

But Jerry's "Before the Parade Passes By" was his own—
reinvented with his own pencil in his own room. We have long
since kissed and made up, and my admiration of Jerry Herman's
talents has grown, not diminished, through the years.

End of film, music up, roll credits.

Funnily enough, years later, the tables were turned when
Arthur Laurents called Jerry Herman to write a new song in
place of one Richard Maltby and I had written for *Nick &
Nora*. Arthur hated the one we had written.

But then again, he hated everything. Stay tuned.

CHAPTER ELEVEN

There's Music in That Boy

ON MAY 1, 1962, *All American* was still running (or hobbling, as the case was) at the Winter Garden (it closed on May 20) when the *New York Times* announced that Hillard (known to his friends as Hilly) Elkins would be presenting a musical version of *Golden Boy* starring Sammy Davis Jr. Ever since the late 1950s, Hilly Elkins had been my manager. For a few weeks, he was vice president of GAC, a then-new theatrical agency that later morphed into ICM, where we had done our inauspicious and humiliating backer's audition of *Birdie*. For a while, Hilly worked at William Morris and handled Sammy Davis Jr. In the early 1960s, perhaps spurred on by the success of *Bye Bye Birdie*, Hilly decided to become a theatrical producer, and so, one day in the autumn of 1961, he called Lee and me with a proposal. "Would you like to write the score for *Golden Boy*?" he asked.

Lee knew the play. "About the Italian boxer who plays violin?" The story was that of a young Italian boy longing to be a classical violinist who sees that boxing might be his only way out of a Depression-era ghetto. The high cost of escaping such a life, though, was the risk of injury to his hands, making him incapable of playing the music he loved so much.

I knew it, too—originally written in 1937 by Clifford Odets, *Golden Boy* had been first performed by the Group Theatre, a prestigious left-wing theater company.

"John Garfield played the title role," I added, "but did you know Garfield's real name was Garfinkle?"

Lee corrected me. "It was actually Luther Adler who played the role. But who played the female lead? Molly Picon?"

"It was Frances Farmer! Then she married Odets," I answered.

Our aimless banter might have gone on, but Hilly interrupted us. "I have in mind another Jew to play Joe."

We waited.

"My Jew is . . . Sammy Davis."

And then there was silence.

At that moment, Sammy Davis Jr. was arguably the biggest star in America. He made sixty thousand dollars a week in Las Vegas as a solo performer and probably double that amount in recordings and films (and those are 1960 dollars). Hilly told us that, as soon as he caught Sammy's act at the Prince of Wales Theatre during a "midnight matinee," he saw the clear parallel between the struggle of a Depression-era Italian and a young black man of the sixties. The plot would move to 1960s Harlem and revolve around an interracial relationship (Sammy was, in fact, married to May Britt, a beautiful white Swedish actress), which was still a crime in certain states. The script just needed some minor tweaking to make this happen, like changing the last name from Bonaparte to Wellington. It was a story ripe for updating, Hilly said, and Sammy was the man to help us do it.

Hilly had it all worked out save one thing. "The one drawback to this plan," Hilly had to admit, "is that I have not told Sammy Davis anything about it."

This, I was to learn, was typical Hilly Elkins. He was a

man who often drove down New York City streets in excess of seventy miles an hour and ran up such large bills at restaurants and department stores that bill collectors were afraid to call in, scared they'd then receive nothing in payment.

This gambit with Sammy Davis Jr. perfectly fit Hilly's style. But that was just the beginning.

Hilly then contacted Clifford Odets, who had as much interest and experience in writing a musical as a rabbi (whom Clifford resembled) would in swimming the backstroke in Syria. But when Hilly told Clifford that Sammy Davis had agreed to do it (which, of course, he hadn't yet), Odets (I imagined his eyes opening and closing to the sound of a ringing cash register in the manner of Donald Duck) said, "Well, in that case, I will write the book." Clifford, it turned out, was usually hard up for cash and, as he told us many times, never felt deeper joy than when he held five hundred dollars cash in his pocket—a leftover from Depression days. This was actually a sentiment he and I shared.

Right after *All American*'s opening in March 1962, Lee, Hilly, and I flew out to Los Angeles to meet with Odets. For several days, the four of us talked over the many aspects of the project. Then we returned to New York to write the songs while Clifford began procrastinating about the book. Hilly tried to get Odets to come to New York, but he was afraid of flying, so we would always go to L.A. Like Mel Brooks, Clifford preferred to talk things through, instead of actually putting pen to paper. But whereas Mel always produced material after his "talk-throughs," it seemed to be that these endless conversations were just Clifford's chosen technique for procrastination.

Nonetheless, with Clifford in place, and Lee and me signed up, the final phone call was to Sammy himself.

"Clifford Odets will write the book, and those two guys who wrote *Bye Bye Birdie*"—which was currently being filmed in Hollywood and was becoming the most-performed musical in America—"have agreed to write the score."

Sammy, as it turned out, had always wanted to be taken seriously as an actor. He had already appeared in one Broadway musical in 1956 called *Mr. Wonderful*, but the show was a slim excuse for Sammy to do his nightclub act. Now, he wanted to be an "actor." Frankly, I don't think he listened as Lee's and my names were mentioned (Tony Newley and Sammy Cahn were his musical deities), but the names Clifford Odets and Group Theatre obviously sang in his ears. They carried the kind of cachet that would make him a real actor.

In any case, Sammy said he would consider doing *Golden Boy* only if he could approve every song Lee and I would write.

This was the kind of agreement I would advise any author or composer to decline. (There should at least be an acceptable payment so that the authors' time is not wasted in the event a temperamental star turns everything down.) And yet, Lee and I accepted, despite not receiving such a cushion. It was a decision that resulted in an odyssey that carried us from Manhattan to Los Angeles, from Atlantic City to Lake Tahoe, to Harlem gyms, late-night parties, and Las Vegas steam rooms—all in pursuit of Sammy's approval of a song.

Traveling so much wasn't the best situation for a newly married man as Barbara and I spent much of the beginning of our married life in the close company of Sammy's agents,

Sammy's bongo player, the Will Mastin Trio, and Sammy's secretary, valet, and bodyguard.

Nonetheless, we leaped into the fray. We were commanded to see all Sammy's shows and spent much of our time waiting around in places like the Sands Hotel and the Copacabana nightclub waiting for him to review our material.

Once, when Sammy was performing at Harrah's casino in Lake Tahoe, we were waiting to play him a new song. The owner of the casino, Bill Harrah, asked me what I thought a suitable closing-night present might be for Sammy. He was being paid sixty thousand dollars a week at the time, but Bill informed me that a closing-night present was a tradition, and that he wanted to do something as a thank you, given the great business Sammy brought in.

I suggested a Rolls-Royce, but Bill said, "I gave him a white one—a convertible—last year. So he already has two."

Taxing my mind, I thought hard to come up with the best present I knew: a Steinway concert grand, and that's just what Sammy got that year.

Sammy sure made a lot of money, and he spent a lot, too. I often saw him drop thousands of dollars at photography shops. He had a need to use everything to the maximum—his money, his vocal chords, his body. It was enough to make one wonder if there'd ever be enough things, girls, and applause for Sammy to fill that void. Frankly, Sammy and I had a lot in common, for I craved those same things—girls, applause, material things. But I'd never surrender my money to buy stuff, for then there would be nothing left. I'd be empty. Would I ever lose that fear?

But for now, it was parties all the time—opening-night parties, closing parties, parties after the show, parties in

Sammy's suite, in local restaurants, even once at a bowling alley. They were excessive but seemingly necessary. After all, Sammy had to unwind!

The idea was that we'd be there with him so that, in the afternoon the day after a show, we'd have meetings in which Sammy could let us know his thoughts about which scenes or songs he'd want written or rewritten. Lee and I didn't write the pop-style, Sammy Cahn–Jimmy Van Heusen songs that Sammy could metamorphose into jazz-sounding phrases, and Sammy wouldn't/couldn't/didn't want to sing our versions of "black." He was bursting to do his 1960s cabaret jazz, so that automatically set us at odds, trying through all these meetings to meet somewhere in the middle.

The problem was that Sammy was often more than an hour late to these meetings. And even when he got there, he was sure to be in a bad mood. In time, we figured out that it was because he felt guilty for being late, so we learned to say, "Glad you were late. We got here late too." That always made him feel better, and we would get to work.

At these meetings, I wasn't always sure of what Sammy said, but everyone else seemed convinced of how perceptive and brilliant he was—that is, until one day when, after a meeting, Lee asked me what Sammy had just said. "I honestly don't know," I replied, so we went and asked the set designer, Tony Walton, what Sammy had said. Tony wasn't sure, either.

We told Hilly of our problem, and he said that, for the next meeting, he would set up a tape recorder, and then hire a stenographer to copy down everything. That way, we could go over the results at our leisure.

At our next meeting, a tape was set up and a stenographer copied everything down. It came out to twelve pages of densely written notes, full of "you're right" and "of course" and "I've been thinking the same thing," said by us. But when we read the words Sammy had spoken, we still didn't have a clue to what he was talking about.

Later it became clear: A smart and charming yet very conflicted man, Sammy often began a sentence in the polished tones of Oxford, but finished it in "down home" talk—a verbal tic that made following his sentences a bit confusing.

𝄢

One night at the Sands, Sammy said he'd meet us at one a.m. in the nightclub. Lee and I both got to the nightclub at one. Sammy wasn't there, but he'd been late as much as three hours in the past. We had to be patient; he hadn't signed his contract yet, even though he assured us that he'd play in *Golden Boy* at twenty-five thousand dollars a week against 15 percent of the gross (a third of his usual weekly salary). So we (Lee, Hilly, Clifford, and I) were still chasing him all over the country to audition the songs and scenes for him.

So we got there that night, and we waited.

And waited.

At three a.m., Sammy came in, trailed by a dozen people.

Surely they weren't all going to stay while we performed.

They were.

We played and sang a new song we'd written. Sammy loved it! He hugged me. He hugged Lee. Several members of his entourage hugged one another.

I didn't believe anyone. But then again, I never believed anyone who told me they'd like something I'd written. On the other hand, I have had no problem believing people who have told me they hated something I've written.

Sammy, having heard the song just once, started dramatically performing it to the chorus girls gathered around the piano. As always, as soon as I was playing a song or phrase, Sammy would start riffing—that is, changing rhythms and melodies. I knew he felt he was interpreting the song in his own way, but I couldn't help feeling hurt. He couldn't have absorbed it all so quickly, and so he wasn't really singing *my* song. I was taught to play notes correctly—to practice, absorb, to polish. Aware that the jazz and African music from which Sammy came grew from different roots, I shouldn't have felt hurt when he changed things to express his feelings, but— hey—I had to express my feelings, too.

No one ever corrected Sammy. His own musical director, George Rose, always just went along, and even later on, when we were in production, my musical director, Elliott Lawrence, had the tendency to just "bop" along with him. I supposed Sammy was more than entitled. He was not that many years removed from the indignities of black vaudeville and from his tenure in the U.S. Army in which, he told me, white soldiers insulted him and urinated on him. Now he was a great star, very rich, and married to a famous white actress. So on I played.

The girls "oohed" and "aahed" as I sat at the piano, sweating out the song, in which we had tried so hard to have every word crystallize the feelings of a young black man in the ghetto and to have every note capture his history and hurt. It was hard to focus now, though, as I was wanting to sleep with at least three of those girls in attendance and was thinking about Barbara at the same time and it was awfully hard to remember what the song was supposed to be all about.

But the hugging continued, set in time to my playing and Sammy's singing.

"Oh, and don't worry, Sam," Hilly said between hugs. "We'll have the new scene tomorrow afternoon." And then there was more hugging and kissing.

Except there was no new scene. Clifford had still not been able to find it in his heart to make changes from his original 1937 version of *Golden Boy*, much less find his way to Las Vegas. And Sammy was starting to get antsy, making noises that if the show wasn't ready, he'd have to move on. The fact was, Sammy's agents would have done almost anything to keep him from signing to do *Golden Boy*; such were the commissions from the immense salaries they'd miss out on from nightclubs, TV shows, and movie gigs.

But "not to worry," Hilly assured me in an aside. Apparently, Odets had just arrived the night before—someone drove him, he still wouldn't fly—and he was "right at this moment" in his hotel room finishing up the new scene. "He'll have it ready tomorrow," Hilly swore. We just had to make sure that Clifford stayed glued to his typewriter until he was done.

The next day, I woke up at six a.m. lying in a circular bed that sat on a raised platform in the center of a large room, exhausted and disoriented. It took me a minute to remember where I was. I looked at the red velvet ropes surrounding the platform—the kind that hold back patrons in a fancy restaurant. I was in bed alone, so just who had been prevented from getting into bed with me that night was unclear. *Of course*, I recalled, as the wheels of my still-sleepy brain creaked slowly into motion. *This is Vegas*. The air-conditioning had turned the room frigid, and even though there were thick blackout curtains over the windows, something in the weight of the air told me it was very hot outside. As I rose from the fog of sleep, images started to slip into the vacuum of my mind: Sammy Davis. Lee. A musical about a boxer.

This schedule and lifestyle were starting to take a toll on me.

I was up at the crack of dawn in order to call Clifford and pick up the finished scene. Oh, but I couldn't yet, the poor guy was working all night—didn't he have enough problems? Money (none), a seriously dependent daughter, and although I had thought that all the *commie* business was over, Clifford was still blacklisted in Hollywood as a former lefty. So I figured I'd kill an hour and let him sleep in.

I dressed, went to the lobby, heard the hum from the casino, and wandered in. It was six forty-five a.m., and it was true: No one slept in Las Vegas. Then I saw Clifford at the "21" table. He had a heavy growth of beard, his hair was wild (it always was, come to think of it—a leftover from his enfant terrible days), his eyes alarmingly bloodshot. For one ridiculous moment I thought, *Poor guy, he's been up all night writing*. Then I remembered how, when we were collaborating back at his house in Beverly Hills, he'd talked of so many things: the Group Theatre, what it felt like the first time he actually had five hundred dollars cash in his pocket, the guilt he felt for selling out to Hollywood. He'd also talked excitedly about flying in Danny Kaye's private plane to Las Vegas to, as he told us with feverish excitement, "hit the tables."

Hilly had given him a thousand-dollar advance the week before to get him to come to Las Vegas. *Could he have been up all night gambling it?*

I went to him. "Cliff, how's the scene coming?"

He turned to me. "You won't believe it, Charles," he said, his eyes wild as he took a slug from the drink at his side. "I was down seven hundred dollars. But I'm getting even now. I'm on a roll." Clearly there was some personal inspiration for the character of the drunken writer in his own play *The Country Girl.*

I called Hilly, who told me that, fortunately, Sammy was still on the golf course (in Las Vegas, one begins playing golf at around five a.m. in order to finish before it gets too hot). After eighteen holes, he'd come back, and then sleep until three or four in the afternoon. "We'll get Clifford to a typewriter before then," Hilly said. Hilly never seemed to panic.

However, at four p.m., there was a call from Shirley Rose, Sammy's secretary, who said Sammy wanted to see me in the fitness room soon as possible. What could it be but trouble?

I arrived there to find the place heavy with security. "Mister, you can't go in there," said a guard who stopped me as I entered the room.

"Sammy Davis Jr. wants to see me," I said modestly but proudly.

The guard spoke into a radio phone, from which he apparently got a word of confirmation, as he looked at me with more respect, turned to the other guard, and said, "It's okay. He's Sammy's composer." I wasn't quite sure I liked the appellation, but it got me past the guards and through a hostile wall of tourists.

Once downstairs, a bodybuilder in the undressing area looked me up and down. Stupidly, I said, "I'm Sammy's composer."

"You'll have to take off your clothes. They're having steam," he said, handing me a towel and pointing me toward a locker. Next thing you know, I was in a steam room, naked, sitting with Peter Lawford and Sammy Cahn as Dean Martin lay dreamily on a rubbing table and Sammy was cracking up at something Frank Sinatra had just said. Frank hit Sammy on the arm—what seemed to me a little too hard—and said, "Now *that's* funny!" I had obviously just missed the joke.

"This is Charlie, my composer," Sammy said.

"He better do something about that rum-tum," said Frank Sinatra.

I don't like to be called Charlie or to have my rum-tum bandied about. Plus, I'd had enough with Sammy always pinching my stomach as he walked by, telling me to take off weight. *Et tu*, Sinatra?

Sammy had called me there to talk of things he could have easily talked about in a phone conversation: "When did Odets arrive in Vegas?" and "Is the new scene ready?" I suspected that he just wanted to show off his new Broadway toy, so I sat there and steamed.

After a while, everyone departed and I was left alone with Sammy. I asked him if he didn't think Sinatra hit him too hard on his arm just to get him to laugh at some joke.

Sammy turned to me and said, "I owe Frank. When I lost my eye in that auto crash, Frank was the first one at the hospital and made sure I was well taken care of."

By five that evening, Lee, Hilly, and I were in Sammy's suite. Clifford walked in, newly typed script in hand. It was almost exactly the same scene as it was in the original play. Fortunately, that's what Sammy had wanted to do in the first place: to be a serious actor, so he liked it, and life went on.

𝄢

Lee and I had wanted to write a musical true to the pain, hopes, and culture of African Americans. So, naturally, everyone involved in the writing was white and Jewish—except Sammy, who was only Jewish. However, Sammy had a constant entourage of four people of color: George Rose, his musical director, and George's wife, Shirley, plus a bodyguard, and a valet, who was always on hand to refill Sammy's glass with Coca-Cola (and, I suspected, something else). Often joining the group were Sammy's mother and father, Will Mastin, Sammy's uncle, and May Britt, Sammy's sweet and adoring blond wife. Usually hovering nearby were at least two agents from William Morris.

To add to the mix, a trio of Brits—director Peter Coe (he had just had a great hit with Lionel Bart's musical *Oliver!*), set designer Tony Walton (then still married to Julie Andrews), and lighting designer Richard Pilbrow—joined the group. Peter and Sammy (Sir Cold and Prince Hot) hit it right off. We had English, Brooklyn, and Harlem accents being spoken, in addition to my own attempts at sounding "street" when singing the songs—in what Sammy called "the worst colored accent I've ever heard."

Being unquestioning of Sammy was the solution we all naturally fell into. There were usually so many people around that to argue with him would have surely stunned his court. Besides, he was so affable, entertaining, and in a rush that one couldn't help feeling like an intruder.

To add to this crazy situation, in the summer of 1963, a little more than a year into our work on *Golden Boy*, Clifford Odets died of cancer at the age of fifty-seven. It was as if he had timed it to warn us of the icebergs ahead.

We'd not known he was that sick. We hadn't seen him in a while and had merely heard he was under the weather. Lee and I were devastated; despite all of his idiosyncrasies, we had grown to love him. A man of strong political beliefs, Clifford had gone to Hollywood, been swallowed up, and spit out. Clifford felt he had sold out. But Lee and I had fond and sad memories of the mornings in his house in Beverly Hills, when he'd boast about the celebrities he knew and about the young starlets who had committed exotic sexual acts upon him. That he would lavish his sexual boasts on two thirtyish songwriters—he, who had captured the poetic language in downtrodden Americans—made it all the more poignant to us. He was a very needy man these last years of his life, and we would miss him a great deal.

Clifford's death left a void in our lives and a void in the show: It wasn't yet completely written. A few weeks before he died, he had handed his second draft of the book to Peter Coe with the admonition to not treat it as a classic.

"If you think something should be changed," Clifford told him, "change it. It's as much your baby now as it is mine."

It was decided that Peter, Lee, and I would write whatever Clifford had not yet finished. We felt up to the challenge. After all, Lee and I had spent time at gyms in Harlem with Sugar Ray Robinson and Gil Clancy soaking up boxing lore. Surely we had picked up enough information to fill in the gaps.

𝄢

It had been months, but in the winter of 1964, finally, we arrived at auditions. Sammy was there with his merry men (a group that had now grown in size to ten). Hilly was there with his beautiful assistant and masseuse of the moment. Peter, Richard, and Tony ("the Brits") were there, as were Lee and I ("the boys").

A single work light dimly pierced the darkness of the Majestic Theatre. (If one asked for more light, there'd be an expensive union electrician's call, which we wanted to avoid at all costs.) Here I was, living the life people dream of. So why did I still feel like I was just a small planet held in the gravity field of a very large star?

The stage manager came out and announced the first person who would be auditioning. A portly white man walked out on stage, and we all quieted down as the pianist leaned into an arpeggio. The man sang: "Niggers all work on de Mississippi, Niggers all work while de white man play." Lee and I sank in our seats as the man continued singing with the clearest diction I'd ever heard, each "Lawd" and "dat" and "Hebbin" as cleanly articulated as if a vocal coach had just drilled him.

You couldn't help but notice a silence and ominous rumbling from Sammy's army as the man sang. After the man left the stage, someone pointed out to them that that was the original Hammerstein lyric to "Ol' Man River," yet I couldn't help but feel our group had lost a bit of togetherness.

We were breaking new ground here. This was to be the first Broadway musical in which a black man made love—not merely touched hands—with a white woman. (Except for *Otello*, the list wasn't too long for opera, either, and at the time, in many states, interracial relations were still illegal.) To score this pivotal moment, we had written the song "I Want to Be with You." Lee and I happened to believe this is how all the so-called races would end up one day, and that is what we worked toward in *Golden Boy*: that each character would be conceived as a *person*, not as a black or a white.

It was, as we found out, unacceptable to many in 1964.

Race relations played out behind the scenes as well as on the stage. For example, if I was drinking a Coke, Sammy liked to take a sip from the same glass. He confided in me that it was really a test to see whether I liked black people.

He never told me whether I passed.

𝄢

Casting was almost complete. Blond, beautiful Paula Wayne, with her smoky jazzy voice, would be playing opposite Sammy, and legendary jazz singer Billy Daniels would be playing the satanic Eddie Satin, but we still had a few roles to fill. Sammy particularly admired a distinguished actor named Juano Hernandez, who had appeared in such films as *Young Man with a Horn* and *Ransom*. He was one of the first Puerto Ricans of African descent to become a major star in the United States. Sammy wanted him to play the father, a role with one song to sing.

There were hidden meanings in Sammy's request. He was convinced I'd turn down Juano for the same reasons

149

Sammy and I usually tussled: the conflict between my desire to have the notes sung properly and Sammy's desire to improvise. Sammy had an exceptionally fine ear, but with it came a jazzman's eagerness to improvise on the music—even before he knew the notes thoroughly. As any composer would, I wanted him to learn the notes as I wrote them. There is a fine distinction between someone who "hears" the music first, then makes jazz of it, and someone who doesn't quite hear it the first time. I could feel a growing divide between us, and although I tried very hard to erase it, I couldn't help but feel my whiteness. I wanted to appease Sammy, but I could only do so without abandoning standards or sucking up.

When someone's had no formal music training, that person's hands can land on the keys where and when they may and "do their stuff." With talent, it comes off as playful, syncopated, infectious—jazz!

But not always necessarily good jazz. I've heard jazz musicians who make great faces while they're improvising and who wear fantastic hats during concerts but who do little else.

In fact, jazz is not unlike composing. Indeed, as Stravinsky said, "The best composers 'mishear' music." Same with jazz players—their hands may play it "wrong," but then they shape something from the mistake. And of course, any jazz player who hears things "too well" faces the danger of being a hack.

Thus, I tried to make it clear to Sammy that I did not want my music performed à la Verdi by rote, that I did want the jazz spirit. But, still, I wanted it be *my* music that was ultimately sung, more or less.

My mother and me at the beach. Her smile
hides the depths of her depression.

Three little urchins from Amsterdam Avenue:
My adopted sister, Lila; my brother, David; and
me grinning in front.

At the Eastman School of Music, toiling on the
Great American Sonata.

Receiving my Bachelor in Music (or a "B.U.M.,"
as Pop jokingly called it).

That's me and Lee Adams sitting in the house. Friends forever.

Gower Champion, me, Ed Padula, Mike Stewart, and Lee.

Martin Beck
Theatre

PLAYBILL

a weekly magazine for theatregoers

BYE BYE
BIRDIE

The *Playbill* from the Martin Beck Theatre production of *Bye Bye Birdie*, featuring our stars Chita Rivera and Dick Van Dyke. Or as I liked to call them, *Tequila* and *Milk*.
PHOTOFEST

Me congratulating Dick in the dressing room of the Martin Beck Theatre on opening night of *Bye Bye Birdie* in 1960. In addition to being a brilliant performer, Dick is a lifelong friend.
BILLY ROSE THEATRE COLLECTION, THE NEW YORK PUBLIC LIBRARY FOR THE PERFORMING ARTS, ASTOR, LENOX, AND TILDEN FOUNDATIONS

Chita at *Birdie*'s opening night party. The very first time I heard her sing, I knew she was a star.

"The Telephone Hour." Gower Champion at his most imaginative.

Chita Rivera (as Rosie) and Dick Van Dyke (as Albert) in the 1960 Broadway musical *Bye Bye Birdie*. PHOTOFEST

Tommy Tune and Ann Reinking in a publicity shot from the 1991 *Birdie* national tour. PHOTOFEST

The "grunts" of *All American*. Stage director Josh Logan always liked some beefcake on the stage. Broadway, 1962.
PHOTOFEST

Me and my beautiful bride on our wedding day in 1962.
STROUSE PERSONAL COLLECTION

Me and Barbara at the Songwriters Hall of Fame in 2007. She's just as beautiful as the day I met her.
STROUSE PERSONAL COLLECTION

Sammy Davis Jr., our *Golden Boy*. Broadway, 1964.

Sammy and Paula Wayne in *Golden Boy*, the first interracial couple in a musical to
kiss onstage. Lee and I both got death threats for being part of breaking the taboo.

Lee, Sammy, and me on the opening night of *Golden Boy*. It took a long time to get there.

Lee, Clifford Odets, and me. Clifford never lived to see *Golden Boy*.

Linda Lavin and Bob Holiday in 1966's *It's a Bird . . . It's a Plane . . . It's Superman.*

Jack Cassidy (who played Max Mencken) and his wife, Shirley Jones, pose with Mayor John V. Lindsay at *Superman*'s opening night party.

Rehearsing. (Can you tell I'm trying very hard not to look at her ample cleavage?)

Lauren Bacall in "But Alive," from 1970's *Applause*. I tried to stay out of her way or I'd get trampled on.

Bacall at the center of the action in "Fasten Your Seat Belts." Joe Mankiewicz, the screenwriter of *All About Eve*, was the one who suggested the phrase as a musical number.
BILLY ROSE THEATRE COLLECTION, THE NEW YORK PUBLIC LIBRARY FOR THE PERFORMING ARTS, ASTOR, LENOX, AND TILDEN FOUNDATIONS

A photo of Andrea McArdle, our brave Annie, and me backstage in 1977, autographed by the star herself.
STROUSE PERSONAL COLLECTION

Andrea McArdle, Sandy, and Reid Shelton.
MARTHA SWOPE

The *Annie* crew: Me, Martin Charnin, and Tom Meehan pose during the show's D.C. tryout.
PHOTOFEST

Another Annie: Sarah Jessica Parker with her Sandy.
MARTHA SWOPE

Bernadette Peters, Carol Burnett, and Tim Curry in the 1982 film version of *Annie*.
PHOTOFEST

Me with Ed Koch at the *Mayor* cast album party in 1985.
STROUSE PERSONAL COLLECTION

The *Rags* family: Joe Stein, Teresa Stratas, Lee Guber, Joan Micklin Silver, and me.
MARTHA SWOPE

We three *Rags* writers: Joe Stein (book), me (music), and Stephen Schwartz (lyrics).
MARTHA SWOPE

The brilliant Christine Baranski, the sly Joanna Gleason, and the gorgeous Barry Bostwick in 1991's *Nick & Nora*.

A Diva Sandwich: me between Dorothy Loudon and Chita Rivera.

Composing is frightening.

Paul McCartney, Joe Raposo, and me.

Carolee Carmello and John C. Reilly rehearse for the *Marty* cast recording in 2007.

A new show: *The Night They Raided Minsky's.* There's Bob Martin, Susan Birkenhead, and Casey Nicholaw, with yours truly at the piano.

When they were little: Ben and Nick, with me and my gorgeous wife.

Me with the grown-up Ben at our former home in Connecticut. (Ben's the good-looking one.)

Barbara and me with (left to right) Nick, Victoria, and Will at home in New York City,
December 2007.

With these thoughts in mind, I was determined not to play *der musik professor* with Juano. If the man could carry a tune and keep reasonable time, he would be in. Fortunately for me, the song the father had to sing (a song that was ultimately cut on the road) could even be partly spoken, as long as it was done with good rhythm and musicality. Think Rex Harrison.

Problem one: Juano lived in Puerto Rico and would be in New York for only one day to meet and sing for us. Problem two: There was no *us* to sing for. Everyone except me would be away—nightclub dates, doctor appointments, meetings. But I was assured that everyone already thought Juano was a great actor. The quality of his singing was up to me to decide.

Okeydokey, I thought. *Sammy wants him, and I've got all the goodwill in the world. This should be a rubber-stamp formality.*

This being a musical, naturally, problems arose.

When I met Juano, he greeted me with a pronounced croak. He sounded like a tenor in orgasm. As nicely as I could, I asked him if there was something wrong with his throat.

"Oh, you noticed," he wheezed, pushing his words through what sounded like a half-closed trumpet valve.

I shrugged, hoping to convey something along the lines of "Yeah, it went through my mind."

He snorted. "I didn't think you'd notice, but I'm glad you did. I was hit in the throat by a tennis ball right before coming up here, but I didn't want to cancel the trip to meet you. I assure you it will be all better by rehearsal time."

At least that's what I thought he said. It was hard to understand him when each word sounded like a sixteen-pound baby being forced out of a very small womb.

But I knew that if I dropped the ball now, Sammy would be convinced I was simply trying to hire "my kind" of singer.

"Do you think you could sing a few notes for me anyhow?" I asked.

"Oh," he grunted, "I can assure you I sing very well."

I didn't know what to say, but I tried again. "Could you try something, anything? Just so I'll know you can carry a tune. Would you mind?"

He was a very distinguished actor, and I was starting to feel as if I were asking Sir Laurence Olivier if he could play the bassoon.

"Not at all," he hissed amiably after a few rounds of my prodding.

With effort, he squeezed from his throat the few notes I played for him on the piano, from the tune of "Happy Birthday." In all fairness, he did sing them in tune, and when I included a four-bar introduction, he came in at the right time and in correct rhythm.

He said, "Charles, I promise you, this thing"—he pointed to his throat—"this unfortunate accident will all be cleared up by rehearsal. I have done many singing roles in Puerto Rico. You're not to worry. Tell Sammy I will see him soon."

At least, I'm pretty sure that's what he said. We embraced and he left.

Later, Hilly phoned to check in. "Well, how was he?"

I explained it all to him.

"Whaddaya think?" he asked. "Can he sing it?"

"When the bruise in his throat clears, I don't see why not—he's performed musicals in Puerto Rico."

Hilly paused. "It's a lot of money. I'm still not all

financed." He was probably thinking about how much it would cost to fly Hernandez back up to New York first class, and to pay off his contract if it didn't work out. "Charles," he continued, "can he sing it?"

I thought for a moment. Sammy wanted Juano—wanted him badly. If he didn't get him, he was going to blame me, convinced that I wanted William Warfield to sing the role so that everything would sound like an oratorio. I had to put my chip down. The wheel was spinning.

"Hilly," I said, "he can sing in tune. He has adequate rhythm. If nature does its thing, his throat will get better. It was only a tennis ball, after all. I mean, who was he playing, Arthur Ashe? I say we go with him."

Juano Hernandez was signed, and rehearsals began one month later, on April 27, 1964.

When Juano appeared for his first day, Sammy stopped everything to greet him. "Hey, baby. How you been?" Sammy said, before quieting down the cast to introduce Juano to the rest of the group. "Everyone—shh! Hold it down. This is Mr. Juano Hernandez." Everyone applauded.

Juano smiled and said, "Hello, how are you?" Only it came out "Aieeo, ow ahr roo?"

Maybe he *had* been playing tennis with Arthur Ashe.

There was a hasty conference between Juano, Sammy, and Hilly. The only words I caught were "etter erry zoon."

I hid for the rest of the day. The actor Roy Glenn was eventually hired to play Sammy's father.

ℐ:

Finally, we started in on rehearsals in earnest. Choreographer Donald McKayle now owned the dancers, and Peter Coe went off with the actors while musical director Elliott Lawrence got started with the singers. (Budgets allowed performers to be hired for a single stage discipline then. There were dancers, and there were actors. Today, of course, everyone doubles.)

My choice of Elliott Lawrence continued the conflict with Sammy. I believed Sammy's musical director, George Rose, didn't have the experience to organize a large, complicated musical like this one. Elliott was white, George was black, and it's only now, writing this, that I look into my heart and ask whether race could have played a part.

But Elliot had conducted *Bye Bye Birdie,* and I knew of his understanding of actors and singers, his experience conducting rehearsals, and more importantly, that he could make music really swing. Truth be told, I went back even further with him than *Birdie.* When I was at Eastman, a group of us used to listen to his orchestra broadcasting from Philadelphia. Not only did his band swing, but—gosh—he'd used a French horn and an oboe in his arrangements, too.

One of the young women in the chorus, Lola Falana, proved to be mesmerizing, and soon she was sharing the stage with Sammy in "Don't Forget 127th Street," a number in which Sammy was at his best, singing, dancing, and joking. The number made bitter fun of Harlem and had some of Lee's sharpest lyrics.

Back when we were writing the show, Clifford had insisted that we cut the song, saying that our protagonist, Joe, wouldn't tap dance after performing an intensely serious scene with his father, who was begging him to give up boxing. Peter agreed with Clifford, but Sammy felt he needed a "Sammy-Davis-song-and-dance moment," and so it stayed in the show. In my mind, I argued both sides, and I felt uneasy when I heard the song rehearsed. It was patently vulgar music with no compositional subtleties.

As it turned out, it was the number that consistently stopped the show.

$$\mathcal{9}\colon$$

We began our out-of-town try-out on June 25, 1964, at the Shubert Theater in Philadelphia, where the reviews were mostly about Sammy's fine dancing and singing. Little was said of his acting.

Our score was well received (after all, Sammy had to be singing and dancing *something*), so Lee and I were mentioned often, though hardly with the accolades saved for the likes of Leonard Bernstein, which was my fantasy. (Years later, when I wrote with Alan Jay Lerner, he said to me, "I'm content as long as the reviews don't humiliate me.") Tony Walton's sets were deemed "brilliant." Peter's staging was appreciated as well. But everything else seemed a letdown. The critics said that it adhered too closely to the play.

Still, as Sammy and the blond Paula Wayne sang "I Want to Be with You," clung to each other and kissed, audiences were really affected.

Reactions were both passionately positive and negative. On the negative side, the amount and the venom of the mail received at the theater frightened us. We were forced to acknowledge a fear that our show seemed to inspire in many people. Two policemen began accompanying Lee and me to our hotel each night, as there was the worry that written threats might turn into something worse.

Representatives of the NAACP were becoming anxious over the racial divide that seemed to be growing over this "kissing" issue, but Sammy and Elkins met with them and convinced them that the tour should continue. And thank goodness, because we were sold out everywhere we were booked. Through some kind of immaculate conception, it seemed that Hadassah and the NAACP had given birth to the perfect child.

I tried to enjoy the full houses and the nightly parties after the show at the Variety Club (a kind of halfway house for performers located on the mezzanine floor of the Bellevue-Stratford Hotel). There was lots of dancing, new friendships (i.e., *show business* friendships: intense, exotic, and short lived), and almost no serious talk between Lee, Hilly, and me of what should be rewritten in *Golden Boy*. It was impossible to have Sammy adhere to a rehearsal schedule anyway, and because he was in almost every scene, it was best to leave everything as it was. Anyway, it was party time, and there was no ducking our social obligations, as Sammy always acted hurt if we didn't come. He hugged Barbara and me whenever there was anyone around and broke up laughing at things I said, even at things I said that weren't particularly funny. He pulled at me like a vacuum, and shamefully, I wanted to be sucked in though I tried to maintain a smile of integrity. William Blake would have recognized it:

There is a Smile of Love,
And there is a Smile of Deceit,
And there is a Smile of Smiles
In which these two Smiles meet.

I couldn't help but feel like I'd become a white Uncle Tom.

𝄢

Then, a stranger drama began. Sammy, who wanted to be taken seriously as an actor, reread the reviews and asked that Peter Coe be fired. Sammy wanted new scenes, new songs, and a new director. And he wanted *me* to do the firing, probably because Peter was my friend (he would later direct *Flowers for Algernon* in London, which I had written with David Rogers). Sammy made it clear: He didn't want to see Peter again!

In a role for which I was particularly poorly cast, I went to Peter Coe's room and told him that Sammy wanted to do the show with a new director.

Peter said, "Well, do you know what you have to do, Charles?"

"No," I replied. "I don't know."

"It's clear," Peter said flatly. "We have to fire Sammy."

My guilt was overwhelming; I knew what Peter meant. Were we supposed to surrender our vision in order to feature a star who could sell a product to a willing and eager audience?

Then I thought of the time we'd already put into *Golden Boy*. Lee and I had been working on it for more than two years; Peter for just four months.

"You may be right," I said. "But I can't go along with that.

Every bit of advance would drop out, and the show would probably fold."

Peter looked at me. "I'm sorry," he said, and then in a scene I could never write, the cold and imperious Peter Coe started crying.

"Me too," I said sadly, and left the room.

Immediately, a carousel of new book writers and directors spun into the Shubert Theatre, where the massive crowds clamoring for tickets didn't care who was doing what as long as the *sepia Jew* showed up. The sold-out shows were largely benefits for Negro and Jewish charities, but they resulted in huge royalties—more money for Lee and me than we'd ever made before. And all it took was for Sammy to walk onstage for the whispers to start: "Look! That's him acting!" or "See, that's Sammy dancing!" They were even thrilled when Sammy cracked up at a missed line or something went wrong onstage.

We still had to replace Odets, so Sammy and Hilly settled on William Gibson (author of *Two for the Seesaw* and *The Miracle Worker*, a great friend and admirer of Clifford Odets's but someone who had never written a musical before) and William brought on Arthur Penn, a sensitive director of actors, who, as far as I knew, had also never directed a musical.

We had our new team, but I couldn't help feeling that, somewhere along the way, my harmonies and rhythms were washed and dried out in that bright-shiny-money-back-guaranteed washing machine known as Sammy Davis Jr.

Was it my imagination, or did it sound like he could have been singing almost *any* song?

𝄢

By the time the show got to Boston, changes were going in every night. New scenes and songs would be rehearsed and thrown in as quickly as possible, but this left us with two different plays playing at the same time. Boston audiences saw a first act in which a character appeared and then never showed up again or a character who would show up in the second act who had never been seen before. And we made all these changes in front of sold-out houses. During the four months we tried out on the road (Hilly had booked the show in Detroit after Boston) our leading character, Joe went from a violinist to pianist to medical student. Songs were thrust in and taken out even faster. Songs called "Poppa," "Playground Songs," "There Comes a Time," "There's Music in That Boy," and "Under the Marquee" were heard in Philadelphia and discarded before the ink was dry on the music.

I still struggled with giving suggestions and musical direction to Sammy, so I went to Bill Gibson, who was known to jump up on the stage and correct Sammy whenever he changed a single word of the script.

Bill, an avuncular man, put his arm on my shoulder. "Charles, perhaps there's something you dislike in Sammy that you're not admitting to yourself, and maybe he can tell," he said. "I suggest you give him no notes for a week, then go backstage and discuss things like a friend."

So I did that for a week and then, after one matinee, I casually dropped by his dressing room.

As I walked in, Sammy said, "What's up?"

"Oh nothing," I said. "I just wanted to chat with you about the—"

"Get the fuck out of here!" Sammy said.

And I wondered why we had problems.

When Lee's wife grew ill and he had to return to New York, I was forced to write a new song on my own, lyrics and all. I remember sitting with Arthur Penn as he told me what he wanted from this new song. It was to come at the eleven o'clock spot. Arthur wanted a song that would reflect not only Joe's devastation and embitterment, but also his vow to not let it happen again, to close himself off to being hurt. Arthur also wanted the song to be general enough so that, when sung by the rest of the cast in a reprise, it would have social relevance. I found it impossible to cram all he wanted into one song. We argued back and forth until, finally, Arthur (who had been nonchalantly smoking a cigar while reading the *Times* as I was becoming more and more passionate) said, "Just write the fucking song!" It startled me, as I had never heard him speak that way.

As soon as he left the room, I sat down and wrote "No More."

"I ain't bowin' down
No more . . ."

I was very proud of that song.

When Martin Luther King Jr. came to see the show in Detroit, Sammy introduced him to me. Dr. King told me that "No More" was his "all-time favorite." I made sure to send him a signed copy of the music.

When we got to Detroit, *Variety* reported that the show was "almost disastrous." Sammy's voice was hoarse and strained, and we had horrible sound problems in the Fisher Theatre. There was even a *Variety* story in which Hilly Elkins was quoted as saying that "the critics could not dislike it anymore than I did."

Still the revisions came. At one point, I just didn't know what to do next. I told Hilly that he had to get another composer in to do some work because my well of music was running dry. It had just been tapped too many times for more revisions. I suggested Jerry Bock, who was not only a friend of mine but also a composer of great quality who had written the music for *Mr. Wonderful.* Surely he would know how to write for Sammy. But they wouldn't let me quit.

Even when the show was in previews at the Majestic Theatre on Broadway, we kept rearranging the score. The Act I finale ("Yes, I Can!") became the first song in the show and then was cut before the opening. Another song, "This Is the Life," was moved from the beginning of the second act to the end of the first, as we moved "While the City Sleeps" to the beginning of Act II. We even put in a brand-new song ("Can't You See It?") the day of the opening. Herb Ross (who had come in to help stage the musical numbers) choreographed it that morning, and when Sammy performed it for the first time at the matinee before the opening, he was accompanied just by piano, bass, and drums because there was no time to orchestrate it.

When the show finally opened October 20, 1964, Sammy was near total exhaustion, but we were as ready as we would ever be. Sammy received raves, while critical reaction to the show itself was mixed. Still, the public wanted to see Sammy and we began selling out and, somehow, without realizing it, I'd become a full-fledged member of Sammy's entourage. I couldn't put my finger on any particular moment when I was sworn in, but before I knew it, the headwaiter at the Copacabana would smile at me and snap his fingers for the front table when I walked in the door, and Cindy Adams would chat me up at parties, asking me for column items. At a party, Jule Styne actually got up from the piano and let me play a song. I played "I Want to Be with You," from that pivotal moment in *Golden Boy*. (Afterward, Billy Rose, the famous, not-too-tall impresario, said to me, "It's nice, but you should write something more like "It Had to Be You." We didn't lack for good advice.)

I made a point not to wear my old sneakers as much.

Governors, senators, Hollywood stars, B'nai B'rithers, and NAACPers all flocked to the show. Marlon Brando came one night. So did Elizabeth Taylor. Martin Luther King Jr. came back again to hear "No More."

Sammy had a special hole made in the curtain so he could peer out. He was stage-struck by the celebrities filling the seats. He photographed everyone backstage, and everyone was photographed with him. It was the perfect case of a celebrity being endlessly fascinated by other celebrities.

I'm still very proud of the show and many people think that it's Lee's and my best score. It contains what remains my most personal song: "Night Song." I wrote it thinking of the evenings I'd spent as a kid laying in Central Park, feeling very lonely as I gazed up at the sky:

> *Summer, not a bit of breeze.*
> *Neon signs are shining*
> *Through the tired trees.*
> *Lovers walking to and fro.*
> *Everyone has someone*
> *And a place to go.*

That song said it all.

Golden Boy was nominated for several 1965 Tony Awards including Best Musical and Best Actor in a Musical for Sammy. But this was the year of *Fiddler on the Roof*, so we didn't win. The New York show ran as long as Sammy was in it: 569 performances. In 1968, with some more revisions, Sammy (who had divorced May Britt that year, following his affair with dancer Lola Falana during the run of the U.S. show) took *Golden Boy* to London's West End where he met a statuesque dancer named Altovise Gore. They married in 1970, adopted a child, and were still together when Sammy died in 1990.

𝄢

Sammy and I actually got to know each other as people for the first time on a flight to Selma, Alabama, on March 7, 1965. We were going to march for civil rights. Barbara had begged me not to go, as there had been a shooting of civil rights workers, and the Alabama National Guard had been called out. New arrivals were being met by Sheriff "Bull" Connor, with his six-guns at the ready. But it was what I believed in, so I went.

It was one of the bravest things I'd ever done—not because I might have been shot while protesting injustice, but because we had to fly on a three-seat chartered plane to get there, and I was morbidly claustrophobic.

Shortly after takeoff, as I sat in the buffeting darkness of the plane, the acute claustrophobia took over. I felt helpless and weak, as if I had been thrust into a small prison with no light. My breath came in short gasps, and I tried to imagine how a poor, imprisoned black man might feel. It didn't help.

The name of the charter company was Harlem Air, and the pilot was black.

"You sure you know all about those buttons and switches, baby?" Sammy joked, in the style of Amos 'N Andy, and then whispered to me, "We sure to crash. Negroes ain't meant to fly." That wasn't helping my fear either.

What did help was the bottle of cognac between us, which we managed to drink half of. No one worried about whose lips were on the bottle now, as the three-passenger coffin cut through the darkness. We'd die together or live to march for civil rights.

We landed after midnight, and sure enough, there was Sheriff "Bull" Connor with his six-guns. He just stared at us, and Sammy turned almost pale. It didn't scare me at all. After that flight, nothing could.

We walked across the deserted terminal building. There was a very old black man mopping the floors. He looked up as we passed, not quite believing what he saw. "Hey, man," he said to Sammy. "You Sammy Davis?"

Sammy looked around with mock concern. Then, speaking in his best "white" voice, he said, "FBI—special assignment. I'm made up to look like him."

For a split second, the man continued to stare, then slapped his thigh, exclaiming, "By God! Who'd believe he'd come here?"

Nobody (that is, none of the white establishment in Selma) would permit a speaker for civil rights the use of any auditorium or platform, so a black undertaker loaned a number of coffins for the occasion. It was raining, and they were placed together in a field, where we, in turns, stood, sat, or knelt during the speeches, prayers, and entertainment.

Kneeling next to me was Leonard Bernstein. I said to him, "What are you doing here?" He turned to me and asked the same. Truthfully, I felt flattered being in the big time. It was only when leaving the fields of coffins that I became frightened. Surrounding us were the troops of the Alabama National Guard. I was never scared "Bull" Connor would shoot me, but these soldiers stared at us with a disturbing kind of blank loathing. They appeared to be eighteen years old or so, had helmets and poor complexions, and their rifles hung loosely down, cradled in that way hunters do. Casually sure of their power, there was no need for them to aim or appear tense. But they sure made me tense.

My bleak hope was that I'd be shot along with Lenny, an event that would make the papers and drive up ticket sales.

A few years later, when Lee and I composed songs for Hanna-Barbera's animated *Alice in Wonderland* called *What's a Nice Kid Like You Doing in a Place Like This?* I asked Sammy if he'd lend his voice for the character of the Cheshire Cat.

He said he would. "I guess I owe you one," he added.

"What for?" I asked, confused.

"You went to Selma for me."

That was the only time I was able to express anger toward him. "I didn't do it for you," I said harshly. "I did it for the cause, and you better know it!"

Sammy looked surprised when I said that, and I still feel angry about it.

𝄢

When I think of vintage Sammy, he's in Detroit performing to a white audience in a nightclub—tie untied, cigarette in one hand, Coke in the other. He is relaxed as he ad-libs (except he isn't really ad-libbing). His hair is straightened, his makeup on, his ghetto jewelry flashes under the lights, and his very expensive shirt is carelessly opened at the neck.

All of this changed upon the assassination of Dr. King. Then, Sammy started wearing his hair in an Afro, traded the glitzy shirts for dashikis, and limited his sexual appetite to girls with darker hues.

Thinking about this change makes me remember a young black singer whom I accompanied in the mid-fifties. She sang great jazz, was featured in *Life* magazine, and had a salary of more than two thousand dollars a week. When we'd travel to hotels, she'd tip the white bellman ten dollars for opening the door for her. *She'd show them* was her attitude.

When we traveled to Miami Beach and stayed at the Americana Hotel, she wasn't permitted in the lobby or even to cross the pool area to get to the public beach before dusk. I wouldn't leave the hotel without her, though she tried to get me to. I told her I'd rather keep her company, anyway. Actually, because of her background (she was raped by her father, she had a drug addiction, and her boyfriend—who was also her manager—was often away), she wanted me to stay with her day and night. Because she wasn't allowed anywhere in the hotel, we wound up in her room.

When she would order room service, she would get two of everything: the steak *and* the lobster. She would eat a bit of both and then leave the rest on the plate. *She'd show them.* How this would have horrified my mother. Like the good boy I was, I usually ordered the tuna salad plate—the least-expensive thing on the menu.

No wonder, years later, Sammy had all that gold jewelry. I could dig that now.

No tuna salad for him.

CHAPTER TWELVE

You've Got Possibilities

IN 1966, MY SON BENJAMIN was born. Dressed in hospital greens, I watched his birth at New York Hospital, trying to share at least a portion of Barbara's pain and fear. It was beautiful, and I cried. Benjamin was pink, and he arched his back as he stared all around the room.

All my self-centeredness seemed to be switched onto another track. I felt useful comforting the tiny Ben when he was colicky and getting up at three a.m. to change his diaper. I carried him and rocked him, sometimes for hours. *Happy daddy.*

But even as I rocked him, other thoughts intruded: Could fatherhood ever be as fulfilling as composing music? A blank music sheet in front of me is an entire mysteriously exciting life. Or what about hearing a full company rehearsing my music? Could parenthood compare to that? Playing with Ben's alphabet blocks and throwing a ball with him didn't seem to do it.

I think about what the great composer Kurt Weill said to his wife, actress-singer Lotte Lenya: "You know you come first. Right after my music."

I have to admit, it was a relief to throw myself into my work.

My first project post-Benjamin stemmed from a connection Lee had made back in 1964, a few years before Benjamin's birth. As a former magazine editor, Lee had worked with Bob

Benton and David Newman. David's son had come up with the idea of doing *Superman* as a musical, and they had come to us to see if we'd be interested. Bob and David were both smart and funny as hell. They were young and connected to the "hip" world. We all clicked.

Lee and I thought the idea was terrific. Superman had been around in comic book form since the Depression, when Jerry Siegel and Joe Shuster, two Jewish guys from Cleveland, came up with *The Man of Steel*. Superman immediately caught on—the world needed a hero just then—and even generated a radio series. It wasn't until 1948 that *Superman* made the transition to the big screen as a Saturday morning serial. When television came into being, *Superman* found a new niche, in the guise of George Reeves. Now, ten years later, we were sure the man of steel was ready to save Broadway in a musical. So, Bob and David came up with a story, and Lee and I started work on a few of the songs.

Before we could go too far, of course, we had to get the rights to the characters that had become so famous in the DC Comics. We put our trusty lawyer, Bella Linden, on the case, and she negotiated a contract, which included a clause (required by DC Comics) saying we were not allowed to use the word "Superman" by itself as a title. Thus, our show was first called *It's Superman* (one of our song titles), before we switched the title to *It's a Bird . . . It's a Plane . . . It's Superman*, which we all thought was catchier.

When we had enough material, we took the show to David Merrick.

At the time, David Merrick was sitting on top of the world as a producer. From *Fanny* to *Gypsy* to *Carnival*, Merrick had hit after hit. Of course, we had had our dealings with him on *Hello Dolly!* and we knew how devious and Machiavellian he could be. But Merrick liked the idea of *Superman* as a musical, and asked that we work up a contract for him to produce it.

It seemed odd, then, when Bella called Merrick to discuss the details of such a contract, and Merrick said, "What contract? What are you talking about?"

I called him, and asked him point-blank if he had changed his mind.

"I never spoke to your lawyer," Merrick told me. "She must be having her period."

Such were the bizarre ways of David Merrick.

Then again, commitment in the theater is tenuous and short-lived. It requires a gambler's instinct, the wisdom and strength of Solomon, plus the artistic eye of the entire Medici family.

Next, we took the idea to Harold Prince, who immediately went for it and gave us a contract.

In 1965, Hal Prince was (and still is) a Broadway phenomenon. He had started as a stage manager under George Abbott. In fact, Hal was one of the stage managers of a show I played auditions for in 1952, *Wonderful Town*. A few years later, along with Robert Griffith (another stage manager on that show), Hal began his producing career with a bang with *The Pajama Game*. He went on to produce such hits as *Damn Yankees, West Side Story, Fiorello! A Funny Thing Happened on the Way to the Forum*, and *Fiddler on the Roof*.

Unquestionably successful at producing, what Hal really wanted to be was a director. He wet his feet on shows like *Baker Street, A Family Affair*, and *She Loves Me* (the latter he produced as well). He was now working with John Kander and Fred Ebb on a musical that took place in Berlin before WWII. The project had them stymied, so *It's a Bird . . . It's a Plane . . . It's Superman* came across his desk at just the right time. Perhaps he needed to get away from the Nazis and do something fun.

It was casting the role of Superman himself that proved to be the biggest challenge. He had to be tall, dark, and handsome, look good in tights, and have the muscular physique so familiar to comic book readers (these were the days before everyone went to the gym).

Not to mention, he had to sing, act, and fly.

He also needed to possess an innocent, naive quality that would make us believe him when he sang about his job of "Doing Good." We couldn't think he was campy in any way. Hal suggest Bob Holiday, who had been in *Fiorello!* He proved to have just the right qualities.

We also searched long and hard for Lois Lane and thought we had found her in Joan Hotchkis, an actress who had done a couple of plays and some TV. Hal replaced her just before rehearsals began, however, with Patricia Marand, who had been the ingénue in *Wish You Were Here*.

Besides the usual Superman characters, Bob and David had invented a few more employees of the *Daily Planet*, including a theatrical gossip columnist named Max Mencken who was patterned after Walter Winchell. Although Max was originally conceived as a secondary character, Jack Cassidy (who got top billing because he had won a Tony Award for his performance in Hal's production of *She Loves Me*) was so funny that we expanded his role in rehearsals.

Mencken's secretary (another new character) was played by the wonderful Linda Lavin. Hal had worked with Linda in *A Family Affair,* and she had made a small splash in an off-Broadway revue called *The Mad Show.* She really got noticed in our show, though, singing "You've Got Possibilities." Since then, she went on to TV fame as *Alice* and won a Tony for Neil Simon's *Broadway Bound.*

We actually had a great time writing material for these characters, including what we thought would be Cassidy's big showstopper: "Dot Dot Dot." The number had Max dictating his column as a parody of the slick, snide style of Walter Winchell. In the song, Lee made fun of Winchell's word-inventing gossip items, his super-patriotism, and his phony poetry.

During our backer's auditions, "Dot Dot Dot" was the hit of the evening. While we were in rehearsals, cast members would show up early just to catch Jack Cassidy's brilliant rendition. Then we got to our out-of-town tryout in Philadelphia on February 16, 1966, and the number bombed. There were no laughs from the audience during its performance and only scant applause at its conclusion.

Everyone involved with the show was in shock, especially Jack. How could the song that had soared in rehearsals suddenly bomb in front of audiences? With no idea of how to fix it, we just cut the number right out of the show and turned to the other things we thought we could fix.

And there was a lot that needed to be fixed. The reviews weren't good, and the satirical tone of the show—which was clear and obvious to us—somehow didn't land with the theater-going public. So we swapped the placement of various songs and scenes, and Lee and I wrote a new song for Jack Cassidy called "So Long, Big Guy," even as Hal was cutting down the rest of his role. Cassidy resented every cut and was always coming up with alternate ideas to replace the ones tossed in the trash. Every day, he would show up with new scraps of paper full of suggested jokes and lines, and Hal would be forced to reject them in front of everyone.

Hal, being both producer and director, also had to watch the budget. We were changing so many scenes so quickly that sometimes there wasn't even time to think about the costumes (beautifully designed by Florence Klotz). One time when a scene changed, Hal suggested simply turning the costumes inside out instead of making new ones. And it worked! I remember thinking how very clever it was of him. My mother would have approved.

It's a Bird . . . It's a Plane . . . It's Superman! opened on Broadway at the Alvin Theatre on March 29, 1966, to mostly favorable reviews. The *New York Times* called it "the best musical of the season."

Still, *Superman* failed to find its audience. Hal tried to reach the youth market by coming up with a creative pricing scheme for tickets in which he split the orchestra into three differently priced sections (twelve dollars for the best seats, ten dollars for the next best, and nine dollars for the fringes) and offered the bargain of two-dollar tickets in the last row of the balcony. During the run, we even played four matinees a week. But it was all to no avail.

Looking back now, we were both too early and too late. When we opened, the TV show *Batman* (which had just premiered a few months earlier) was at the height of its popularity, on air twice a week. Why pay to see the same kind of thing you could get at home for free? As David Newman said, we were killed by "capelash."

Of course, twelve years later, Bob and David wrote essentially the same script for the movies, and had an incredible success with *Superman: The Movie*, which made gobs of money. Lee and I didn't share in any of that, as we never had the film rights to the show, but we never begrudged David and Bob; we were, in fact, very happy for them. Still, I can't help thinking that if our show had opened just before the time of the movie, *It's a Bird . . . It's a Plane . . . It's Superman!* would have been an extraordinary success.

The show closed on July 17, 1966. I went to the last performance so that I could be with the cast. I felt awful. We all did. How do you feel when you watch your best friend die? By this time, Hal Prince had moved on, gone, as he was every summer to Greece or Switzerland or some other exotic vacation spot. He had his next show, *Cabaret*, on his mind now. I understood. But I never forgot. It hurt like hell.

9:

In late 1966, Barbara and I took a vacation to Europe (where we now had a beautiful flat in Filimore Gardens) to recover, and when we returned, we got a phone call from Hollywood.

"It's Warren Beatty," the voice on the other end of the line said.

Yeah, sure. Warren Beatty was calling me. I was sure it was a joke.

He told me he was producing a movie, and he wanted me to write the background music. He asked my price, and I quoted him a high one.

"Can you do any better?" he asked. "It's not a high-budget film."

"No," I replied. "That's my price." I stood firm because I didn't really believe it was Warren Beatty on the line, and yet, I couldn't say to him "prove to me you're Warren Beatty." A matinee idol, the star of 1961's *Splendor in the Grass,* calling me? It didn't seem likely.

But then he said, "Arthur Penn is going to direct, and he recommended you."

So it *was* Warren Beatty after all.

Arthur Penn, of course, had been the final director of *Golden Boy,* and it turned out that Bob Benton and David Newman, my *Superman* collaborators, were writing the film Warren was talking about, which he told me was called *Bonnie and Clyde.*

Sure, I had gone to Hollywood to write the title song for the film version of *Bye Bye Birdie,* but *Bonnie and Clyde* was to be my first major film experience. I was excited to do it and thrilled it was going to be directed by Arthur and produced by Warren at Warner Bros. The only problem was that I didn't see that much in the script: It seemed to be just your standard 1930s gangster film with a dollop of homosexuality thrown in. That is, until I heard bluegrass banjos flying along in the background. It was then I knew I could do something with this.

The experience was notable, too, for being my first encounter with sound editors who inanely believed that the chirping of birds or the squeal of tires were more important than my oboe solo.

I had a lot to learn.

This was also my second near-physical fight with a collaborator. The first had been with Mel Brooks during *All*

American (nothing came of it), and this time it was with Warren Beatty himself.

He had said he "really loved" everything I'd written when he'd first heard it. Then, at the recording session, after nearly everything was played to him, he'd say, "Can I hear that with a tuba and a piccolo added?" For some reason, those instruments seemed particularly fulfilling to him. I don't know whether it was artistic or personal, but little by little, Warren started to make all sorts of changes during the recording session.

As the producer, he certainly had the right, but at the point when we verbally clashed, he physically pushed me.

So I pushed right back.

Now, Warren was lean and six-foot-something, and I was flabby and five-ten (almost), but the next thing you knew, we were at it, until Arthur Penn, who was four-foot-nine, finally pulled us apart. (Arthur is actually taller, but that's how I remember it.)

Looking back, I think it was my inexperience as a film composer plus Warren's restless imagination (along with his frustration at his inability to express himself) that set us off. In any case, standing up for what I believed had a positive result. We made up and had a great Chinese meal at a restaurant called The Shanghai, where Warren did all the ordering. The food was great, and so was my inward satisfaction that I had become someone who fought for what he believed in—a strong and confident man.

Warren was much too handsome for me to think of him as possessing an intellectually superior mind, but oddly, he had one. We chummed around a bit and he took me to parties, at which I noticed he always chatted first with the most unattractive woman in the place. Brilliant!

Once, Warren, Julie Christie, and I went to Mexico for the weekend. (Hey, man, you can't leave *that* out of a memoir.) When we walked into a restaurant, the mariachi band played "Lara's Theme" from *Doctor Zhivago*, and Warren didn't look too happy. It wasn't from one of his movies. But a good tune beats 'em all.

Following the first screening of the movie, Jack Warner, the head of the studio, said, "Not bad. I had to get up and piss only once."

One of the sound engineers informed me that Mr. Warner's getting up only once to urinate was considered, by those in the know, on par with receiving four stars in a New York newspaper.

Warren and the others decided to have the first public screening of the film in a college town because of the abundance of violence in the film. He had an instinct that students from USC would appreciate the movie more than, say, farmers from middle America. So, the first time we all saw *Bonnie and Clyde* in front of an audience was in a theater in Brentwood, California. I sat near an elderly couple and paid close attention to them. I knew what was coming, and they didn't. This, not the film itself, was the dramatic moment for me. I watched the couple closely out of the corner of my eye, and when the gunshots began, without a word or glance at each other, they got up and walked out. It was too much for them, but the kids loved it. Warren seemed to have a real instinct for the youth market, and I was learning.

𝄢

I was still constantly spun about by career choices and aesthetics, but finally I was becoming financially secure. *Bonnie and Clyde* led to other film scoring work.

Walking on the beach at Fire Island in 1967, I met Norman Lear, the producer for whom I'd later write the theme song for his hit show *All in the Family*. Norman had cut his teeth in live TV back in the 1950s, writing *The Colgate Comedy Hour*, *Four Star Revue*, and *The Tennessee Ernie Ford Show*. He recently had a hit with his film *Divorce American Style*, but his great successes were ahead of him on TV with such innovative sitcoms as *All in the Family, Maude, The Jeffersons, One Day at a Time,* and *Good Times.*

Norman knew my work from *Golden Boy* and *Bonnie and Clyde* and mentioned he was writing and producing a new film called *The Night They Raided Minsky's*. He wondered if Lee and I would be interested in writing some songs for it and if I'd write the background score as well.

I immediately found Norman to be one of the most approachable guys I'd ever met. To this day, he has a wonderfully warm, considerate way of dealing with people. The same is true of others, of course, but given Norman's gigantic success and position in the entertainment and political world, one would expect a warping of spirit—but not at all. His producing partner, Bud Yorkin, turned out to be a sterling copy of Norman as well. Given the kinds of experiences I'd had in the theater, this was something new and wonderful. This was like *family*.

I didn't know it at the time, but the film was to touch my future in ways I couldn't have imagined.

The Night They Raided Minsky's told the story of an innocent Amish girl, played by Britt Ekland, who, in a rebellious fit, leaves home to become a dancer and ends up inventing the striptease at

Minsky's Burlesque in 1925. The movie turned out to be brilliant, but the production of it was plagued with all sorts of problems.

Attention to detail was paramount. A great deal of effort was made to keep everything true to the spirit of the story and the time, so much thought was put into everything from the kind of young woman who might strip at Minsky's to the look of the 1920s in New York City.

But it was only director Billy Friedkin's third film experience (he'd only directed a quickie comedy starring Sonny and Cher and a stagy film version of Harold Pinter's *The Birthday Party*; *The French Connection* and *The Exorcist* were in his future), and he ate up a lot of time reframing shots and fussing with musical rehearsals. To save time, Lee and I wrote four songs ("Perfect Gentlemen," "Take Ten Terrific Girls," "The Night They Raided Minsky's," and "You Rat You"—the last of which, a few years later, I slowed down to waltz time, changed a few notes, and gave to Daddy Warbucks to sing to Annie as "Something Was Missing")—and recorded them before any filming was done, which was not the usual method.

Then, with very unfortunate timing, one of the film's stars, Bert Lahr, best known as the Cowardly Lion in *The Wizard of Oz*, died during the start of shooting.

When Bert died (itself a great tragedy of the theater), it was decided to scrap the whole film and lose the money already invested. But Norman and the brilliant film editor thought it was possible—by cutting around Bert's scenes, filming a double from the back, and using the music as a kind of glue—to "retexture" the movie. Amazingly, they did it. A magazine photographer had been doing publicity filming during the rehearsals—grainy and not suitable for 35 millimeter—but

Norman decided to use it, and it ultimately gave the work a grainy and authentic feel.

Altogether, *The Night They Raided Minsky's* was a film I was proud to be associated with.

And, for you trivia fans, it starred Jason Robards, which makes Lee and me the only songwriters to have written songs for both Mr. and Mrs. Robards (as Lauren Bacall, our future star of *Applause*, was married to Robards for most of the 1960s).

$$\text{𝄢}$$

Nineteen sixty-eight was also the year for another big production: our second son, Nick. Unlike Ben, who was born calm and inquisitive, Nick screamed at his birth. He was named after my friend and TV producer Nick Vanoff, who had been the stage manager of *What's the Rush*, Lee's and my first show, at the Pittsburgh Playhouse.

I imagine Nick absorbed my "conflicted" genes, as he's been an actor, a rock and roller, and finally, a psychotherapist. He was successful as an actor (he replaced Matthew Broderick on Broadway in *Brighton Beach Memoirs*), and starred in a movie and a TV series; yet he's happiest as a therapist, deeply involved in the treatment of his patients both at a big hospital in Connecticut and in private practice.

As for Ben, although I tried to coax him into being a musician, he didn't take to it, and instead went off to law school at New York University, where he readily passed the bar examinations. But he hated being a lawyer and now writes musicals.

I guess genes'll get you every time.

$$\text{𝄢}$$

My old friend Bill Flanagan had continued dating Edward Albee for years, but Ed's success in the theater was hard for Bill to take. With each play, Ed was getting more and more famous, and Bill was drinking more and more, until he and Edward finally broke up. I wanted to be there for him, and often invited Bill over for dinner, but I was now married with children, and it was hard to be that support he needed. I loved him, and he was always welcome, but it just wasn't right that he was spending this amount of time with a straight couple.

Meanwhile, Edward's picture appeared on the cover of *Time* magazine.

Bill became friendly with Judy Garland at one point and spent much time at her apartment. She was, of course, a well-known favorite of homosexual men and a woman with a disproportionate share of suffering in her own life. Rumor had it that drugs and excessive drinking were part of her scene.

I could tell by looking at Bill when I saw him that he started to look more and more "used up," so it shouldn't have been a surprise to read in the paper that he had died in 1969, at age forty-six, but it was. I hadn't seen him in months.

This kind of death, I read, is not uncommon: large consumption of alcohol mixed with drugs. Was it suicide? Jesus, I couldn't even believe it. I used to trail him around, copying his moves, his attitudes. We all did. But how he must have suffered.

I couldn't help but feel at the time how little I knew him. I felt as though I had used him. No one else knew me as he did, and I needed him to reflect the "me" that I might be someday. But me, me, me . . . was I truly a friend to him? Could I have helped save him? The guilt eats at me even now.

CHAPTER THIRTEEN

Fasten Your Seat Belts

WHEN HAL PRINCE AND I were working together on *Superman*, I told him a notion I had carried in my head for years: a musical based on the classic 1950 film *All About Eve* starring Ethel Merman as Margo and Carol Lawrence as Eve.

"Charles," Hal said to me after I told him my idea, "no one is interested in the emotional problems of actors."

A year later, in 1967, when I was on the Warner Bros. lot working on the score for *Bonnie and Clyde*, my office just happened to be near that of playwright Sidney Michaels (who, coincidentally, was later to be one of the screenwriters of *The Night They Raided Minsky's)*. Sidney had written the plays *Tchin-Tchin* (which starred Anthony Quinn on Broadway in 1962) and *Dylan* (on Broadway in '64) and the book for the musical *Ben Franklin in Paris,* a '64/'65 season show which starred Robert Preston in the title role.

When I told Sidney my idea of a musical *All About Eve*, he flipped over it. Upon our return to New York, we got in touch with producer Lawrence Kasha, who had co-produced *She Loves Me* with Hal Prince and directed the musical *Bajour* (which starred Chita Rivera). Before too long, Larry quickly became the driving force behind the project.

The brilliantly witty screenplay for *All About Eve* had been written by Joseph Mankiewicz, who also directed it. But as Joe had been employed by 20th Century-Fox at the time he wrote *All About Eve,* he didn't own the rights. 20th Century-Fox did. And 20th Century-Fox did not want to give us the rights.

With some digging, Larry found out that Mary Orr, the author of *The Wisdom of Eve,* the story on which *All About Eve* had been based, retained the stage rights to her story. At least we had something to work with, but using the earlier version meant that many of the characters Mankiewicz had invented (including the acid-tongued critic Addison DeWitt and Margo's sensible ex-vaudevillian dresser Birdie Coonan) could not be used in our version.

Still, it was the main story that had attracted us, and we began work in earnest on what we called *Welcome to the Theatre.* (The title was from the Act I curtain line Sidney had written.)

We were sorting things out and forging ahead, but truthfully, there was a time in 1968 when I temporarily lost interest in our musical. The reason: Theater critic Clive Barnes had written an article in the *New York Times* after *Hair* opened that said henceforth *every* American musical would be a rock musical. (This judgment would be made again—as it was after the 1996 debut of *Rent and* 2006's opening of *Spring Awakening*—by other theater critics, a group not always noted for its prescience.) It seemed to me that it was equivalent to saying, at another time, that "all opera should henceforth be written like Wagner."

I did not think that our show should have a rock score.

Musicals are a bastard form. Jewish composers got into the picture after being largely shunned in Europe; then immigrants in America flocked to burlesque with its base humor; while at the same time, the Yiddish theater sank roots in New York City's Lower East Side. Tap dancing sprang from the poorest

New Yorkers (the blacks and the Irish), who lived and danced on the mud flats in lower Manhattan—a jumble of Irish clog dancing and black jazz mixing it up.

Looking back, I see now I couldn't help wanting to swim in this stream. From my earliest days—hearing of my father's experiences during the Depression, my accompanying black performers through the South, my mother's stride piano—all of it was coursing through my veins. I've always loved music, but figuring out my own place in it took a bit of time.

Rock music has been *the* popular music in America, and now the world, for more than sixty years. Lee Adams and I first used it on Broadway in *Bye Bye Birdie,* and since that time, rock has become serious, worldly, expressive, and more finely crafted. It's still relatively simple, though, usually relying on harmonies derived from one, three, four, and five chords and often repeating one of these chords for many measures. To be fair, much rock has ventured outside this scheme, and yet, as I see it, most of it still involves instrumental accompaniments consisting of guitars (acoustic, electric, steel, or bass), synthesized or acoustic keyboard, and drums. (For a more country sound, harmonica and solo fiddle can be introduced.) And then this rock—as delivered by (usually) male rock musicians who are young, have great hair, and have equally great bodies—is greeted by wild reactions in kids. It's similar, I guess, to what the Charleston and Black Bottom brought to my grandmother's generation and Sinatra brought to my own.

The most exciting rock music has very loud percussion accompaniment, electric guitars, and synthesizers and is sung in a very high register. This type of music can create a problem in musicals with varied characters as they tend to require other moods as well.

I'm not about to do a history of the subject—much has been written about it already. And although *Birdie* had rock music, basically, most of it was satire. Lee and I were not about to be mistaken for Led Zeppelin. (We do, however, like to remember that we were the first to do it on a Broadway stage.)

So, perhaps due to critical pressure, as I wrote the score for what would wind up being titled *Applause* (after we tried *Make Believe* and *Applause, Applause*), I found myself trying to be who the "critical sages of the day" wanted me to be. I never thought it my best score, for that reason, but in retrospect, it taught me a great lesson: Be me!

𝄢

Right from the start, we knew that the role of Margo Channing, so brilliantly played by Bette Davis in 1950, needed a powerhouse star of a certain age. In the film, Margo admits to forty or, as Bette Davis's Margo said, "Four-Oh!"). Very early on, we all decided that Lauren Bacall would be ideal.

After being a very youthful film star and Mrs. Humphrey Bogart, Bacall had made great strides as a stage actress appearing first in *Goodbye Charlie* and then in the hit play *Cactus Flower*. At this time, she was coming to the end of her eight-year marriage to Jason Robards, who had starred in the aforementioned *The Night They Raided Minsky's*, and she was ready for a challenge. So, in early 1969, we got an introduction to her, played her five or six songs, which she said she liked, and she agreed to play the part.

It was that simple.

I later found out that this directness was one of her strongest characteristics. She was always straightforward whether she was supporting you or hitting you over the head.

When I first met Bacall, she confided in me that, not only had she gone most of her life without singing in front of anybody, but also that when she finally did get the courage to try—at a party in Hollywood—she made sure it was dark and smoky, and that the room was particularly noisy, and only then would she sing, quickly and quietly, so that no one would pay too much attention to her. Even then, she had a close friend accompanying her, who followed all of her tempo changes, waiting for her to take time finishing a phrase if she took it slowly or rushing to catch up whenever she sped ahead.

When I explained to her that, onstage, she would be accompanied by an orchestra, and she would have to come in on a cue, she asked, "Why can't the orchestra follow *me*?"

It didn't give me a barrel of confidence, but how couldn't you like her?

Bacall's decision to play the character of Margo was a first for her—her first performance in a musical. Right away, I worked with her on three songs, to get her comfortable with singing. She was an instinctive musician—good intonation and good rhythm. The vocal sound itself? (One didn't use the word "timbre" with her!) Well, it was unmistakably "Bacall."

The first person she sang these songs for was the avuncular and perceptive orchestrator Phil Lang. He was very complimentary, and she started to gather more confidence—enough so that, one afternoon when her son Sam came home from school, she agreed with my suggestion that she perform these three songs for him. He was, I believe, about thirteen at the time.

She sang the songs and when she finished, he grimaced and said, "Yuck! That's the worst thing I ever heard!"

Betty (for that was her real name: Betty Persky, and by this time we were getting friendly enough for me to call her that) was crushed, but remembering my own childhood, I told her how embarrassed I had been when my mother did anything out of the ordinary—particularly when she wore her silver fox jacket to pick me up at school.

I assured her it was a common rule: Mothers are embarrassing to thirteen-year-old sons. No matter what they do.

Interestingly, when Hal Prince found out that Lauren Bacall had signed on for the role, he changed his mind about the viability of the show, already imagining what she could do with the role onstage. Hal was no fool.

But Hal Prince was not to be our director. The man who choreographed Hal's last two hit shows was.

When we were doing *Superman*, I had tried to convince Hal Prince to hire Ron Field as the choreographer. Ron had been strongly recommended to me by Fred Ebb, who had worked with him on Liza Minnelli's nightclub act, but Hal wouldn't accept him then because Ron hadn't had a hit Broadway show (though he had choreographed two flops: *Nowhere to Go But Up* and *Café Crown*). I had seen some tapes of Ron's previous work and felt he was "the man," but the money behind Broadway is often timid, so I was unable to bring him on board. Ron Field did later team up with Hal, choreographing *Cabaret* and *Zorba* (I guess Fred Ebb had some influence there). After winning a Tony for *Cabaret*, Ron felt he was in a position to ask to be the director of *Applause*, and Joe Kipness and Larry Kasha (who had worked with Ron on an off-Broadway revival of *Anything Goes)* and Ron had made the bold decision to hire this first-time director to direct the great star Bacall.

I've worked with quite a few choreographers: Bob Fosse (*The Girls Against the Boys*), Gower Champion (*Birdie*), Donald McKayle (*Golden Boy*), George Faison (*A Broadway Musical*), Peter Gennaro (*Annie*), and even Michael Bennett for a month or so on Sammy Cahn's and my *Bojangles* (before Michael switched to *Dreamgirls* and Cahn died). There were others I'd played for in dance classes, rehearsals—and, hell, I'm even married to one. To say I've loved them all might be misunderstood. But there's a quality about them—like racehorses that have been whipped often—that turns most of them into excellent whippers, and I like that. They're high-strung, organized, confident (sometimes), and wicked (often).

Ron Field had all of these traits except for confidence. He was insecure about his hairline, and went almost every day to a salon where his thinning hair was replaced strand by strand. He saved all the theater reviews from the *New York Times* so he'd be sure to please the first-string critic then. He told me he would rather have dinner with Hal and Judy Prince than with friends or relatives; his point was that he only wanted to be where *it* was happening. But *it*—life—was happening, he was convinced, only where he wasn't.

I recognized this, of course, from my mother.

With a director and star on board, we were suddenly faced with "the book problem." The problem was that Lauren Bacall didn't like Sidney Michaels's book. She didn't feel that he wrote the way she spoke. Because she was the linchpin—the one who was making the show happen and was so positive about the songs—we had to listen to what she wanted. And what she wanted was to bring in Comden and Green to write a new book.

By this time, Betty Comden and Adolph Green were already legendary. They began their Broadway careers in 1944 writing the book and lyrics for (and playing two of the leads in) *On the Town* (music by none other than Leonard Bernstein). Their subsequent hits included *Wonderful Town*, *Bells Are Ringing*, and *Do Re Mi*. Their Broadway success translated to Hollywood, where they concocted the screenplays for several of MGM's best movie musicals (including *Singin' in the Rain)*. Most of the time, they wrote both book and lyrics (sometimes just lyrics) but never had done just book. Until now.

In the spring of 1969, after Sidney Michaels departed, Betty and Adolph came on board. They were welcomed by tough-guy producer Joe Kipness saying to Betty, "I hope you're going to fix this book. But if you don't, I'll break your legs." Although he was not beyond punching someone out, I'm sure he was kidding. The ladylike Betty Comden just blanched.

Meanwhile, Larry Kasha went to David Brown, who was then in charge of East Coast operations for Fox, and with his help, got us the right to use a "limited amount" of material from the film. Still, we were still prohibited from using any character that wasn't in the original Mary Orr story.

We spent the summer collaborating on a new draft with Betty and Adolph. Instead of Margo's dresser Birdie (played in the film by Thelma Ritter), they came up with Duane Fox, Margo's gay hairdresser. The acid-tongued columnist became the acid-tongued producer Howard Benedict, which actually improved the plot in my opinion, because a producer could certainly be more helpful to Eve than a columnist ever would be.

This whole time, I kept thinking to myself that if anyone had told me back in the early 1950s that one day I would be collaborating with Betty Comden and Adolph Green, I would have thought they were crazy. And yet, here we were.

Late in the summer, Fox granted us full rights to the movie script. It was sudden and unexpected and likely because we had just announced that Lauren Bacall would be our star. By that time, however, we had solved most of our problems, and the show didn't need to use the movie script. In the end, I think there were roughly a dozen lines taken from the film. Ultimately, as Betty and Adolph put it, with the show starring Lauren Bacall, it would be more *All About Margo* than *All About Eve*.

We gathered a great team (including Don Pippin as musical director, Phil Lang on orchestrations, and Mel Marvin and Marvin Hamlisch doing the dance arrangements), and as usual, the shaping of our musical was an endless process. Everyone— the producer, his spouse, the business manager, the star, and the star's agent (and the agent's partner)—were all "helping" by crit icizing and suggesting changes. Seeing this led me to the observation that Darwinists would surely agree with: Throughout history, the strongest drives in human beings are the seeking of food, shelter, sex, and the rewriting of someone else's musical.

To give you an idea of theater people's insecurities, let me tell you a story about the show's title.

It came from a song Lee and I wrote late in the day (and even that almost didn't happen, but that's a whole other story). When we wrote that song, it was suggested that it might be the title of the show, and we all were pleased with that possibility.

Then, one afternoon, Ron Field came to my apartment straight from his hair-transplant appointment. "Bad news," he said. "I showed the title to my hair consultant, and he said, 'You cannot use that title because the printed word looks like "applesauce."'"

A few of us laughed at first, but Ron printed the word out, and in a moment, we all saw what his hair guru had seen. We were certain that everyone in the Western world would call our show *Applesauce*.

It was only when a handyman working on a radiator in my apartment didn't see anything but "applause" in the word "applause" that we all came down to reality and stuck with the title.

Bacall got to sit on the casting calls and read with all the candidates for the role of Bill Sampson, her romantic lead. We finally cast a newcomer with a great voice named Len Cariou. He and Bacall had what Frank Loesser in *Guys & Dolls* called "chemistry, yeah chemistry." In fact, soon, like Bette Davis and Gary Merrill before them, they emulated their characters and started a May-December romance.

For the all-important role of Eve Harrington, we cast a twenty-one-year-old girl named Diane McAfee. Brandon Maggart was cast as Buzz Richards, the playwright (his name in the film had been Lloyd Richards, but by this time, there was a famous director by that name). Diane and Brandon fell in love during rehearsals and had four children. In fact, their two daughters both went into show business: singers Maude Maggart and—yes—Fiona Apple.

Although we began rehearsals with Garrett Lewis as Margo's hairdresser, we wound up replacing him with Lee Roy Reams, who gave a performance of great subtlety in what was probably the first out-of-the-closet "positive" gay role in a

Broadway musical. Rehearsals began a few days before Christmas 1969, and on January 19, 1970, we opened at the Morris A. Mechanic Theatre in Baltimore. It was then that we began our real work.

Fortunately for us, Bacall kept her eye on the ball. A strong woman, she gave all her strength to *Applause,* and she expected the same from everyone else.

One recollection of Bacall is still firmly in my mind: the night that we opened in Baltimore. An out-of-town Broadway opening is exciting under any circumstances, but this was Lauren Bacall in her first musical! As it that weren't enough, *Look* magazine had sent a photographer and a critic-reporter who was to write a major article for the magazine, which had a circulation in the high millions.

After the curtain fell, we went backstage to congratulate the cast. Following that, we were supposed to all meet in Bacall's suite at the hotel with the theater critic and photographer. All of us (both Bettys—Comden and Bacall—Adolph, Lee, Ron, and I) were going to be photographed and were expected, I suppose, to say something pithy. I couldn't focus on that, though, as I knew something that no one else knew: A small local magazine had already written that we were a bomb. I convinced myself that the audience's laughter and applause that night was somehow not *that* enthusiastic.

My gray mood followed us back to the hotel, where Lee, Betty Comden, Adolph, and I scrambled to entertain the reporter Louis Botto, who was already looking bored.

Lee plastered a smile on his face. "Would you like a drink?" he asked cheerfully, while Betty and Adolph scrambled to make Louis comfortable. At a loss for anything better to say, I chattered, "I really like Baltimore although the weather is cooler than I expected." I felt like I was in the masterful Comden and Green "Conversation Piece" number from *Wonderful Town* in which everyone sits around, trying in vain to make conversation.

We had to impress him, and so it wasn't a good thing when the conversation seemed to have run out. Nobody said a word. I remember walking to the window, looking down at the lights of Baltimore (which was not exactly the Manhattan skyline), thinking of jumping, and then thinking that we were only six floors up, so I might not die but just be crippled, and maybe Baltimore doctors wouldn't be up to Mount Sinai's standards.

I collected myself, turned back to the room, and said, "I thought the audience tonight was pretty darn . . ."—I paused, and mustered up my most confident smile—"Well, for a first-time audience?"

But I was interrupted by the appearance of the glamorous Lauren Bacall, who walked in with her new best friend (just like their characters of Margo and Duane), Lee Roy Reams.

Botto said, "Oh, hello, Miss Bacall. I'm Louis Botto, from *Look* magazine."

Did I imagine it or was it *he* who was the one bowing now?

"We're delighted," he fawned, "that you could give us a few minutes."

A photographer appeared from nowhere and began snapping pictures.

Betty and Adolph were leaning in to get into the photographs as Lee Roy brought Bacall a drink. After taking a sip, she spoke. "What'd you think of the show?"

My heart stopped. We waited.

"Well," Botto started, and then paused. "I thought"—he paused again—"it was"—another pause—"very interesting."

"Go fuck yourself!" Bacall said.

I could have kissed her.

Even with all the time I'd spent in therapy, I could never have spoken like that, but of course, it was exactly what I felt. And after she said it, Botto magically became her slave. Oh, God, if someday I could learn to do that!

Well, we got awful reviews in Baltimore. This was the time when the men were to be separated from the boys. I definitely still felt like a boy, but Betty—*damn!*—she strengthened me every inch of the way.

We made change after change to songs, dance numbers, and dialogue. Our original ending to the show had Margo actually dumping Bill in favor of her career in the theater, which we felt was very true to life and very true to Bacall herself and to the kind of star who is married to her career. When it became clear the audience liked the show, but didn't love it, we decided to try the sentimental ending in which Margo gives up the theater for the love of a good man. Well, the audience leaped to its feet, which says a lot about Americans in the 1970s. If we were redoing it today, I would opt for the realistic ending instead of the romantic one.

Betty performed the old version of the show every night, and then, every morning, she would arrive a half an hour early, warm up, and then rehearse whatever changes or new material was to be put into the show that night.

One day, I gathered the courage to ask her to lunch during the rehearsal break the next afternoon. She said yes, and I didn't sleep well the entire night before.

When the time came for our lunch break, it started to rain, and I don't mean just rain—it poured and poured. And, of course, there were no cabs.

Next door to the theater was a five-and-ten (the same kind I had bought sheet music at with my mother) advertising a special: Tuna fish salad plate with potato chips, pickle slice, and a Coke for ninety-nine cents. We dashed in there, and Betty had the special, with the tuna fish, pickle slice, potato chips, Coke, and all.

After, when the rain had stopped, we walked out and she said, "Thanks for the worst fucking lunch I've ever had!" Classic Bacall candor.

And then it was back to work. During our eight weeks in Baltimore and our two in Detroit, Lee and I and Betty Comden and Adolph Green never stopped working, tinkering and changing. A new opening number went in, and Ron Field polished the dances. We were living the cliché of clichés—the scramble to the finish line on an out-of-town Broadway show that you always see in the movies. Only the bleeding, the pain, and the fights were all real.

During the Baltimore run, we found that we had to replace our Eve. Diane McAfee was a talented singer, but Bacall, with her powerful presence, just wiped her off the stage. Everyone was very upset about letting her go, including Betty.

"You're too young and rosy to scare Margo Channing," we assured Diane. "Especially Lauren Bacall's Margo!"

Ron Field was so upset over having to let her go that later on he made sure she got the role of Eve in a touring company of the show, for which Bacall did not reprise her lead role.

Penny Fuller was brought in to learn the role, and with her experience (she had played Sally Bowles in *Cabaret*) and added years (she was thirty to Diane's twenty-one), she was able to be a real threat as Eve to Bacall's strong Margo. The show began to work.

We opened in Detroit on February 19. The reviews were much better, but that didn't stop us from making improvements. A few days before the end of the Detroit run, we gave Len Cariou a new ballad ("Think How It's Gonna Be") to replace his first song ("It Was Always You"), and we replaced Bacall's eleven o'clock number ("Love Comes First") with "Something Greater," which used much of the sentiment of the great Joe Mankiewicz speech in which Margo talks about "a woman's career" and how it's no good at all "unless you wake up and there he is."

Then, at last, we were on to New York!

March 30, 1970. The Palace Theatre.

Whenever possible, I've ducked opening nights, but Betty said that if I didn't show up, she wouldn't either. We locked eyes and stared at each other for a moment. It was just enough time to conclude that she really meant it, so I sat there with Barbara on opening night, in a theater filled with the smart, rich, hypercritical people known as "a New York audience."

In a season in which nothing exciting had caught on, we received nearly unanimous raves (though Clive Barnes thought that my music wasn't up to snuff).

A day after our opening, on the backstage bulletin board, somebody posted the front page of an English-language Hong Kong newspaper. In bold letters, it read: LAUREN BACALL TRIUMPHS ON BROADWAY! It fascinated me, and still does, the long reach of Broadway. A hit was international as well as national news. It was all pretty heady stuff.

𝄢

Applause won four Tonys, including Best Musical and Best Actress in a Musical. (That year, just like the year *Birdie* won, they didn't have a Best Score . . . was it a conspiracy against me?) Ron won two Tonys (for direction and choreography) and promptly went to Los Angeles, where he had stamped on his license plate "2 Tonys."

I always thought that a large part of our success was due to the Joe Mankiewicz's screenplay for *All About Eve*, which I considered a masterpiece. I had gotten to know Mankiewicz while *Applause* was still being written when I composed the music for a film he directed called *There Was a Crooked Man* (which starred Kirk Douglas and Henry Fonda). When I told Joe that I was working on the show, he told me to make sure to use the line "Fasten your seatbelts, it's gonna be a bumpy night" in a song. And of course, we did. Because he was under contract to 20th Century-Fox when he wrote *All About Eve*, Mankiewicz had no financial participation in any further rights. My respect and affection were such that I asked all connected with *Applause* to share something with Joe—if not money, at least a small acknowledgment.

At the Tonys that year, it was decided that Lee would make the acceptance speech on national television were we to win, which we did. I asked Lee to at least mention Joe's name, but, by the time Lee got up to make the speech, he was dead drunk. Not only did he forget my request, he also nearly forgot Lauren Bacall's name. Fortunately, a commercial break came and Lee was steered away from the camera before he started singing the Ohio State fight song. Bacall told of the night Mankiewicz (an old friend of hers) came to see the show. He told her he had been apprehensive about seeing the show. After all, he had written and directed the film; it was his brainchild, and he was rightfully possessive about it. After the show, he told her he was happy to see how much of his work had been kept in it and that he liked it a lot more than he anticipated. Betty was relieved and grateful. Joe Mankiewicz is gone now, but his family should know the depth of gratitude we all felt.

♪:

Applause ran for two years on Broadway, and when Bacall took it on a national tour, she was replaced on Broadway by the original Eve from the film, Anne Baxter, who in turn was replaced by Arlene Dahl. Actually, Bacall was supposed to be replaced with a very different and equally exciting ex-film star: Rita Hayworth. (I spent two exciting weeks coaching her.) But Hayworth, the screen's sizzling sex goddess of the 1940s, couldn't remember her lines or retain any staging. At the time, the press reported that she was drunk, but the truth was that she was exhibiting a disease that didn't have a name in the early 1970s: Alzheimer's disease.

♪:

Odd to say, but history and memories are not always in neat little rows or chronological order. Most times, events in your life run parallel or crisscross over each other, and our memories either mush them together or separate them.

I have found that memory is seldom reality.

In reality, Lee and I were writing two shows at the same time. One was the very American and very contemporary *Applause*, which was begun in 1967, and the other was intensely British and historical *I and Albert*, which we began a year earlier.

I and Albert began life when Lee and I approached a wonderful playwright named Jay Presson Allen (*The Prime of Miss Jean Brodie* and, later, the screenplay for *Cabaret*) about writing a musical concerning Queen Victoria. It turned out that Mrs. Allen, a Victoria buff, found our idea very interesting, and our collaboration began. We all agreed that we didn't want to do a saga of "sixty glorious years," but to tell a human story in which Victoria and Albert would emerge as real people as they had never been portrayed on the stage before. As we began to write, we found our source material was so rich and the people so fascinating that we just didn't know what to leave out.

By 1969, when *Applause* was going into production, we had a working script and score but couldn't find our Victoria or secure the authentically British cast we needed in New York. *Applause* opened in triumph, and the producers of *I and Albert*, as we had entitled our musical, decided that we had to do the show in London, where the action took place.

And this is where the parallel shows converged.

Lauren Bacall had agreed to make her London debut in *Applause* in November of 1972, and after enticing John Schlesinger to be our director, and casting Polly James and Sven-Bertil Taube as our title characters, *I and Albert* was scheduled to open one week before *Applause*.

John Schlesinger was a brilliant Oscar-winning film director, who, by 1972, had directed *Darling, Far from the Madding Crowd, Midnight Cowboy,* and *Sunday Bloody Sunday.* Lee, Jay, and I were to spend the summer of 1972 rewriting, trimming, and sharpening to fit the show to the vision of Schlesinger.

In the spring of 1972, Barbara and I brought our two sons with us to London and rented a house on Mulberry Walk, where now-five-year-old-Benjamin could often be found teaching a policeman the songs from *Applause.* The poor policeman couldn't escape Ben's tutelage because he was walking back and forth guarding a minister's house on the street, and we were all more than amused to see this bobby gamely singing, "I feel wicked and wacky and mellow, / Firm as Gibraltar and shaky as Jell-O / But alive! But alive! But alive!" with my son Ben prompting him.

As I looked forward to two London openings, it was hard for me to not feel optimistic.

And yet, as Benjamin sang "But Alive," I couldn't help remembering a relentless tune my mother always sang in my head: "Be careful, Buddy. The world is not your friend."

CHAPTER FOURTEEN

It Would Have Been Wonderful

THERE ARE FAILURES and there are *failures*, but few failures were as hurtful to me as *I and Albert*.

After a summer of exciting and fruitful work with Schlesinger and our creative team and an encouraging rehearsal period with a great cast, we opened at the Piccadilly Theatre in London's West End on November 6, 1972, ten days before *Applause* premiered at Her Majesty's Theatre.

I and Albert celebrated the hundred-year reign of Queen Victoria—the love story, the imperialism of her government, and the devotion of her people. I thought it one of the finest scores Lee and I had written and felt the book by Jay was literate and poetic. To be sure we were authentic, the producers had engaged Lady Antonia Fraser as our consultant, and we were convinced we were British to the core, with a musical reflecting reverence for the queen and her empire.

But there was an artistic and cultural conflict that, in retrospect, helped to kill us. Our director John Schlesinger was openly gay, and gays in London at this time were openly satirical about Queen Elizabeth and the Royal Family (think of many Americans' attitudes toward President Bush in 2008). Queen Elizabeth was generally referred to around the West End pubs as "Miss Beige," and many of the actors and dancers thought of her as a "hoot." Thus, from the beginning, there was a stylistic conflict, as Lee, Jay, and I attempted to portray Queen Victoria and Prince Albert with reverence, and the director and *his* queens tried to paint a satirical edge on it all.

In addition, our Albert, Sven-Bertil Taube, caught the flu and couldn't perform for our first nine previews. An understudy stood in for him, but there is a British law that once you have had ten paid performances, you *must* open to the public and the press. So, we opened with a leading man who had never performed the role in front of a paid audience.

We were screwed.

If you speak of musical failures, to most people, it's as boring as hearing about "the four hours I spent waiting for a plane at the Buffalo airport." Everyone's been there, so no one wants to hear about it. (Oddly, in a later production *in* Buffalo, at Artpark, *I and Albert* was termed a "masterpiece" by a theater critic there. All failures in theater are painful because they are public, and so added to one's own feelings are the feelings of everyone witnessing it—both friends who can't help but feel happy it's not they who failed and enemies who revel in schadenfreude: the tears of the crocodile.

We were crucified in the British press, though the *International Herald Tribune* and some American magazines gave us excellent reviews. A very wonderful man who loves musicals, John Yap, recorded the entire score (including Sven's still-sick voice), so should any reader happen upon the recording, know that Lee, Jay, and I felt it represented some of our best work.

℘:

Mingled with the sadness of the closing of *I and Albert* was great joy: Our daughter, Victoria, was born.

Barbara was too far along in her pregnancy for her obstetrician to permit her to go back to America for the delivery, so it was decided to have the baby in London. Barbara gave birth at the King's College Hospital, a rather sad-looking place (it was a teaching hospital and very nineteenth-century looking) compared to the zippy New York Hospital.

It's hard to be honest about my feelings, when (in retrospect) the most *unimportant* one—the closing of a show that I had labored so long and hard on—overwhelmed the most *important* one: the birth of our daughter. And I don't expect anyone to sympathize or comprehend that the death of a musical—something I'd created out of notes—could in any way have been as important to me as something created from my genes—a beautiful baby girl. That I felt that way then, is inconceivable now. But tears of failure and tears of joy don't mix into a satisfying or nourishing cocktail. The bitter taste of one, sadly, overcomes the sweetness of the other. Today, it shames me to have felt those conflicts. Watching Victoria turn into the feisty, talented, and amazing girl she became did a great deal to teach me what success and what failure truly mean.

But Victoria's delivery scared me at the time.

I was somewhat experienced in dealing with my own fears during the birth process as I'd been through it twice before, but the alarm at Barbara's pain, the shock of the bright lights, the "foreignness" (an Indian doctor oversaw the birth), and I suppose, my empty feelings after the demise of *I and Albert* all left me short of breath and close to fainting.

I turned to Barbara, who was in the midst of terrible pain.

"I have to go outside for a moment," I said, as I bolted for the door. "Don't worry. I'll be all right."

Looking back on it, Barbara still thinks it's hilarious. It's a lucky guy who has a wife with a sense of humor.

𝄢

We took our new baby girl and our two sons back to Richard Nixon's America. Despite the deep economic depression and the sense of hopelessness and distrust that many Americans were feeling, Nixon had been reelected by a landslide—in large part due to his brilliant strategic timing—ending the Vietnam War three months before the election.

Applause had ended its two-year run on Broadway, and I had no show on the boards. Broadway just wasn't knocking on my door. Post-*Golden Boy*, Sammy Davis was still killing them in Vegas and on TV, but instead of my tunes, he was singing "Who Can I Turn To," "Candy Man," "If I Ruled the World," and "The Lady Is a Tramp." I confess I was jealous that our score doesn't live on in Vegas or Atlantic City.

When several of our songs were bought for television commercials, helping to sell soap, razor blades, and Kool-Aid, I felt good about it. *After all*, I thought, *I'm part of the American economy. And didn't Verdi enjoy hearing his tunes on a hurdy-gurdy?* And though I'd never asked Aaron Copland how he felt about his music accompanying John Wayne on a horse, he had, after all expressed something like delight upon returning from Europe to find out that I had written *Bye Bye Birdie*.

So, because a lot of Kool-Aid had been sold using "Put on a Happy Face," I was asked to head the music department of a large advertising agency.

At first, I found it demeaning. "Hey man, I studied with Nadia Boulanger," I wanted to say. But then I remembered Barbara's advice for finding coins on the street. She has a talent for spotting coins, but I have no knack for it, so one day, I asked her how she did it. She said, "You're looking too hard. You should look down only when there's a coin there."

I accepted the job.

I took a stroll to think about my decision, and as I walked on West Fifty-seventh Street and turned toward Central Park, I felt that I had sunk low.

"And what does that feeling remind you of?"

There he was at the Fifty-ninth Street entrance of Central Park. The fat little boy: Buddy. I thought he was gone. I mean, I hadn't seen him around in a long time. But I guess he's never really far away.

"What does the feeling remind you of?" he repeated.

I felt compelled to answer. "I don't really need the job," I ventured. "It's like when I overeat?"

"Yes...?"

"I have enough," I responded, "but I want more. Always more."

We started walking together in the park. It was chilly and the trees were bare, but Buddy wasn't wearing a coat and didn't seem cold at all. It didn't seem odd to me at all to be talking to this strange kid in knickers.

"Why do you want more than you actually need to sustain your body?" he asked.

"But didn't Beethoven accept commissions for music he didn't want to write?" I countered, thinking to myself, *I've got him now.*

"Did he have the money you have?"

"But I have children—schools...you know..."

"Any other reasons?" He was pushing now.

"I love to write...anything," I admitted. "Connecting notes gives me great satisfaction."

"What do you think that means?"

The reason—the real reason—I just couldn't say out loud.

As if he could read my mind, which of course he could, he whispered, "Try."

I bent down and whispered in his ear so that no one else could hear.

"If I don't do it—write music, I mean—I'd be lonely. I'd die of loneliness."

𝄢

I had never worked in an advertising agency before. People who had worked there for a long time seemed to disparage their own lives, but I seemed to command a kind of celebrity because of *Applause* and *Bye Bye Birdie*.

I learned quickly that this was not to last.

They offered me a corner office and a secretary to set up appointments and answer my telephone. I was told that I could, if I wished, orchestrate and write jingles myself or hire other composers and orchestrators and tell them what to write based on ideas generated by copywriters and sketched out on storyboards.

I declined the corner office and asked instead for a closet-sized room with no windows that was as far as possible from the other executive offices (so no one would hear me when I sang loudly) and a piano.

During my first meeting, I was introduced to all the heads of different accounts and even the owner of the agency, who bid me welcome and then quickly left.

We got down to business, and I swiftly became frightened as all the old doubts seeped in. *What have I really accomplished in my life?* I thought as someone introduced the next item of business: one of the agency's bigger accounts—Pabst Blue Ribbon beer.

A very sophisticated-looking girl turned on a TV monitor, and a film played without sound. It showed two clenched hands in white gloves. One hand touched the other, which then opened, revealing a very small can of Pabst Blue Ribbon beer.

Everyone turned to me.

Oh, Jesus.

A kindly man explained: Pabst was putting a six-ounce can of beer on the market along with the usual eight-ounce can and launching it with a major advertising campaign. I immediately thought, *why don't people drink less of the eight-ounce can?* But I wisely decided to say nothing, which I came to learn is a cardinal rule of advertising.

The kindly man continued. "It's a magician doing a magic trick. The smaller can seemingly appears, like the traditional rabbit out of a hat."

Everyone was still staring at me, and although various kinds of music were passing through my head, the simplest yet most economical way to project this idea would be a snare drum–roll crescendo ending in a struck cymbal. It was a banal idea, but I'd played in enough clubs and strip joints to know the universality of it. So I told them the idea.

I swear two people applauded. Others nodded or said, "Terrific!" or "Of course!" and the sophisticated girl who turned on the monitor smiled at me. I seemed to have passed with flying colors.

When we disbanded, I went to my closet, called my secretary, and asked her who hired musicians for the agency. She quickly gave me the number for the contractor, and I called him. "I need a good percussionist, sit-down drums, and a cymbal on a stand."

The contractor said, "I have the very best—he plays with the New York Philharmonic. He charges double, but he happens to be free this week. Just tell me where and when you want to record and how many other musicians."

One was all I needed, so he set up the studio and the date. Now, because I had about a week with nothing to do, I called my old friend and lyricist Martin Charnin to set up a meeting to discuss an idea he had.

A musical based on the comic strip *Little Orphan Annie*.

CHAPTER FIFTEEN

I Think I'm Gonna Like It Here

I HAD MET MARTIN CHARNIN back in 1959, when he was appearing and understudying Dick Van Dyke in the short-lived revue *The Boys Against the Girls*. Since then, Martin had given up performing and started writing lyrics for such musicals as *Hot Spot* (with Mary Rodgers), and, in 1970, he collaborated with Mary's father, Richard Rodgers, on *Two by Two*. That same year, Martin also won an Emmy for producing an Anne Bancroft TV special.

One of the writers on that TV special was a fellow named Thomas Meehan.

He was also there that day when I met with Charnin about *Little Orphan Annie*. The truth is, I thought the idea was pretty terrible. Tom Meehan thought it was even worse than I did.

I took an immediate liking to him.

Tom was extremely mild-mannered, even permitting someone else to speak before offering any words of his own. It was obvious he hadn't worked in the theater before.

Tom and I had even more to complain about right off the bat. It seemed Martin had had a mock-up poster made for this yet-to-be-written show; the poster prominently featured Bernadette Peters in the starring role.

Tom asked, "Wasn't Little Orphan Annie ten years old?" He was obviously as surprised by the Bernadette Peters poster as I was.

"I believe she was eleven," Martin said with some authority.

Tom nodded, then paused. "And, didn't she have a dog?"

"Yes, she had a dog," I answered. "Also, a father whose name was Warbucks, who was cue-ball bald and wore a plum-sized diamond in his shirt."

"He was in the munitions business and made a penny for every bullet manufactured," Martin added.

"Every bullet?" Tom asked.

"War-bucks. Get it?" I responded, then continued. "Didn't he also have a servant named Punjab, who is Hindu or Muslim?"

"Muslim?" Tom asked.

"It was the Great Depression and everyone was out of work," Martin explained.

"I should add," I went on, "she has no eyes."

Tom was flabbergasted. "She's blind?"

Martin laughed. "I know it sounds *meshugena*, but that's the way Harold Gray drew then. No one in the strip has any eyes."

While Tom, our token non-Jew, tried to figure out just what *meshugena* meant, Martin went on. "Trust me," he said. "I saw a collection of *Little Orphan Annie* cartoons in a bookstore as I was buying a present. I realized then and there this could be a giant hit!"

It sounded crazy, but Martin, who had never been known to wear clothes that were more than a week out of fashion, seemed to know what he was talking about. I figured *Annie* could be shown as a TV show and—who knew—maybe my Pabst beer commercial could be used at the station break.

(Though with *Annie* being a kids' show, beer advertisements weren't all that likely.)

But as we went on, I started to realize that Martin was hitting on something Hal Prince said to me years before, after *It's a Bird...It's a Plane...It's Superman!* had closed. Despite generally positive reviews, the show, also based on a comic strip, had failed to get the audience it needed to stay alive, closing after just 129 performances.

"Write a children's show that kids can bring their parents to, and you may be okay," Hal had told me. "But write a grown-up show that parents can bring their children to, and you've got a hit."

Later on, I realized that a comic strip is an ideal basis for a musical comedy because they are similar forms of popular American culture. That is, both deal in broad stroke, telling simple stories in as few words as possible.

At this first meeting, however, I was not totally convinced.

"This will run on Broadway for years," Martin said, interrupting my thoughts. "Across the country, in films!"

"But this is for TV," I said, turning to my ally. "Tom?"

Tom's thoughts had been drifting. "Suppose the dog does its business onstage. What do we do then?"

But Martin's enthusiasm couldn't be checked. "Let's meet next week! I have an idea for the opening!"

♪:

But, before that could happen, it was back to work for me: the Pabst Blue Ribbon beer recording.

The recording studio was cavernous, and the engineer, Ed Rice, was knowledgeable, fast, and experienced. I connected with him right away. Martin had given me a lyric for *Annie*, but I had to do the music—or, more specifically, the drum roll—for this commercial first. Actually, it was lovely being pulled in two directions like this. It meant I was wanted. Plus, this commercial shouldn't be too bad to bang out.

I explained the concept to my colleagues: The drum set in the big studio was merely for a snare drum roll and a cymbal crash, as though an act were being introduced in a nightclub or circus. Ed set up a click track (a series of audio cues used to synchronize a sound recording with a moving image) that would coordinate the start of the drum roll and the cymbal crash at the end, and as he did that, his assistant set up four microphones.

When the musician came in—this hallowed drummer from the Philharmonic—Ed asked him to sit at the drums and hit the cymbal. Then Ed changed the microphone and went through the same process with the snare drum. Next, there was a discussion about whether the bass drum on the foot pedal should be struck simultaneously with the start and end of the cymbal crash or whether it should be a tom-tom. Or perhaps it should be both. Microphones were set up for all of the various possibilities.

Getting antsy, the drummer asked me if I thought we'd go into overtime, because he had another rehearsal. He could call someone to sub for him at the other gig, but he needed to know in fifteen minutes. And then he handed me the union contract and a tax slip to save time later if he had to split fast.

Finally, the microphones were all set up. Each one was tested, and the click track was added to the film.

"You wanna run it once?" Ed asked.

"Go," said the drummer.

"I give you four for nothing," Ed said.

But the drummer couldn't hear anything, so Ed had to send out an assistant to change two plugs. The click track began with the monitor in sync, and four slash marks coordinating the final cymbal crash. We were set.

"Wanna practice once?" Ed asked.

The drummer said, "I have to call Sol. He's covering me on another job."

"Say hello for me," Ed said coolly as the drummer went out to the hall to arrange for his sub. I began to sweat profusely.

"Will this go into overtime?" I asked. Ed didn't answer, so I continued, "I just started as director of music up at the place, and I don't want to run up a big bill."

"Nobody looks at bills there," Ed responded.

At last, the drummer returned and resumed his seat. Ed started the film and the click track.

"Take one," he announced.

"One?" I said. "It's a damn drum roll."

"Let's try it again," said Ed to the drummer and then to me, "Try not to talk."

The whole procedure was repeated.

"I think we got it," Ed pronounced, but the drummer wanted to try one more time. He felt he hadn't dampened the cymbal quickly enough, and because we were on overtime already, he wanted another shot.

"The commercial will be over," I said to Ed. "What's the difference?"

"Let him try one more. He's a perfectionist."

The drummer tried one more. It sounded as good as the last one. Ed put it all on an audiotape.

I felt as though I'd created a masterpiece and called the agency. A meeting was scheduled for three days later.

"Why three days?" I asked.

Apparently, the Chicago-based client wanted to hear it, too.

Three days went by. Various people would pass me in the hall, saying, "I hear your new commercial is great!" or they'd make a clicking sound, smile, and stick up a thumb—a traditional sign for well done.

On the fourth day, I couldn't help but notice that the clicking sounds and smiles had stopped. No more thumbs-up, no more passing praise.

I was told to report at eleven a.m. the following day in the head of the account's office. He was the same man who had been so kind to me at the first meeting, but the very first thing I noticed about this meeting was that the ebullience of our last encounter was no more.

"Charles," said Mr. Kindness unsmilingly, "the Pabst people listened to your commercial in Chicago."

"And?"

"The wife of the head of Pabst said that the drum roll before the cymbal crash sounded like someone had 'gas.'"

There was a hollow silence.

"Is she a gastroenterologist?" I whispered to the fellow next to me. He turned away as if he had never heard me or even seen me before.

Everyone in the room looked down at their laps; some tightened their lips and shifted uncomfortably. Otherwise, there was nothing but the muted sound of traffic from sixty floors below.

I'd let everyone down and, more than that, sullied my reputation. My mind raced. That drummer was one of the best in the world. The New York Philharmonic!

"Perhaps I made an error in getting such a fine percussionist," I ventured to the now-silent room. "What I should have asked him to do was play a 'cheesier' drum roll."

The sun dimly peeked through the clouds. I observed several small nods.

"Better yet, suppose I hire a bad drummer, one that's played in nightclubs—mainly for magicians or strippers."

Two nods, one hint of a chuckle.

"Could be a solution," Mr. Kindness said, and a few more people nodded. "Okay, let's get on that." Then he turned to his assistant, and said, "Air-France has just signed Gene Kelly. He's going to do a pitch on the airline. Get Charles a storyboard; he may have to go to the Coast and work with him. Kelly's contract says no more than an hour for rehearsing and shooting."

I rushed to the phone, called the music contractor, and asked for the worst drummer he knew. I fixed a recording date, and then looked at the storyboard for Air-France. I felt a rush—everyone needed me! I had no time to think

As it turned out, I didn't have to go to the Coast. Instead, I learned Kelly's vocal range, wrote and recorded some music in New York, and hired that bad drummer.

That Pabst commercial was never put on the air. They decided to stick with the eight-ounce can.

The cost of the commercial? Twenty-five thousand dollars. Meanwhile, the Gene Kelly commercial turned out just fine, and I never even saw the man.

𝄢

In my spare time, I was still meeting with Tom and Martin, and we decided to deal with the cartoonist Harold Gray as if he were Charles Dickens. Gone was the character named Mrs. Mean. Gone was Bernadette Peters. Gone were the hollow holes for eyes, and Punjab, and "penny for each bullet" for Warbucks.

The dog stayed.

With eyes.

Martin and I worked closely on the score. When he liked a melody I'd written, he went off and wrote a lyric. The first—and it turned out the only—lyric Martin showed me *without* my writing music beforehand, was for "It's the Hard-Knock Life." Not a word in that song did we change. I had never heard that expression "hard-knock life," but he assured me it was used. And even if it weren't, it would be.

For every other song, I composed the music to what I thought the scene would be. Tom, bless him, had never written a musical, and so he liked practically every tune I came up with. It made it really easy to work with him as he wrote the book.

As for Martin and me, if I had any criticism of a lyric, he staunchly defended it. It was a very different working relationship from what I'd had in the past with Lee, who was much more amenable. In this case, as always, sometimes I was wrong, and sometimes I was right. But the discussions between Martin and me were a little more—what's the word?—"salty."

Martin was determined to direct *Annie*, but because he wasn't a "name" stage director (he would actually win another Emmy that year for co-directing a Gershwin TV special. But that was TV!) and because he had little reputation, I refused to agree to his demand at this point that he would automatically be the director. I was worried that without a big-name director we'd never attract investors. We let the subject pass in the early stages, but it surfaced and again and again and, as it turned out, nearly sank the whole venture.

With each passing week, it became clearer that no one was particularly eager to hear *Annie* or to even try to imagine it as a musical. Early auditions for friends and possible producers had induced blank looks—not unlike the empty eyeballs of the Harold Gray cartoon itself.

As Martin, Tom, and I met, our memories of the early *Little Orphan Annie* began to focus on what now seemed an obvious fact: that it was drawn in shades of gray with black shadows. It was, after all, the time of the Great Depression. And another thought arose, too: America of the 1970s was also a land in trouble. Once we began thinking more about FDR, out-of-work stockbrokers, parched land, hungry farmers, and not Bernadette Peters, the show started to take shape.

At long last, two investors surfaced, but we found out they were "tax shelter" specialists—a somewhat iffy branch of accounting, we were told—who tried to attract rich investors, usually to get high deductions on their income taxes (e.g., investing in an exhausted coal mine).

This didn't give us much confidence, but they had come up with option money, and I supposed one should never look a gift horse in the mouth. Or a coal mine.

But there was no one else. I went back to those "friends" who, after *Applause* opened and was making lots of money, had said to me, "Next time, tell me when you have a new show." I tried telling these friends about *Annie,* but no one was willing to get on board with us.

That shouldn't have surprised me. Tom and I hadn't liked it either, at first; but as it was starting to take on a new shape, I was beginning to think we had something there. If only someone could just see it.

In 1974, we played the score for Michael Price, the new artistic director of the Goodspeed Opera House, in East Haddam, Connecticut. He had recently taken the reigns of the little jewel box of a theater from Al Selden, who had produced *Man of La Mancha* there.

Michael Price liked the show but, agreeing with me, said we should pursue other directors. Martin was angry, but I begged him to go along, saying that we had to at least speak to other directors to please Michael. I favored Martin if we could get investors willing to agree, and I told him so.

Anyway, it turned out that either other directors were uninterested or the three of us disliked *their* ideas (one of which, surprisingly, was to cast Bernadette Peters in the title role). After hearing this, Martin said, shockingly, that if he couldn't direct it, he would collaborate with another composer.

I was given no choice. After all, he had come up with the idea, so I reluctantly took back my music.

Martin continued to write *Annie*—now with someone else's songs. I felt awful about it, of course, but Martin couldn't wait. I particularly remember playing what had been the music for "Tomorrow" for a number of lyricists I had then started working with, but no one could hear anything in the melody. Martin and I remained friends; I respected his opinion, but he couldn't see mine.

Of course I was curious about who his other composer was. It couldn't be Steve Sondheim, who wrote his own lyrics. And

John Kander was too wrapped up with Fred. I decided it was Cy Coleman, because when I asked him one day if he was going to an ASCAP luncheon, he looked at me in an odd way and said, "Tomorrow?"

𝄢

A year went by, and then in 1975, I was still turning out advertising jingles when I got a phone call from Michael Price.

"I'm calling from London," he said. "My wife and I are in Piccadilly Circus, and I'm singing a song and Johanna is singing another song, and neither of us can figure out where we know these songs from, and it finally occurs to us that they're both from that show you played for me last year—*Annie*."

Of course, I was flattered, but I explained that there was no more *Annie*. Martin was doing the show with another composer, and the songs that Michael remembered had been disbursed into other projects or put in a drawer.

"Well, you have to get it back together!"

"I'll do what I can."

I phoned Martin and told him of the call. I asked him to please meet me for coffee, which he agreed to without much emotion. I brought my wife, Barbara, with me, because she's so good at finding those coins on the street and in life, and because, over the years, she's shown me that she's more calm, more sensitive, and more astute than I.

I laid out the whole thing for Martin: Michael's phone call after a year, the fun we could still have. I asked about his wife and children. I drank two cups of bad coffee, and waited. Martin was dressed in a big furry coat that meshed with his gray bear beard, and I felt somewhat like I was talking to a bear.

He sounded reasonable enough, but I was still somewhat worried about an attack.

"I've been thinking about this lately," he said, which I took as a good sign—one that his other *Annie* was either unfinished or not living up to his expectations.

"I would agree to not be the director, if one of three other directors agrees to take the show on."

I knew what was coming and held my breath for the inevitable.

He continued: "Jerry Robbins, Gower Champion, or Michael Kidd."

I should have been relieved that he didn't say Sir Laurence Olivier.

"But, Martin," I jumped in, "they're all unreachable, untouchable! This is not a play by Harold Pinter or a Bertolt Brecht opera. It's a comic-strip character with a mop of red hair, a man who has no hair, and a dog with no eyes."

"I'm sorry, that's where I stand."

"Can we at least speak to a few other directors? Michael Price is ready, and if Tom and you and I mark time, I feel it could go your—our—way, and you could direct. Let's at least start auditions, work on the show, and force Michael into a decision."

Barbara refilled Martin's coffee, and all the time I'm thinking, *if Michael Price can remember two tunes over a period of a year, maybe there* is *a diamond buried under the mud.*

Well, of course Kidd, Champion, and Robbins were unreachable, unavailable, or uninterested. So as the summer of 1976 approached, we began auditions anyway, and two things happened: The first was that Martin took over running the auditions, and as Michael Price saw, there was no use fighting the inevitable: Martin became the director.

The second was that, of all of the young girls who turned up to audition, only seven had the vocal range I'd written into the score. (I tested them thoroughly by having them sing the last part of "Happy Birthday," working their way slowly up in different keys so they'd have no verbal or rhythmic challenges.) By coincidence, seven were exactly how many orphans we needed. How convenient, then, that there were only seven girls, in the northeast of the United States who could sing the leaping phrase "'Steada kisses, We get kicked!"

It's very strange to think now, that, in a few short years there would hardly be a young girl in America, Asia, or Europe who could not sing this leap of notes: an octave and a fifth! It's like when track's five-minute-mile record was broken—suddenly everyone was breaking it and even four-minute miles became not unheard of!

Well, the magnificent seven orphans in *Annie* did it first.

𝄢

We were to have a ten-week run that bicentennial summer of 1976, beginning on August 10.

During the rehearsal period, Tom and Martin and I wrote and wrote. Then we rewrote what we'd written. The night of our first run-through at Goodspeed, there was a hurricane, and all the lights went out. Trees and power lines had been knocked down when I got a call from Barbara, who was carrying our fourth child, the one we wanted to call Annie, if the baby was a girl.

Barbara had told me she had been bleeding, but I didn't know about miscarriages, so I just left Martin working through both acts of the show and rushed back to the house where Barbara and I were staying temporarily. By the time I got there, Barbara's bathrobe was full of blood.

I got her into the car and drove her to the Yale New Haven Hospital. Although I didn't know how to get there, Barbara gave me directions. As usual, Barbara knew just what road to take.

As Barbara was brought her into an operating room, I paced, my thoughts tumbling like a washing machine. I was so worried about Barbara and about our baby, but the damn show kept eating at me, and my mind still clung to the unwritten second section of "Easy Street."

What kind of a husband was I?

How could I be thinking of a new song when Barbara was bleeding?

I paced into an anteroom, thinking about how we had planned to name the baby Annie. Finally, the doctor came in and told me we had lost the baby. It was male. God seemed to have mixed up everything.

I cried then, my tears just as much for my frustrations about the show as about our baby who was not to be.

Barbara remained in the hospital. She was more depressed than I'd ever seen her, but even after we began performances on August 10, all the work that still needed to be done on *Annie* tugged at me. Every morning, Martin, Tom, and I would wake to write a new scene or a new song. And all these new scenes and songs were rehearsed and tried the same night. How the cast did it, how Martin and Tom and I wrote it all, I don't know. Songs were put down in such a fever that I relearned the process of composing. Or maybe I was practicing an important compositional technique: letting go.

After one week, we decided to replace our Annie, thirteen-year-old Kristen Vigard. Kristin's genuinely sweet interpretation was not tough enough for the street-smart character, so a tougher girl, who had been one of the orphans, was promoted to the lead. Andrea McArdle, our new Annie, learned the whole part virtually overnight.

Things were getting better. Michael Price would stand at the bottom of the stairs at the end of each performance, greeting the audience as it left. The people didn't look that happy, but *Annie* was getting tighter. Audiences were laughing more, and I even heard a few "not bads," and the girl at the confection stand told me she'd sold a few more chocolate bars.

Our hopes rose, not a lot, but a little, until one day, we were informed that Walter Kerr, the first-string critic at the *New York Times* (a man for whom a theater would be named one day), was coming to Connecticut to review *Annie*.

Didn't he have anything better to do? A man like that could go to Paris. Or Barbados. *A man like that could kill your brother!*

Or your show!

Now, even the dog, Sandy (a foundling who had been rescued from the pound by the then-stage manager, Bill Berloni), had formed an unquenchable ambition to be a star.

What are you gonna do Mr. Kerr, break a little dog's heart?

Yet . . . Kerr *could* like it, couldn't he? Couldn't he like the story of a redheaded orphan who finds a stray dog?

We were about to find out.

𝄢

Because there were only two performances before Kerr arrived, and we couldn't make any more changes before he came, I decided to return to New York for two days—after all, the advertising agency had been paying me a salary, and I had been absent for seven weeks.

To my amazement, no one at the agency seemed to have noticed I was gone. People said hello as though they had seen me yesterday, and one man said, "Don't forget the eleven o'clock meeting."

"Right." What the heck was the meeting that about? "You mean for the, uh ... "

"Yeah, the new root beer."

"Of course," I lied, "the new root beer. Remind me of where the meeting is?"

Seven weeks, and no one had missed me.

The meeting concerned a new root beer that the Coca-Cola Company was putting out. It was called "Razzle Root Beer," and they needed a jingle. I got together with the account people, and they explained the positioning of the new product (not as traditional as Hires Root Beer—bet you didn't know root beers had "positions"). I wrote a jingle, and everyone liked it. What a relief from writing for that little redheaded orphan girl!

And Barbara was feeling better, though still depressed.

Later, in a recording studio, a groovy choral group sang the jingle to exhort all to buy this root beer, and it bounced and jingled. *Annie,* for the moment, was off my mind. The feeling of relief was like a wonder drug to a sick patient. I had done something everyone liked! Take that, Walter Kerr!

The account people came to the recording session, along

with an executive from Coca-Cola itself, and everyone bounced and jingled along with it.

"Great!" "That's it!" "He's got it!"

But there was one small request from the Coca-Cola executive: "Could you please use a little less 'tiffany' on the word 'cola'?"

Somehow managing to keep my face straight, I turned to the percussion player and, in all seriousness, said, "A little less 'tiffany' at measure twelve."

"Got it," he said and, without changing expression, he made a mark in the music.

It's amazing what a little love and praise can do. I felt thinner, stronger, convinced the little blond singing alto really admired me. We went for a final take when suddenly the control room yelled, "Hold it!"

What could it be? A haggard-looking lawyer had just gotten off the phone with the news that the word "razzle" was subject to some kind of copyright infringement and could not be used.

There was a huddle, and then all heads turned to me.

Should I have known?

I had an idea, so I said, "I have an idea."

The faces that turned to me were a mix of impatience, desperation, and antagonism. Jobs were on the line. And millions of dollars in revenues.

I took a deep breath, then spoke. "Why not change the name of the root beer?"

My suggestion was greeted with sneers.

"Let him talk," someone said.

"Change it to what?" someone else asked.

I took a deep breath. "How's 'ramblin'?"

There was a long pause.

Someone nodded. "No 'g' at the end? Just 'ramblin'?"

Someone else spoke, "Easygoing, but does it zing?"

Another executive chimed in. "Homey, but modern," he said.

The lawyer was on the phone talking intensely but not quite as grimly now. The air began to lighten in the control room.

"How long would it take to re-record?"

"Just one more take," I said. "It's just that one word we change."

I did another take, using "ramblin'?" instead of "razzle." They all cheered. Oh God, such pleasure! One word and a room full of smiles. Millions of dollars for everyone!

Ramblin' Root Beer became a best seller. Coca-Cola built a new factory to produce and distribute it.

I went back to Goodspeed to work on *Annie,* knowing I'd helped the American economy.

♪:

The Saturday night that Walter Kerr came to the show, Martin and Michael Price paced the hallway. Tom went to a nearby restaurant and drank martinis. I went to the same restaurant and ate a small salad and a basketful of buttered rolls.

The applause at the end of the show was un-tumultuous.

The next day (a Sunday) we read the *Times* and on the front page, center, of the Entertainment section, was Walter Kerr's review.

The headline read, T'AIN'T FUNNY BOYS!

He hated it.

Kerr said in no uncertain terms that we were *not* Broadway bound. We were crushed. Even Martin, ever optimistic, looked defeated. Tom was broke. And I felt exposed, naked, untalented, and fat.

My mother had triumphed at last.

But Tom—sweet and mild-mannered Tom—had, as it turned out, a stubborn streak. And Martin, Bronx born, had been a gang member in the original cast of *West Side Story*, which meant he'd been in the ring with Jerry Robbins. Neither Martin nor Tom would lie down easily! Had a composer ever been so blessed? They had faith in me, in the idea, in the three of us.

So we sat down the next morning on a sunny knoll in back of the theater. Martin and Tom came with their cartons of coffee, I brought lots of forced cheer, and we pored over each word Kerr had written. We parsed his sentences and discussed his background. We were like rabbis deciphering the Talmud, imams interpreting the Koran.

Why does Warbucks use such-and-such phrase? Is Annie too sugary sweet? How come the audience laughs when FDR enters a room? Etc., etc.

We spent the day analyzing the show, arguing, and rereading Kerr's review. We did the same thing the next day and that night. And then it hit us: Kerr was a traditional Roosevelt liberal, a man of the 1930s, deeply influenced by the Depression. In that respect, he was like my father. I know how my father loved Roosevelt and how the Depression frightened him.

At first, it didn't seem that important, then it slowly sunk in. Perhaps we had made the Depression too inconsequential and had turned Roosevelt into a clown. Perhaps we'd made

Warbucks too kindly, made Annie too sweet. Had bucolic Connecticut audiences lulled us? During the time of our show, millions of Americans were out of work, on breadlines. Perhaps my early love for Shirley Temple was still fluttering in my heart. It seems simple now, but the surgery that followed was anything but. Arteries had to be removed, bypasses cleared. We left no sentence, song, or bit of direction untouched. We were fired up.

And the audience started to leap to its feet!

Michael Price said he had no money left for rehearsals, so Martin and I spent our own. (Tom had been broke from the start.) There were three weeks remaining before we closed in Connecticut.

Probably forever.

And then . . . an incredible bit of luck happened.

Jay Presson Allen—my *I and Albert* collaborator, a close personal friend, and a remarkably honest woman—came to see *Annie*. I had asked her to come because I knew she would tell the truth. I knew that she was likely to say, "Close the show," if she didn't like it.

I also knew, from having shopped antique stores with her in London, she often managed to find a magnificent piece others would have never noticed on a half-hidden shelf. Tough, but with a heart that could melt at a moderately warm temperature, she had the hauteur of a film star and a mouth like a cobra. I trusted her.

She came to see *Annie* with her husband Lew (who had co-produced *I and Albert*), and afterward, she said, "I think this is a hit."

I could have kissed her.

"Mike lives nearby," she continued, "and I'm going to call him."

Mike was Mike Nichols, the superstar director I obviously didn't have the guts to call, so Jay called him from the backstage phone.

"Mike, I'm down here at Goodspeed, and there's a musical you should see," she said into the phone. "I don't care if your wife is having a baby. Get your ass down here!"

And Mike did come down to Goodspeed to see it (Jay is hard to refuse), and after the show, he said, "It's good, really good."

"It's not yet," I responded, "but we're going to keep working on it."

"Don't give me that crap," he said. "I want to produce it!"

Not once did I ask how his wife's pregnancy was going or think of my wife's miscarriage, for that matter, or the baby we were going to name Annie—it had all flown from my mind.

"I want to produce it!" he had said. The words echoed in my ears.

Someone, and not just any someone, but Mike Nichols, wanted to produce *Annie*!

The orchestra in my head played loud and clear.

And it was playing "Tomorrow!"

CHAPTER SIXTEEN

Tomorrow

FIVE YEARS AFTER Martin bought a book of comic strips, four years after he revealed his hopeless idea to Tom and me, and two years after another composer musicalized a different *Annie*, Tom, Martin, and I—*Annie*'s original Drs. Frankenstein—had stitched together a new redheaded orphan.

Slowly, slowly the bandages were removed, and with a partially deaf choreographer named Peter Gennaro leading the company in new songs and dances, a crippled dog practicing new tricks, and Tom, Martin, and I doing much patching, cutting, and praying, finally, one night, it moved. Slowly, slowly rising from a mountain of smudged music paper and retyped scripts, wearing a bright red dress by Theoni Aldredge, hair gussied up, and sounding like a whole brass section, we heard, as if for the first time:

"The sun'll come out . . ."

Our butterfly had emerged from its Connecticut cocoon.

We were thrilled to have Mike Nichols on the team, though we soon learned he didn't actually invest his own money. What he liked to do, he told us, is to say, "Change those shoes from the blue to red." That was his conception of how a producer acts, but I soon learned he did a whole lot more.

Soon after Mike came on board, I made an important and unusual decision: I wanted no billing for any of us at the beginning. Not for my collaborators, nor the producers, choreographer, myself, anyone.

No one except Mike Nichols.

Hal Prince's words were still ringing in my ears: "If a musical appears to be a children's musical, and the children can bring their parents to it, it probably won't be a hit. But if it's an *adult* musical that parents can bring their *children* to, you've got the possibilities of a smash!"

A poster that reads "Mike Nichols Presents *Annie*" would scream "Adult!"

"That's impossible," everyone said. "What about Tom's contribution? What about Martin as lyricist and director? The choreographer, the cast, the dog? "What about all the money invested in this by people who want their names tied to it?"

I felt certain about this. I was going to stand up, and I was not going to be afraid.

And if I didn't get my way, I would take away my music.

Most of this went on behind closed doors. No one except Mike's agent, Sam Cohn (and, I expect, Mike, who didn't object), and my wife knew of this roadblock I had erected, but it seemed I *had* the power because I *took* the power.

And you know what? It worked.

One of the biggest losers was, of course, Martin, who had directed the show and now whose reputation might be obscured by the fact that another name, another director, would be forever linked with the show. It would always be "Mike Nichols Presents . . ."

Nevertheless, I felt it was an important choice, which would enable people to hold *Annie* up to a different standard.

The argument Martin and I had from the beginning regarding his directing the show really came home to roost.

Recently, Gerry Schoenfeld, chairman of the Shubert Organization, approached me. "Really, Charles," he said, "between you and me, *Annie* is too good. Nichols really directed it, didn't he?"

I told Gerry the truth as I tell everyone, and as I do now: Martin Charnin directed every word and note in *Annie*.

𝄢

We were in fairly good shape in terms of the show itself, but at that point, the financing was still incomplete. Because Mike was in the picture now, the two original "tax shelter" investors refused to drop their option, but one of the pair was now in jail, and they'd apparently exhausted their nominal backing contribution. With Mike Nichols being Mike Nichols, it took four or five phone calls from his agent's office for the rest of the money to become *almost* all subscribed.

But there was still a large hole—more than a hundred thousand dollars—that needed filling before legal papers could be drawn up. The law required that all financing be complete before production (e.g., designing and building sets, sewing costumes, hiring choreographers, etc.) could begin. It's been described to me as a "widow's law"—its purpose being to protect old ladies from being chiseled out of life savings by a producer who might not be fully financed.

At this moment, the only ones capable of completing the full backing were "the Shuberts"—affectionately named that in honor of the real Shuberts, J. J. and Lee, who used to own virtually all theaters in New York. Although they were dissolved as a monopoly by the government into a smaller entity, they were still the owners of largest number theaters in New York. Now, Gerry Schoenfeld—whom I had known since he was a lawyer working for Lawrence Shubert, who owned the Majestic Theatre where *Golden Boy* had been a hit—and Bernie Jacobs (since deceased), a dour-looking but sweet man, were usually referred to collectively as "the Shuberts."

I scheduled a meeting between Mike Nichols and the "Shuberts" at my apartment on West Fifty-seventh Street. Barbara served coffee and Entenmanns's coffee cake. I ate a lot of the cake as I listened and tried to appear calm. Neither Bernie nor Gerry, as I recall, bothered to say if they actually liked *Annie*. My presumption was that they *did* like it, or we wouldn't have been meeting at all. But who knew?

Mike opened the meeting by saying that *Annie* should open at the Eisenhower Theater in Washington's Kennedy Center. "The Shuberts" controlled booking for that theater (a friendly space given its modernity, which held eleven hundred seats) and for its much larger sibling, the Opera House, which holds about two thousand seats or more.

Mike said flatly that we wanted the remaining financial backing in order to open *Annie* at the Eisenhower Theater. Bernie said no; he had gone through the show's budget carefully, and even if every seat at the Eisenhower Theater were sold, *Annie* would still lose $110,000 a week. But at the Opera House, even at less than 100 percent capacity, the weekly profit could be substantial.

Now, I had never seen Mike Nichols go to the mat. He was (and still is) a reasonable and soft-spoken man. But Mike wanted the smaller, more intimate theater, the Eisenhower. He knew it would be better for the show and refused to see it any other way.

I've seen Mike whisper into actors' ears and—almost without seeming to take sides—settle a steaming fight between them. I've known him to suggest most sweetly that perhaps a trumpet player wasn't hitting all the right notes, and should I defend the trumpet player, then ask me with perfect innocence, "Have you a death wish?"

So he responded to Bernie and Gerry in his way. "In that case," he declared, "we shall lose $110,000 a week."

The moment was tense. The Entenmann's coffee cake lay in a lump in my stomach as Gerry and Bernie left.

I don't even remember them putting on their coats and going to the elevator (we lived on the seventh floor, so they must have), but I do remember hearing the beating of wings as my career flew out the window. Should I have said something as I used to do when my parents quarreled? "Dad didn't mean to say that. His feelings were hurt and his blood sugar's low."

What I do remember is meeting the next afternoon in Sam Cohn's office. Sam was on the telephone while Mike was suggesting people to call, adding up what we needed, what we had, suggesting that we turn down a certain investor who would come with strings but suggesting another smaller one who would be influential in bringing in other investors.

Mike was a major-league player—the one who, when I was a kid, I was scared would drop the high fly, but who always just stood there calmly waiting until, sure enough, the ball fell right into his mitt.

My admiration for Mike was intense. He seemed so modest. Jokes he told were always on himself. He told me when he first became famous, at that level when you're recognized by others, he got off a plane in New York wearing a new camel-hair coat, threw up in the center of the floor and, as he tried to regain his footing, kept slipping in the vomit as people pointed him out.

I'm told he had only a small amount of his own money invested in the show. Smart. My mother would have loved him.

Sure enough, we got the Eisenhower Theater.

𝄢

Dorothy Loudon had agreed to play Miss Hannigan. Dorothy was a remarkable woman and a great singing comedienne. For years now, Dorothy was used to getting great reviews in unsuccessful shows, such as *Nowhere to Go But Up*, *The Fig Leaves Are Falling*, and *Lolita, My Love*. Dorothy had also been a regular on *The Gary Moore Show*, replacing Carol Burnett, who would later take her roles in the film versions of *Annie* and *Noises Off*.

Dorothy had made her stage debut in 1962 in *The World of Jules Feiffer* directed by Mike Nichols, but when Mike called her up to find out if she was interested in being in *Annie*, she hesitated. "Don't you think I'm too old to play Annie Oakley?"

Her husband, Norman Paris, a great arranger and the man who had many times employed me as a substitute pianist after college when I had no work, convinced her that the songs were good. So, she took the role.

"And not because of Mike Nichols," she assured me later in our relationship.

The night of the first preview, I spent the whole lead-up to showtime trying to convince Dorothy that the audience would not hate her because she was mean to little girls. She was convinced everyone would despise her and that she'd made a giant mistake.

About twenty minutes into the show, I wasn't really sure how it was going. Tension does that. The audience seemed attentive but hardly transported. Then, near the end of the first act, there was a hair-raising scream from backstage. Dorothy's foot had gotten caught in a winch. The house lights were turned up, and the entire audience stood, applauding.

Tom caught my eye: "Do we have to use the second act?"

Martin joined us to watch the cheering audience. "Dorothy's okay. It's just a bruise on her ankle. Why is everyone standing?" I had figured out that they were applauding the actress whose foot had been caught—like in a football stadium when they carry out the wounded tackle. Could it be that the standing ovation was for the show itself? At intermission? Unheard of.

In the midst of everything, the stage manager reminded us that we had committed to go to the White House directly after the show and sing for the president, and we rushed through the second act. How meetings with presidents are arranged, I don't know (I imagine Nichols had something to do with it); nevertheless, we were hustled aboard buses to go to the White House.

The audience was still cheering. (Or were they asking for their money back?)

Everyone was a wreck—everyone except Andrea McArdle, our Annie, the little girl who never seemed to get upset over anything. The leading lady had gotten caught in a winch, and Andrea, moments away from singing for the president of the

United States, was calmly chatting away while Tom and Martin and I were in utter panic.

The next day, the box office phone lines were semi-busy, which made me semi-happy. It seemed at least we were less than a disaster. I forced myself to remember wise words from Alan Lerner: "All I ask at my age is that I'm not humiliated by the reviews."

We were doing okay, but we all knew the show had major holes because (a) the audience seemed to break out coughing during our brilliant opening number (featuring apple sellers in the Depression), and (b) "N.Y.C.," practically the only number in the show that used the entire company, had turned into a numbing "stage wait."

In most musicals, if a choreographer or director doesn't like a song or can't stage it successfully, the composer and lyricist are asked to change it. This they invariably do because most composers and lyricists have murky opinions of themselves or they wouldn't do what they do in the first place. (They'd be tap dancers, lawyers, or hedge-fund investors.) But there is (sometimes) a great advantage in having your lyricist double as director.

Martin was a never-give-up kind of guy. Instead of just rewriting the song, he did everything to try to get what was already written to work. In Martin's and Peter Gennaro's various versions of the song "N.Y.C.," it had been sung by firemen, movie ushers, tourists—even Sandy made it into the song. There were moving sidewalks, stationary sidewalks, nurses pushing strollers, policemen chasing purse snatchers, and I wouldn't have been surprised if one night Nazi storm troopers had come out to sing it.

Every night Sam Cohn, Mike Nichols's agent, would say to me, "When are you going to change the 'N.Y.C.' number?" Sometimes he would say it while he was passing by, not looking at me, sometimes he'd mime it across a crowded room, and sometimes he'd whisper it in my ear.

That's musicals. Everyone cares too much. I know I did.

Part of the problem with the number was an ill-timed moment in the middle, when one singer's note landed much too prominently. That singer was an intense girl with a huge warm voice whom I had found while at the advertising agency. Her name was Laurie Beechman, and she'd never been on the stage before, but when I brought her to Martin's attention, she not only became a member of the ensemble but also won a featured spot as a character we called "star-to-be."

During all the myriad of changes that kept the number in flux, Martin decided to place Laurie in a very strong position on stage, resulting in her note in the vocal arrangement ringing out too strongly. During this moment, she was in the ensemble, but, seconds later, she was to become our "star-to-be," and we couldn't have her debut too soon. To me, it all seemed musically unsound.

One night, in a restaurant with most of the cast looking on, I confronted Martin about this and we almost came to blows over whether to change her note or his staging. Fortunately, Mike Nichols, in another example of his statesmanship, broke up the fight.

Was I quick to anger because I was subconsciously jealous that Martin had taken over my discovery? (It was rumored that he and Laurie were having a fling.) Perhaps. But the truth was I was right about the music.

In the end, Laurie Beechman was removed from the earlier part of the number, and got to shine brightly in her Broadway debut. Still, it was clear that we were all very nervous and this "almost-fight" in front of the cast just added to the strain on everyone. Although we hadn't officially opened, word of mouth seemed to be growing. Important Washington figures attended. One night, Henry Kissinger came to a preview. When I was introduced to him during intermission as the composer of *Annie* he looked past me, offered me a limp hand, and didn't even try to conceal his boredom.

I felt like a third world country with no oil.

I was trying not to count my chickens before they hatched, so it was with stunned surprise that I greeted the incredible explosion when the Washington press unanimously and wholeheartedly took *Annie* to their collective hearts.

When the papers hit the stands, eight telephone lines in the box office blew out due to the immense demand for tickets. Classified ads for new apartments mentioned properties being "near *Annie*" as an inducement. The head of the Kennedy Center recognized me in the hallway. I was personally called by two senators' offices begging for house seats.

Still we kept working. Mike was especially vigilant, observing and changing a great deal more than the "blue shoes" he imagined would be his due as producer. Along the way, he had become a watchful shepherd—good-natured but keeping the sheep in line nonetheless.

Despite the positive feedback, we were forced to admit that the very beginning of the show didn't work. All right, it's the Depression; men are selling apples, and the orphans are suitably wan and tough.

"So what?" we felt like the audience was saying each night. Something else was needed, and someone (Martin remembers it was he, I remember it was I, and perhaps Tom remembers it was he . . . I'm sure the usher from the mezzanine takes credit for it as well) pointed out that we weren't hearing Annie's problem soon enough. Whoever's idea it was, Martin and I came up with a song called "Maybe," and Tom preceded it with a clever and touching scene from the orphans. The moment it debuted in the show, you could tell by the intense quiet of the audience that it was working!

What is there about a melody and lyric expressing loneliness and longing that can convince us more of emotion than any talk that says the same thing? ("I'm lonely, I'm lost.") It's as magical and surprising to me as it must be to any amateur.

And the melody hadn't just "come" to me. It was the first four measures of a melody I had written for a beer commercial that the advertising agency had rejected. What didn't work for beer certainly worked for *Annie*.

During our D.C. run, there were editorials in the Washington newspapers, and an especially gratifying one in *Time* magazine, about how *Annie* had caught the mood and needs of our country, helping to salve our post-Watergate wounds.

My father had loved *Time* magazine, and I wished he were alive to read the review.

$$9:$$

And then, on April 21, 1977, *Annie* moved to New York, to the Alvin (now the Neil Simon) Theatre. Everything I'd dreamed of was given to me. Even Walter Kerr apologized in a column.

Could my mother's view of life been wrong? Could Buddy have left town for good?

It's this memory that's the hardest to describe, for it's been in my dreams too many times to be really true: double lines of people stretching from the front of the Alvin Theatre on Fifty-second Street, curling around the corner to Fifty-third and Eighth Avenue, and back again. But it was real, and I stood on the opposite side of the street breathing it in: the admiration, the love, the money. Beautiful women in Oscar de la Renta dresses smiled at me. And there I stood, well dressed (no sneakers), slim, given immediate seating at expensive restaurants.

Charles Strouse. A composer.

I turned. Standing next to me was Mike Nichols. He couldn't possibly share these silly, mundane, childish thoughts. Could he?

He looked sheepish and glanced at me with an embarrassed smile on his lips. I said to him, with a rare feeling of authority, "Mike, do me a favor and stand across the street near the line of people and make a silly face. I want a photograph."

And he said, "Don't be an idiot." But you know what? He crossed the street, made a face, and I took the picture.

Then I noticed, by coincidence that I was standing near the Musicians Union Hall, where, thirty years ago at this very same time of day, I used to go to put my name down for a job as a piano player. And then time whooshed backward, and I thought I could see that fat and frightened kid—me with dark circles under my eyes, and Mike Nichols who had just come from Europe looking like a young, sad Warbucks.

But now, we were both standing here—a couple of misfits from P.S. 87.

𝄢

Annie won six Tony Awards that year, including Best Musical, Best Score, Best Book, and a very well deserved Best Actress statue for Dorothy Loudon, who finally got a hit show. It was a show that started with adults bringing their children, but over the course of the 2,377 performances, it started to seem like legions of little girls in Mary Jane shoes were dragging their parents to see it.

In 1978, London welcomed the little red-haired girl for 1,485 performances. Andrea McArdle got to do the first forty performances before British Actors' Equity got one of their own girls in there. Back in New York there was an assembly line of aspiring leather-lunged belters begging to fill Andrea's shoes.

One of them was my own discovery.

In 1977, the same year *Annie* premiered on Broadway, the Manhattan Theatre Club produced a revue of my songs entitled *By Strouse*. In that cast was a plucky and talented nine-year-old named Sarah Jessica Parker, whom I recommended when we were casting for *Annie* replacements.

With the exception of me, everyone connected with the show was against casting Sarah Jessica as Annie. She was "too sad looking," they said, and "too dark." But I had worked with her in my revue, and knew how talented she was, so I insisted.

And I won.

Sarah Jessica joined the cast as one of the orphans, before stepping into the lead role in March of 1979. She played Annie for a year. And just think: If I hadn't insisted on her, how many millions of women today would be without their manual of how to be single and sexy in the city?

Annie spawned four national touring companies and just as many bus-and-truck versions, and the movie rights were sold to Columbia Pictures for nine million dollars, a record amount of money.

We were certain from the start that the huge fee they were paying us was meaningless unless we all could have a part in the making of the film. In fact, Mike Nichols refused to get on board at all. I personally suspected that he had wrung all he could from the little orphan. But I, along with Tom and Martin, had never seen this amount of money. We believed it would give us all the kind of security we had never enjoyed before, so we signed on.

Our suspicions peaked when John Huston (Oscar-winning director of such great films as *The Maltese Falcon* and *The African Queen* who had never directed a musical and I suspect hadn't even seen one) was made director and a hip London choreographer named Arlene Phillips (she was later to choreograph the roller-skating trains in *Starlight Express*. Enough said.) was put in charge of the musical numbers.

When we spoke to producer Ray Stark (he had produced *Funny Girl* on stage and screen), he told us not to worry. "We'll get every kid in the world anyway. Now I want to make the movie sexy."

Annie? Sexy?

When we wanted to talk further about the script that we were shown, we were refused any access to the set or to any performers. The only actor who even talked to me was Albert Finney, who was playing Daddy Warbucks. I was even denied access to my good friend Carol Burnett, who was being asked to play Miss Hannigan more and more drunkenly.

It was only when we threatened to give an interview to the *New York Times* about how the original creators were being shut out that we were suddenly granted access to the movie set.

There was John Huston on what looked to me like a throne, sitting above the goings on. I watched as he directed the little girls with no emotional connection between him and the children at all. There seemed to be no sense of reality.

When I again said something to Ray Stark, he replied, "That's the trouble with you New York writers. You want to make everything you write into *Hamlet*."

The film's reviews in 1982 ranged from positive to extremely hostile, and in spite of a $57 million U.S. box office take (making it the tenth highest grossing film of the year), the film still did not turn a profit on its theatrical release.

In 1999, a new film version of *Annie* directed by the brilliant Rob Marshall was presented on television. This production went back to the tone of the show and made all the authors and millions of viewers very happy.

𝄢

To be a part of someone's memories, to bring joy—what a gift I'd been given! Sad Ethel and sick Ira—they gave me their genes, but I was able to orchestrate a small piece of people's lives.

The tape rolls in my mind to one of those telethons that collect money to stamp out infantile paralysis. A little girl in a wheelchair was brought out and the emcee (I think it was Jerry Lewis) said, "Let's see if this child will walk tonight. The money you've pledged, plus a little something the orchestra is going to do, may show the way."

And the orchestra started playing, and a shapely woman in a sequin dress began singing, "The sun'll come out . . ." and the little girl struggled to raise herself from her chair. And, as the sequined singer reached "Tomorrow, tomorrow, I love you, tomorrow," the little girl worked her way up and fell into Jerry Lewis's arms. The audience screamed.

Was it possible Martin Charnin and I had achieved sainthood? And would we be notified of it like a Tony nomination?

I think of the time a man said to me at a party, "When our little boy was killed in a car accident, your song 'Tomorrow' pulled us through." I thanked him as earnestly as I could with my mouth stuffed with a hot cheese ball.

(Then again, at another party, a different man said to me, "If I have to hear my daughter sing 'Tomorrow' one more time, I'm going to kill myself—and you!")

Be that as it may, when *Annie* opened in Tokyo in 1978, thousands of little Japanese girls climbed out of buses, subways, and airplanes, and astoundingly, they all knew every song from *Annie*—in English—and the cast recording hadn't been released there yet.

In fact, for the last thirty years, every spring, the cherry blossoms and *Annie* bloom again in Tokyo. With Nippon Television Network behind it, she might be there thirty years from now as well.

It's nice to know there will always be tomorrow.

CHAPTER SEVENTEEN

Dance a Little Closer

IT TOOK US OVER FIVE YEARS to get *Annie* up on the stage—from my first meeting with Martin and Tom until the show landed at the Alvin Theatre. During those years, Tom had done part-time work at the *New Yorker*, gotten remarried, and treated himself to a Jaguar. Meanwhile, Martin had staged four benefits, two very successful revues, two less successful musicals, and had bought five new fur and/or leather outfits.

I hung on to the advertising job, continuing to peddle Pennzoil, Air France, Pabst Blue Ribbon beer, and Chrysler cars because I enjoyed it. I'd also written the music and lyrics for *Charlotte's Web*, a winning dramatization by Joseph Robinette. Because film rights were held by others and no New York producer would invest in a show that didn't include screen rights, it was produced—and produced very often—in regional theater. After a while, I wound up making as much money as I would have for many a Broadway production. I also spent those years focused on my role as a father, trying to do the best job I could. (The reviews are still out on that, but I believe I helped conceive four great hits!)

They were years full of luck waiting in the wings—both good and bad. We were still writing and rewriting *Annie*, hoping for it to someday see the spotlight (and Mike Nichols hadn't even come into the picture yet), when one day, our publisher Buddy Morris asked us to audition it for ABC/Walt Disney TV. Because I had always thought that *Annie* was not really a stage piece, this audition represented the height of my ambitions. And, because NBC owned the rights to *The Wizard of Oz* (which, at Christmastime, wiped out all the TV competition), this would be an important chance for the orphans to go toe to toe with the Munchkins.

It was a very tense audition. Martin, Tom, and I read, played, and sang our strongest songs. I remember how polite and beautifully dressed the movie and TV people were. But, they seemed to share one thing with New York producers: the lack of time to read a script.

It must have gone better than we anticipated, for in a few days we received a call offering us $65,000 for the rights to show *Annie* on television for ten years. Martin and I were thrilled—that is, until Tom, who had been sitting there with a pad and pencil, pointed out that if we accepted this offer, it would mean that, from the time we started working on *Annie* to the time this decade-long contract lapsed—eighteen years in all—we would have each earned just over three dollars a day.

We decided to raise the stakes and boldly asked for $85,000. I don't think any of us could conceive of a higher sum. When *that* request was made, curiously enough, no one was available to speak with us. The executives were all in London, and when we contacted them, we were told by their secretaries that they had not been given any messages to pass along to us.

It took us about a month to realize no one was interested.

I've mentioned before the advent of luck, and here was a perfect example: We turned down the $65,000 offer from ABC, and then, a few years later, rights for a movie were purchased for almost $10 million. It's a wonderful peculiarity of the theater, as it is in composing music: the note that surprises you is often the one you never thought of but just "happened."

What most know-it-alls are convinced they know, they often don't. This was a lesson I'd learn over and over: Success may arrive when you don't know what you're doing. It holds the same for composing: The last note you need is elusive, and you don't know where you're going, and then you hit a note you didn't mean to, and that one note brings out the sun.

Our fourth child, William, was a little like that: sunshine, unheralded, as if he had hopscotched in, to fill the emptiness of Barbara's miscarriage. We had expected he would be a girl, whom we would name Annie, but *Annie* anticipated him by arriving first on Broadway. Yet, far from being lost in the shuffle, William, from the start, exhibited a unique star personality. He was not going to play second string to the three preceding him. No, he would make his entrance in his own way! And, like the star he would soon become, when the time came for his entrance, the delivery room was hushed and expectant as he decided he was going to damn well make us wait. The lights shone fiercely down, the audience (basically Barbara, the obstetrician, a nurse, and me) couldn't understand why he was taking his sweet time, but then the nurse said, knowingly, "Oh, we got a star here!" And she put her hands together, lifted them high, and brought them down on Barbara's stomach with a *whomp*, and out he came: an original, crazy, funny, hard-to-pin-down, unique, and talented son.

𝄢

With *Annie* an undeniable success, I turned toward my next projects, and the old insecurities began to seep in: Does such success make the gods angry?

The truth is, no one sets out to write a flop musical—not unless they're a character in a Mel Brooks show. Yet, while *Annie* was packing them in at the Alvin, my next show—*A Broadway Musical*—opened four blocks south at the Lunt-Fontanne Theatre on December 21, 1978, and closed the very same night. Despite its brief life on stage, *A Broadway Musical* is a show that I'm proud of. Lee Adams and I had wanted to make a musical from our experiences with Sammy Davis Jr. We envisioned our musical about white people writing a musical for a big black musical star as funny, ironic, racially charged, and filled with life's imbalances. We certainly knew the territory.

We had a terrific director-choreographer in George Faison. George had won a Tony as Best Choreographer for *The Wiz* in 1975, and like Ron Field at the time of *Applause*, was now directing as well. Our book writer was William F. Brown, who had written the book for *The Wiz*.

We did an unorthodox workshop/tryout at the Theatre of the Riverside Church on Manhattan's Upper West Side. It wasn't exactly like going out of town. Unfortunately, the first time it got on its feet, the show was imperfect, and the powers-that-be (in this case a pre-Livent Garth Drabinsky and Norman Kean, who was one of the producers of *Oh! Calcutta!*) replaced Faison with Gower Champion.

Gower never saw eye to eye with us on the show. He brought a whole different attitude and choice of recasting to the work that deeply hurt the show. Dealing with race elicits complicated reactions in people, revealing their buried biases at war with their sense of "morality." I like to think that, particularly after writing *Golden Boy*, Lee and I were mostly free of these conflicts. Yet—thanks in part to Gower's wrongheaded razzmatazz—by the time we got to the Lunt-Fontanne, *A Broadway Musical* was not the show we had intended it to be. Some of the New York critics saw racial bias and all sorts of misperceived things in the content of the show. That's not at all what we had meant.

By some strange theatrical coincidence, the same night *A Broadway Musical* opened and closed, *Flowers for Algernon* (book and lyrics by David Rogers) had its world premiere in Edmonton, Canada.

I had been friendly with David Rogers, a prolific playwright and actor, since before I married Barbara. He had been one of eight shareholders in a summerhouse on Fire Island that I went in on because I'd broken up with a girl and then desperately wanted her back and thought that sharing a house with these guys might blunt my heartache.

David had been commissioned to create a stage version of *Flowers for Algernon* by Dramatist Play Service, a play licensing company. The piece had started life as a short story by Daniel Keyes and then become the 1968 movie *Charly,* for which Cliff Robertson won an Oscar for playing a brain-damaged man who, through a breakthrough surgical technique perfected by research on a mouse, becomes a genius. The success of the procedure is short-lived, though, as the mouse's facilities begin to decline, and Charly realizes that his mental loss can't be far behind.

I read David's stage adaptation and thought it unusual and moving. The subject fascinated me, so we began to collaborate on a musical version. After our premiere in Edmonton (featuring the wonderful Christine Ebersole, who would one day play Margo Channing in the 2008 *Encores!* production of *Applause*), the show opened in London on June 14, 1979. It starred Michael Crawford (who was a dream to work with—always an hour early to rehearse and wanting everything to be perfect) and had original and intriguing staging by Peter Coe, the original director of *Golden Boy* and a man I consider a genius.

Despite a seeming recipe for success, the London production lasted only twenty-eight performances. What I found such a fascinating subject—the Frankenstein-like scientific manipulation of a retarded man's mental capability—wasn't so thrilling to British audiences.

Still, Charly was down but not out. We retitled the show *Charlie and Algernon* (Algernon was the white mouse on whom the scientists had first experimented) and opened in the spring of 1980 at the Kennedy Center's Terrace Theater. The reviews were so good that it was remounted that fall at the larger Eisenhower Theater (where we did *Annie*) before its transfer to Broadway. *Charlie and Algernon* opened at the Helen Hayes Theatre on September 14, 1980, and met the same critical fate as the London production. It ran for only seventeen performances. The public just wasn't buying it. It seems that a show about retardation, brain surgery, and animal experimentation just wasn't what people wanted: another *Annie*. I prefer to think it just was ahead of its time.

𝄢

By 1980, *Bye Bye Birdie* was still the most produced musical in America and a top moneymaker for the company that licensed the amateur rights (community theaters, schools, camps, etc.). But how many times could the same schools do the same show?

Tams-Witmark, the company who licensed *Birdie*, came up with the idea of writing a sequel—but just for the amateur market. We agreed to do it in the belief that it would be limited to those aforementioned community theaters, schools, and camps. No one but doting parents would ever see it.

Our meager plans were derailed when somehow Lee Guber and Shelly Gross—producers of the 1977 *The King and I* revival, among other shows—got ahold of Michael Stewart's book and decided that a *Birdie* sequel just *had* to go to Broadway!

I honestly don't know how we got talked into it, but I suspect the same devil that convinced Lee and me to write the title song for *Bye Bye Birdie* was sitting on our shoulders that day:

DEVIL ON MY RIGHT SHOULDER: *Do it! Do it! Think of the money!*

ANGEL ON THE LEFT: *But what about the integrity of the original show?*

DEVIL AGAIN: *Forget it! This is Broadway! Integrity? You've gotta be kidding me!*

Mike, Lee, and I—normally the closest of friends—fought all through the incubation of the show, which we called *Bring Back Birdie*. A point of particular contention was the wall of TV screens brought in by our director-choreographer Joe Layton. Joe said it was to make the show more "cutting edge," but we just thought the TVs should have been cut.

Chita Rivera played Rosie once again—stopping the show

again more than two decades later—but Dick Van Dyke wisely turned us down. Donald O'Connor now played an older Albert Peterson, dancing his heart out in front of all those damn "cutting edge" TV screens.

We opened at our original theater, the Martin Beck, twenty-one years after *Bye Bye Birdie* became the sleeper hit of 1960.

History didn't repeat itself in 1981. After thirty-one previews and four performances, the show closed.

As Alan Lerner wrote in *On a Clear Day You Can See Forever*: "Why is the sequel never the equal?"

(I'm compelled to add one exception to Alan's maxim: I reserve a warm and affectionate spot in my heart for *Annie Warbucks*, which I think has some great work from Tom, Martin, and me and which I believe is a good show!)

♪:

The first time Alan Jay Lerner and I worked together, I had a stressful backache, and Alan said to me, "Dear boy, I used to have the same kind of backache. Take this pill, and it will disappear."

I took the pill, and within ten minutes, I was begging for my wife and children to be brought to me so I could die in their presence.

Once I'd recovered, Alan's assistant Bud Widney advised me, "Never take a pill from Alan Jay Lerner." This might be called a cardinal rule of the theater and should be written in every medical textbook.

My collaboration with Alan, *Dance a Little Closer*, began its life in 1978 (just after *Annie* opened in London) when one day, the phone rang, and it was Alan Jay Lerner. We had met a few years earlier when I was flying to L.A. to score a film. While disembarking from the plane, I casually reached into my pocket and realized I had forgotten my wallet, which contained all my money and credit cards. I started to panic. What if the studio car didn't show up? I didn't even have a change to make a phone call.

Luck intervened, for there in the front of the plane was Alan Jay Lerner. We had never met, but I was familiar not only with his work as the lyricist-librettist of *Brigadoon*, *My Fair Lady*, *Camelot*, and *Gigi*, but also his face, from hundreds of photos in the newspapers. I figured he'd be a good bet to help a composer in need, so I introduced myself, explained the situation, and he loaned me forty dollars. (Later, in typical Lerner style, he told the same story during an interview but said he had loaned me ninety bucks. This describes Alan as well as I ever could.)

I'd paid back the forty dollars he'd loaned me years ago, so I was surprised when the phone rang that day in 1978, and he was on the line, calling from London.

"Dear boy," he said, "I have a new musical that I'd love to show you. Would you be interested? It's based on the Pulitzer Prize–winning play *Idiot's Delight*, by Robert Sherwood. I've always thought of it as a great musical, and I think you'd be perfect for it."

I said I didn't know the play but would buy a copy right away.

"Don't!" he commanded. "I will send you my adaptation by next post."

Three days later, an envelope arrived from London. Right away, I tore into his adaptation.

I didn't get it.

Here was a famous lyricist-writer's adaptation of a Pulitzer Prize–winning play, and I didn't get it. Obviously, it was me. So I reread it. Twice. And then I called him in London.

"Alan, there are a couple of things in your play that I'm not sure I understand," I began hesitantly. "I'm sure I'm reading it wrong and I—"

He interrupted me. "I'm taking a plane tomorrow. I'll meet you at your place. Let me read it to you then."

Lerner was taking a plane to read it to me? Incredible.

I told Barbara, who had danced in *My Fair Lady*. She seemed unimpressed. "If you don't like it, don't do it," she said.

How was I supposed to know what I liked? For God's sake, others always had to tell me. If I played a song in an empty room, I'd have no idea whether it was good or bad. I needed someone to tell me. It's a curse—a never-ending refrain of doubt courtesy of my mother.

When Alan arrived, I sat on the sofa, and he stood before me and read the entire script.

It now seemed brilliant! The story took place at the outbreak of a great war when two people meet and rekindle an old love affair. Alan had updated the original play from just before WWII to what he called "the avoidable future." It was fascinating.

"But where can we find a leading lady who can play this part?" I asked once everything had sunk in. "She's mercurial, mysterious, and glamorous."

"That's the best part," Alan said. "We have her. Well, I have her—she's Liz Robertson!"

"Who?" I asked.

"My next wife!"

The tiniest bell rang. Was it the door or a faint death knell?

"She was in *My Fair Lady*," Alan continued. "She is brilliant, she's gorgeous, and she sings like a bird."

"That's great," I said. "When can I meet her?"

"She's at the hotel. We'll meet for lunch."

Alan had been married eight times, and though I didn't know it then, he had an insatiable hunger for women. The sheen of a woman's lips, a skirt that was partially slit so that her legs showed when she walked—his eyes practically bulged when he spoke of these things. Mutual friends later told me they had advised him that he might try going to bed with a woman and not committing right away to marital vows, but during the writing process, Alan confided in me about the many women he had slept with whom he did *not* marry. (One tends to speak of intimate things on the path to collaborating on a song.) Alan also said that he had never loved a woman as much as he did his new fiancée, Liz.

Friends told me Alan said that of every one of his wives.

But that early day, we met for lunch with Liz, who had played Eliza Doolittle under Lerner's direction in a London revival of *My Fair Lady*. Liz *was* quite beautiful, but I immediately felt she wasn't right for the part. Lynn Fontanne, who originated the role in *Idiot's Delight* (and whom I'd never seen except in movies and photographs), had a dark glamour and subtly veiled humor. Fontanne's looks were so iconic that when Norma Shearer played the role in the film version, they made her up to look just like Lynn Fontanne, wig and all. Liz's beauty was more obvious, and her speech rang of elocution lessons.

Alan could read some doubt on my face, but before I could say anything, he said, "Dear boy, I want you to know that, during rehearsals, if either of us finds Liz wrong in any way, she's out—and I'll make the first move because I'll be the director."

Now, there's not much anyone can really teach you about how to write a musical. You simply have to write it and let the audience guide you. Of course, the great conundrum is that no one actually wants to produce them once you do write them. But that's neither here nor there. Musicals *do* miraculously get made sometimes. And, sometimes, they become a hit, and the person who has written it can make a fortune and get invited to parties in East Hampton.

But, there *is* one injunction, which you might call the injunction of injunctions, never to be disregarded, and that is: Never write a musical in which one person is the director *and* the book writer *and* the lyricist. If, in addition, that person should be engaged to, intimate with, in possession of carnal knowledge of, or deeply in love with the leading lady (or man), in no case shall the musical be given life.

We seemed to be headed for disaster right from the get-go with these circumstances, and the creative process didn't begin any better. Alan insisted on sitting near me while I was composing, an intensely private activity for me. He said he did that because when he worked with "Fritz" (his nickname for Frederick Loewe, his collaborator on now-classics such as *Brigadoon, My Fair Lady*, and *Camelot*), Loewe would always try to leave if Alan didn't keep on top of him. (Alan claimed this was because when Loewe was a young boy, his mother would chain him to the piano to make him practice. Knowing

Alan's distant relationship with the truth, I couldn't help but wonder if this was true or not.)

Alan was a man who was often fast and loose with the truth. I had heard him say he had lost his eye while on the boxing team at Harvard. He had also told people that when he was in England, everyone thought he was Sammy Davis Jr. He also claimed he never paid taxes, instead keeping his money on the Isle of Wight in the English Channel, where it was retrieved when he needed it by sending his lawyer there with an empty suitcase. I have no idea if any of these things were true. I only know that when I queried my accountant asking if I, too, could leave my money on the Isle of Wight, my accountant wisely said, "Pay your taxes!"

𝄢

Friends like Leonard Bernstein, who had collaborated with Alan on the disastrous *1600 Pennsylvania Avenue*, warned me about Alan and his habits of procrastination. But perhaps because he was writing this show for the woman he loved or perhaps because it was his "lucky 13" (the thirteenth show he had written), Alan and I got along beautifully once we settled into a routine, and the work came quickly. I also felt that I understood why Alan might not show up to a meeting. He was a perfectionist and wouldn't hand a composer a lyric unless he was happy with it.

Alan taught me one of the most significant lessons of my life: Somewhere there is a word, the right word, the *explicit* word, that will convey all of the meaning, color, and tone of what you want to say. (And, often in our business, it must rhyme, too.) And you must never rest until you find that word, and you must never be satisfied with anything less than that word.

Alan lived that ethic. Often, after I questioned a certain phrase or word of his, Alan would be up all night (Liz would tell me)—headachy, sick, tossing, walking—but by morning somehow he'd have found the right word. Deep in his heart, Alan had a poet's conviction that the *one* word was there, somewhere, to describe any event or emotion. It was a terrible path that he was doomed to follow, but he taught me a valued lesson.

Instead of going out of town, we workshopped the show in New York at 890 Broadway. In the rehearsal space, the show seemed to be going well. Once we got into the Minskoff Theatre, everything changed.

The set was supposed to represent a modern European hotel, but the hotel was dominated by giant sheet of Plexiglas or Saran Wrap or something. It was supposed to denote a great window overlooking the Alps (Alan's war was apparently in Switzerland), but it couldn't be hung without the stage lights blinding the entire audience. The ill-conceived set had been Alan's idea, and it was a massive task to change the material and the angle of the "window." It also shook whenever actors walked by it. People in the cast would refer to the hotel as the "Jell-O Arms."

The cast was splendid: Len Cariou, who since *Applause* had won a Tony for *Sweeney Todd*, George Rose, Brent Barrett. I feel I wrote some good music for it. One song, "There's Always One You Can't Forget," remains, to me, one of Alan's finest lyrics. And still, *Dance a Little Closer* opened and closed May 11, 1983, leading Broadway insiders to dub it "Close a Little Faster."

It was to be Alan Jay Lerner's last Broadway musical. He died in 1986, still married to Liz Robertson. At the time of his death, the IRS was in pursuit of him. I guess my accountant was right about the Isle of Wight.

About his financial legacy, Liz was reported to say, "The only thing Alan left me was a taste for champagne."

He left me a lot more.

CHAPTER EIGHTEEN

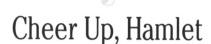

Cheer Up, Hamlet

THOUGH I'M BEST KNOWN as a composer, I have occasionally written my own lyrics as well. As far back as 1956, I wrote both music and lyrics for a song called "I Lost the Rhythm," which was performed by Joel Grey in Ben Bagley's *The Littlest Revue*. In 1964, when *Golden Boy* was trying out, and Lee Adams was unavailable, I was forced to come up with the lyric for "No More," which, as I've said, became a favorite song of Dr. Martin Luther King Jr.

The notion of joining words to my own music has been an ambition that I'd largely kept under wraps, but I was thrilled when, in 1981, Meridee Stein asked me to write a piece for her First All Children's Theater. I decided to take the plunge and write both music and lyrics for *Nightingale*, a short opera I based on a story by Hans Christian Andersen. For the first time, I was totally responsible for *all* the material, and it felt good.

Following its New York premiere, *Nightingale* was produced in 1982 in England at the Buxton Festival. There, a British director named Peter James heard it and asked to direct it in London at the Lyric Hammersmith Theatre. That production starred a pre–*Phantom of the Opera* Sarah Brightman and received excellent reviews.

It was just the encouragement I needed to continue.

While *Annie* had been on Broadway, Ed Koch was one of seven candidates running for mayor. His campaign office called me and said that it would be interested in using "N.Y.C.," one of the *Annie* musical numbers, as their campaign song.

There were five other candidates running for the office (among them was women's movement leader Bella Abzug), and a few of them asked for the use of that song. At the time, I had never heard of Koch, but friends (particularly Congressman Stephen Solarz) told me that Koch was a good man. I checked with Martin Charnin, who said, "A plug is a plug," and thus "N.Y.C." became the tune to which Koch won the election.

I'd never met the man, but when we were at the same benefit one evening, I introduced myself.

"I'm Charles Strouse, Mr. Mayor," I began. "I wrote the song—'N.Y.C.'—that you used in your campaign."

He shook my hand warmly and said, "If I have to hear that song one more time, I'm going to kill myself." How could you *not* like him?

In 1984, while still installed in Gracie Mansion, Koch wrote a book called *Mayor*. Despite the fact that many of his constituents (including me) somehow managed to avoid reading it, the book became a bestseller.

Soon after it was published, Koch phoned me.

"Charlie," he said, "would you like to make a musical out of my book?"

"I have to be frank, Mr. Mayor," I replied. "I haven't read it."

But I thought about Koch's invitation. After the excellent reviews *Nightingale* had received in London, I really had the itch to take a crack at lyrics again. But a musical about Koch himself? The man's conceit had no boundaries! This was a terrible idea.

Little by little, the concept began to grow on me. Koch *was* New York and I'm a New Yorker down to my socks, so at least I'd be writing about what I knew. (In addition, it would only be a little off-Broadway show so, at the very least, if I failed, it might be little noticed.)

When Koch agreed to have a "no approvals" clause in the contract, I decided to give it a shot. I paired up with a book writer, Warren Leight, who had authored a cynical and snappy tome called *The I Hate New York Guidebook*. Warren and I wrote the show, played it for a couple of producers who raised the money, and hired a talented director (Jeff Moss, best known as head writer for *Sesame Street*) and a talented choreographer, Barbara Siman, who also just happened to be my wife.

Ordinarily working with one's wife would be a no-no (I had learned my lesson on *Dance a Little Closer*), but everything went right with this production. Warren's monologues were special, skillful, and funny; the direction and choreography were a perfect fit; and the cast (Doug Bernstein, Marion J. Caffey, Keith Curran, Nancy Giles, Ken Jennings, Ilene Kristen, Kathryn McAteer, and Lenny Wolpe as the mayor) was from heaven. My lyrics were even singled out as being especially good and funny by some tough New York critics. We had a nice run at the Top of the Gate at the Village Gate (sadly, now a drug store) and then moved uptown to the Latin Quarter (now a hotel).

I guess, like me, New York keeps changing.

The downside of all of this success was the realization that, when anything goes particularly well, my depression hits me the hardest. I don't know why this is, but it was particularly hard on my family. Could it be (*yes it could*) that I felt I just didn't deserve to win?

$9\colon$

In 1983, Lee Guber, who had produced *Bring Back Birdie* in 1981, told me of a screenplay written by Joseph Stein that he believed would make a fine work for the stage. This work, *Rags*, was, he told me, a continuation of the story of *Fiddler on the Roof*, which Joe had written with the fabulous Sheldon Harnick, brilliant Jerry Bock, and genius Jerry Robbins.

How could I possibly follow in those footsteps?

But I read it, and it took my breath away! The poor people from Anatevka in *Fiddler* had immigrated to America only to be met by prejudice, fear, and cynicism from Americans.

Remind you of today?

It was a moving and very timely play, which focused on the story of an immigrant woman—her loves, her traditions, and her indestructibility. I was definitely interested in it, and even better, the evolving music of those times particularly suited my ambitions as a composer.

In the early 1900s, music was bubbling in the streets, in brothels, in barrooms, and at Bar Mitzvahs. Irish clog dancing met black rhythms, and suddenly tap dancing was there. In New York, in particular, immigrants were jammed in tight. Everyone fought to get out, and it was the fighting that made all those sounds happen. I heard music in all of this.

I wanted to write the lyrics as well, but Lee Guber wouldn't have it. In spite of my successes with *Mayor* and *Nightingale*, it seemed I was indelibly stamped as a composer (not that I was complaining). As lyricist, Lee suggested Hal David, who had written all those pop hits with Burt Bacharach, as well as *Promises, Promises*, Bacharach's only musical.

I began writing some songs with Hal, but no one felt they struck the right tone. Our partnership just wasn't working, which sometimes happens. It was like those couples that break up because they say they love each other, but they're just not "in love." (Later, Hal and I would collaborate on another musical, *Lady for a Day*, and for that, the chemistry worked.)

Lee then suggested Stephen Schwartz to replace Hal, and I was flattered by the idea. Stephen is twenty years younger than I, a composer as well as a lyricist with such huge hits under his belt as *Pippin*, *The Magic Show*, and *Godspell*. (Later he would go on to write the smash hit *Wicked*, winning three Oscars along the way for songs he wrote with Alan Menken.) Stephen also had written words for Leonard Bernstein's *Mass*, and I thought that credential might lend the right tone to this new project. What surprised me was how funny he was, too.

In 1984, we did a workshop at 890 Broadway, which Stephen directed. At the time, the show had no star and most of the roles were of equal size. Two years later, we went into production with much larger show and a new director, Joan Micklin Silver, who had written and directed the film *Hester Street*, also about Jewish immigrants on the Lower East Side. It seemed a good fit.

For three weeks, Silver rehearsed the actors around a table, refining the dialogue for days without ever actually blocking any scenes. Actors would stagger out of the room in which these readings were being held, their faces wracked with boredom, still utterly confused about what they'd do once they got up onstage. This clearly wasn't working, so Lee decided Joan had to go.

Stephen and I took over the direction, but we were clear to emphasize that we were only doing so temporarily, as we knew how crazy it would look opening in New York with the lyricist and the composer listed on the playbill as "directors" as well.

We had a stellar cast including Larry Kert, Terrence Mann, Judy Kuhn, Dick Latessa, Lonny Price, and Marcia Lewis. Our leading lady, Teresa Stratas, one of the Metropolitan Opera's great stars, was making her Broadway debut in *Rags*. After twenty years of Menotti, Puccini, and Weill, she was now singing Strouse. Stratas was such a dedicated musician that if I had written a song starting on an F-sharp, she wouldn't permit me to transpose it even though her voice might be stronger in another vocal range.

"You must have felt something about the F-sharp when you wrote it, Charles," she'd say to me.

I loved Teresa, but she was a true diva. Over the course of rehearsals, this tiny woman had thrown a chair at me (something to do with that F-sharp I mentioned before) and hit me with her fist (I pushed her back). To protect her vocal chords, she kept pots scattered all over the floor of her nine-room apartment (where she lived alone) to keep the air suitably humid. Every time I went there, I felt I was on a strange, faraway planet.

The problem was, Stratas showed up to perform only when a cold wasn't impending—which was infrequently. In fact, she missed a whole week of performances in Boston, including her opening night.

And yet, even minus Stratas (her standby Christine Andreas went on), the show opened to rave reviews in Boston. Hordes of people came to the show, and my wife and I used to take great pleasure walking by at eight in the morning to see students sitting on the sidewalk waiting for standing-room-only tickets.

The music and lyrics were particularly praised (in fact, I think Stephen's lyrics are still his very best work), so I felt happy. But as friends came up from New York, word somehow leaked that there was trouble with the show. Maybe having no director's credit in the playbill wasn't such a good idea.

Teresa called Jerry Robbins, who came and saw it. He was complimentary about the staging, particularly the opening, which Stephen had cobbled together with benches. But *Fiddler on the Roof* had been Robbins's last Broadway show, and as we had suspected, he decided he couldn't take over, claiming he had other commitments.

Other directors who came from New York gave us vaguely positive, but somewhat foggy, reactions. There was no clear path, so Stephen and I kept directing, making cuts and rewrites here and there, until we all decided that another director was absolutely necessary if only for cosmetic reasons.

We tried out another director recommended by Teresa, but he and Stephen clashed (and, let me tell you—Stephen is *some clasher*). Finally, Guber came up with what would seem to be the perfect solution: Gene Saks, the man who had saved *I Love My Wife* after Joe Layton had to drop out and also directed *Brighton Beach Memoirs* (which happened to star my son Nick at the time).

Gene took over once we got to New York. We wrote a new first act number for Larry Kert (he had been the original Tony in *West Side Story* and played most of the run in *Company*) called "What's Wrong with That?" Gene seemed to like the song itself, but we hit an artistic snag when he made it clear that he did not like songs being sung in either high or low registers, as he felt they were "understood better" when spoken. It was a curious prejudice when dealing with singers of this caliber.

Gene Saks cleaned up the loose ends of the plot, but in cutting down and explaining things, he took away some of the show's charm and musical substance. None of us were happy—in particular, Stratas, who one afternoon literally went down on her knees in a hallway backstage and begged me to get rid of him.

Still, Gene stayed on as director, and *Rags* opened at the Mark Hellinger Theatre (today a church) on August 21, 1986, to tepid reviews for the show but to great notices for Teresa and for my music. Ticket sales were slow from the start and getting worse. These were the dog days of August—not the best time to open a show.

The fans we did have were fervent, and our cast was incredibly loyal. Following our third performance, a Saturday matinee, the cast marched down Broadway in an attempt to catch the excitement that *Rags* engendered and drum up publicity and business. Unfortunately, their efforts proved fruitless, and the producers threw in the towel after four performances.

Eight months after we closed, the show received five Tony nominations, including Best Musical, Best Score, Best Book, and Best Choreography.

As my father used to say, "That and a nickel will get you in the subway."

Gene Saks was not nominated for Best Director.

I am very proud of my music for *Rags* as I feel it expresses a great deal of what I feel about America, immigration, and the changing styles of European music and jazz.

𝄢

"They're really good, Buddy," a sadder, older, and progressively drunker Lenny Bernstein proclaimed to me one afternoon at lunch. "I can't write them like that." He had just seen one of the run-throughs of *Rags*; and he, Barbara, and I had gone for a bite at a nearby Japanese restaurant.

And, after hearing them just once, he sang *from memory* three of the most complex songs from the show. He sang them loudly, calling a great deal of attention to himself and drawing stares from the other diners.

Lenny seemed very unhappy; he smoked a lot and ordered more drinks when Barbara and I hadn't even finished our first ones yet. In his drunken state, he continued to hand me lavish compliments about my "tunes." I could only hope he meant what he said, but knowing him as I did, it was hard to imagine he was giving up the high ground for me. I had the feeling perhaps he was just acting "lordly."

But, as he kept singing and laughing drunkenly, I came as close to loving him as one could. Not for his compliments— but because I was moved by his sadness.

Lenny? Sad? The idea left me feeling down. Audiences had cheered him, and he was handsome enough to have been a movie star (I have read it was something he considered). But now his hands shook, his skin sagged, and his hair—that glorious hair that shook when he conducted Mahler or Beethoven—had grown thin and gray.

Here was my hero, showing the cracks in what always looked like such a perfect façade.

𝄢

After *Rags* closed it seemed that there was little on the Broadway horizon for me. Instead, a mélange of animated films came my way. I wrote *Lyle, Lyle Crocodile* for HBO (adapted from the children's book), and *The Worst Witch* for the BBC. I also wrote the music for *All Dogs Go to Heaven*, which starred a singing Burt Reynolds—as close to an oxymoron as you're going to get from me. These were followed by *Alexander and the Terrible, Horrible, No Good, Very Bad Day* (adapted from the Judith Viorst book), and HBO's *A Child's Garden of Verses*, which I wrote with my old *Annie* cohort, Tom Meehan.

But nothing was happening with my career stage-wise, and I felt like there was a new boatload of younger composers arriving in port daily. I could see them all coming down the gangway, their banners unfurled. Tisch School of the Arts, Northwestern School of the Arts, the BMI Workshop.

Oh, yes. I was feeling "older."

But was it age or greed or that same old devil that sat on my shoulder back in 1980 when I wrote *Bring Back Birdie* who now appeared in the guise of Martin Charnin?

"Hey, Charles," the devil/Martin said. "I've got a great idea."

"What is it?" I asked.

"How about doing a show? Not really a sequel, but a *continuation*."

"What are you talking about?"

"I'm talking about *Annie 2*."

CHAPTER NINETEEN

As Long As You're Happy

BY THE TIME *Annie 2: Miss Hannigan's Revenge* had officially opened on January 4, 1990, at the Kennedy Center, Martin Charnin (again the lyricist and director), Tom Meehan (still on board as our book writer), and I had written enough material for three shows about the little red-haired girl. We certainly had enough money thrown at us to do so. I remember moneyed people lining up to invest after a first audition at my office. Perhaps another maxim of this tinseled world ought to be: The easier it is to acquire backing, the more likely the show will fail.

Previews began on December 22, 1989, with high hopes. By the time the curtain came down, we knew we were not in Kansas anymore.

Martin's idea for the "continuation" was to pick up the story six weeks after the plot of *Annie* ended. Because of Dorothy Loudon's great success in what was really a supporting role in *Annie*, we made her our star, centering the story on Miss Hannigan's escape from the Women's House of Detention in order to seek revenge on Annie.

The audience, who had come to see what became of Annie, sat in stunned silence.

The opening was postponed, as we rushed to rewrite. Missing were the orphans everyone had loved so much, but even more significant was that Annie herself had somehow been pushed into the background. We immediately wrote a song for her called "Changes," and put it right at the top of the show, so the audience would know her desires right from the start. The song had lovely shades of "Maybe" in it, and it remains a favorite song of mine because it hinted at a young girl's reaching puberty as well as the more obvious changes in Annie's life at this point.

Songs and situations came and went in this insane period of a few weeks. We moved scenes from Wall Street to Yankee Stadium and changed numbers featuring FDR to ones featuring Babe Ruth. Miss Hannigan's initial plot was changed and tempered from killing Annie to only kidnapping her. Also, Miss Hannigan's ludicrous disguise as southern belle Charlotte O'Hara (don't ask!) changed into the tragic Fran Riley. This gave us a chance to write what I thought was a fine song for Dorothy called "But You Go On" that, in hindsight, also unfortunately deprived her of the chance to be comic, which was one of the reasons we had wanted to do the show with her in the first place.

By the time we opened, the show was better, but the reviews were bad.

We continued to work on the show throughout its month-long Kennedy Center engagement, which was very hard on Dorothy, who decided she wanted out. I couldn't blame her, but to lose her at that point would have meant the end of the show. Dorothy and Martin had massive blowouts as he tried to get her to stick with it.

Their fights were for nothing, though, as the closing of *Annie 2* on January 20, 1990, was very public. The news made headlines all over the country. It was as if we had taken everyone's favorite orphan and killed her in D.C.

Martin and Tom are nothing if not tenacious, though, and they were determined to make the show work. We went back to the drawing board, doing a bare-bones production at Goodspeed's Norma Terris Theatre in May of 1990. The producers kept up pushing for a transfer to Broadway, but, by 1991, unable to raise the money, they gave up hope and surrendered their option. The rights to the show reverted to the authors. The story would seem to have a sad ending, except *Annie 2*, now with her adopted name of *Annie Warbucks*, rose from the ashes and opened off-Broadway on August 9, 1993. Gone was Miss Hannigan, gone was Charlotte O'Hara. *Annie Warbucks* arose and then actually flew. The show was recorded and is a staple of schools and community theater groups, and the movie rights were sold to Sony. I wrote some good tunes, but Martin and Tom are the real heroes for stitching the thing together again.

As our logo said, "tomorrow can come true."

𝄢

"Is anybody who they seem?" asked Joanna Gleason as Nora Charles.

The line was written by Arthur Laurents for our musical *Nick & Nora*, but it could have been the slogan of our collaboration.

Arthur, as the world knows, was the librettist of *Gypsy* and *West Side Story*, as well as the screenwriter of both *The Turning Point* and *The Way We Were*.

Collaboration, like marriage, should mean a desire to support your partner, but at the same time, you have to cling to your own vision or you're no artist. It's a tough nut to crack for someone who is, like me, unsure of himself. I found it very fortunate, then, that Arthur Laurents and I seemed to connect. We had long talks about the show and about our careers over leisurely dinners. Heck, we even watched the Gay Pride Parade together. He was charming. And witty and bright . . . *and I pity anyone who isn't—*

But I digress.

I knew little about the history of the show's production but soon found out that it had had a lot of trouble getting off its feet. *Nick & Nora* had first been conceived in 1980 as the musicalization of *The Thin Man*. Laurents, who had just had a great success directing *La Cage aux Folles,* came on as director in 1985. Playwright A. R. Gurney had taken a crack at the book but quit after a short time (for reasons I can now easily imagine but had no idea of at the time), leaving everything in Arthur's hands. It was in May 1988 when I climbed aboard the luckless vessel.

At first, I was surprised to hear rumblings from others who had sailed with our captain. A mutual friend told me, "Arthur changes stripes." Someone who had collaborated on three musicals with Arthur added, "Watch out. He gets nervous when rehearsals start." I disregarded these signals, sure we'd end up lifelong friends, as I liked and admired him so.

There were further disquieting signs, one of which happened when I arrived at Arthur's house on St. Luke's Place one afternoon. As Arthur opened the door, he was giggling—barely able to suppress his laughter, as though he'd just heard the funniest joke in the world.

"What's so funny?" I asked.

Once he was able to stop chuckling, he said, "Tony Perkins has AIDS."

I had two thoughts of this odd reaction of his. My first was that he wanted me to know that he knew Tony Perkins. The second was that he must have then been so distraught that his emotional wires were crossed, causing a kind of short-circuit in the brain—like when one can't help but laugh at the most serious of moments. I never imagined he was capable of actual cruelty, and I thought little about it at the time.

Besides working with Arthur for the first time, *Nick & Nora* was my first collaboration with lyricist Richard Maltby Jr., the director of *Ain't Misbehavin'* and lyricist of *Song and Dance*, *Baby*, and *Miss Saigon*. We had met while we were both "dramaturging at the O'Neill Center" (a song title if there ever was one). One night when we were both roaring drunk, we found we had an affinity for each other. We had never worked together, but I knew that Richard was one of the finest lyricists working in the theater.

At the beginning of our collaboration, when Arthur and I were still in the honeymoon phase, Arthur said the following to me:

1. "No one has ever understood me like you, Charles."

2. "Your ideas for underscoring some of the dialogue will give 'movie reality' to the plot."

3. "Will you and Richard stay for lunch?"

Giving Richard and me lunch was a sure bet to win our hearts and minds. We both had, as mothers everywhere used to say of their children, "healthy appetites—God bless 'em."

In any case, a series of lunches—sandwiches (with the crusts cut off the bread), served on fine bone china with silver cutlery by a motherly Spanish maid every afternoon—had wooed us into a cozy lovefest.

The lovefest started to show signs of wear and tear when Richard took a yellow pad and diagrammed Arthur's script, showing us that the very complicated who-done-it plot (for this was a murder-mystery musical) made little sense.

Perhaps this put in a chink in Arthur's armor, for the next thing I knew he was telling me that the last song I wrote was "awful."

Not knowing what to say, I let it slide and tried to keep the peace, even when Arthur started hinting that we had eaten too many sandwiches at lunch. Hell, I do tend to eat too much. It just wasn't worth fighting over.

𝄢

Working in New York can be distracting, and because Arthur didn't think we were progressing quickly enough on the score (there was a certain accuracy there, for Richard is a perfectionist and very slow), he suggested (or rather informed/ordered) Richard and I sequester ourselves for a week at his house in Quogue, Long Island. This, Arthur told us, would give us uninterrupted time—no wives, no phone calls, a refrigerator stacked with goodies—to write the new songs that had to be written for *Nick & Nora*.

Richard and I went right to work, excelling, in particular, at consuming the cheeses, sausage, crackers, and fruit from the fridge. Arthur would call every morning to check on how the songs were coming. There was never a word allowed about how his script might possibly be shortened or changed; the hint of any such suggestion was caustically swatted down. (I'm not sure swatting can technically be caustic, but like a pitcher with a hidden screwball, Arthur had his ways.)

The daily phone calls from Arthur were frightening, especially when he called to check on my progress on one particularly difficult song.

"It should sound like a song by Irving Berlin," Arthur ordered, "but with the snap and cynicism of Lenny."

Quite a tall order.

I'd finished the music, but there were still no lyrics, and we were nervous, as Arthur's tongue both floated like a viper and stung like a viper. (Although, one song—"Is There Anything Better than Dancing?"—turned out quite good.)

There were hardly any funny things about the process of working on *Nick & Nora*, but there were two—and both of them had to do with that week in Quogue.

If I was frightened of Arthur's daily phone calls, then, Richard was positively terrified. He rarely finished his work on time and so bore the brunt of Arthur's tongue-lashings. There were three reasons for this:

1. Richard was a meticulous craftsman who worked—well—meticulously.

2. Richard was poorly organized, and his latest lyric most often ended up on the back of an old sheet of paper and had three alternate words for each "finished" line, which made it difficult to figure out what he had intended.

3. Richard was constantly falling asleep. (I believe this was his reaction to tension. I happened to like him, but it was annoying to be slaving away at a promising melody, only to turn and see him snoozing happily on the sofa.)

The phone rang one afternoon while Richard was boiling

water for tea. It was, of course, Arthur (we had been instructed: "no outside calls!"). I was desperate not to talk to Arthur myself, so I shouted, "Richard! It's Arthur for you. He wants to know how that lyric is coming."

Richard was so rattled with anxiety that he picked up the boiling kettle, spoke into the phone, and leaned on the counter, unconsciously holding the scalding kettle against his stomach. He spoke sensibly for about two seconds, at which point the searing heat on his stomach reached his brain, and he burst forth with a bloodcurdling scream.

Of course, there must still be a scar on Richard's stomach (I haven't looked recently), but imagine Arthur Laurents's shock to have heard that scream after delivering one of his dictums! That does offer one a smile.

The other funny thing was something Arthur said to me when Richard had to go back to the city because his wife was ill.

"David Merrick had the right idea," Arthur proclaimed. "Everyone in his office is gay; this is the last time I work with heterosexuals."

𝄢

We began rehearsals on August 12, 1991, and the corn was really starting to pop. We'd had a few walk-throughs of scenes and I noticed that, afterward, Arthur would meet with a small group of people that included Steve Sondheim. Richard and I were never invited to participate in these conferences.

Part of me wanted to just walk over and say, "May we join you?" But, still bearing the brand of my mother, I simply felt left out and let it go at that, convincing myself that they were probably just talking about last night's Yankees game.

Coincidentally, after these powwows, Arthur would come to us with suggestions that we get rid of one song or another. There was still never anything mentioned about changing one word of Arthur's book.

I wasn't the only one unhappy. There had actually been a meeting called at the producer Jimmy Nederlander's office (Terry Allen Kramer and Liz McCann were among the attendees), where Arthur's dismissal was brought up for the first time. I objected, and defended him, saying that, good or bad, the ship couldn't sail on with a new captain.

In retrospect, wasn't I just doing what I had done my whole life? Refusing to stand up for myself? When was I ever going to be a man?

𝄢

Arthur came to dislike me in a way I'd never felt disliked since I encountered the southern man who spat at me for being with Butterfly McQueen. At least with *him*, I knew the reason for his hatred. With Arthur, I had no idea. (Our songs couldn't have been *that* bad. After all, Richard and I both received Tony nominations for *Nick & Nora*.)

But the problems continued.

One day at rehearsal, Joanna Gleason, a wonderful talent, was rehearsing the same note incorrectly over and over. I went to the pianist, Patrick Brady, to see if the note was actually written wrong on the page or if Patrick was just letting it go by. (These things happen in the first days of rehearsal.) I was just saying to Joanna and Patrick that the note should have been an E-flat when Arthur hissed at me, "I don't want you talking to my actors *ever again*."

Like on that long ago day in 1950 when I played my Gertrude Stein settings for Virgil Thomson and, instead of a compliment, he said, "The *prosody* is very good," I wanted to say, "Fuck you!"

Here was the perfect time. It was *my* show. But I didn't stand up. I just mumbled, "Sorry, Arthur."

Things hit a new low for me at the first orchestral rehearsal, when the performers sang the songs with full orchestra for the first time. The Jonathan Tunick orchestrations had all been done with their usual fine quality, and I was pleased. During the break, several performers came over and complimented me on how good my songs sounded. Arthur, quite audibly—so all the cast could hear—said, "Charles's songs aren't good. Jonathan's orchestrations make them sound that way." And then he left the studio.

I was humiliated, and to make matters worse, my son Nick was there to witness this. My anger grew inside me. I jumped up and ran out to find Arthur.

I imagined killing him and being brought to trial. I could picture the judge peering down at me.

"Are you the man who killed Arthur Laurents?" he'd ask.

"Yes, sir," I would say, "I couldn't control myself."

And the judge would smile and say, "I want the mayor to meet you and to shake your hand."

These thoughts took place as I dashed toward the theater, Nick on my heels, grabbing my jacket and trying to stop me. I finally found Arthur in Christine Baranski's dressing room, and I burst in, fist raised, my son clutching me around the waist.

Before I could say a word, Arthur seeing the murder in my eyes, held up his hands, and said, "I apologize."

I was breathing heavily but managed to say, "Don't ever speak to me like that again!"

My mother would hardly have recognized me.

𝄢

Nick & Nora opened on December 8, 1991, after a brutal nine-week gestation period of seventy-one New York previews. The Broadway vultures were out in full force. No one survived.

In 1993, I received a note from Arthur saying he had finally listened to the CD of *Nick & Nora* and "was impressed." This was two years after the show had closed. He wrote nothing to Richard Maltby.

A year later, in 1994, I received a call from Richard Maltby, who told me that he had been asked to write the lyrics for a stage version of *The Night They Raided Minsky's* that was to be directed by British director Mike Ockrent (famous for *Me and My Girl* and *Crazy for You*) and choreographed by Ockrent's wife, Susan Stroman. Richard wanted me to collaborate with him on the score.

It seemed like an odd request because, although I'd written the background score for the movie, Lee and I had written the songs together. Plus, I couldn't figure out why a Brit was to direct this very American piece. Furthermore, Chris Durang, an extremely talented American playwright, had written the book, and Chris was well known for writing about Catholicism whereas this story has a Jewish background.

Still, I was never one to turn down lunch, and moreover, Susan Stroman (or "Stro," as everyone called her) was not merely smart, funny, and good-looking, but she also gave great Chinese food.

I met with the principals and read Chris's script (which I thought was charming, even though New York's Lower East Side now had more priests and nuns than I'd recalled), and I fell in love with Mike Ockrent.

Mike was a cockney Jew, and had a most cheerful, warm, and generous presence. Also, he was attractively childlike, a man who never outgrew his love of pantomime, a uniquely British form of theater (mostly performed at Christmastime) in which men dress as women and visa versa. Mike had never seen our movie and knew nothing of Lee Adams, so why he liked the story so much puzzled me.

I could have declined then and there, but I'd enjoyed working with Richard on *Nick & Nora* (despite Arthur Laurents's peculiar blend of acid and charm) and thought I'd do it. First, though, I called Lee Adams (after all we *had* worked together on the film) and asked how he felt about my composing the score with someone else. He said that because Maltby was signed there wasn't anything he could do anyway and—besides—he wasn't *that* interested. (A somewhat contradictory answer but knowing Lee, one not out of line with a growing disinterest he had in working in New York theater.)

Complicating matters further, in a few days, Richard called me and said he couldn't write the type of humor being called for, and he was resigning. I quickly phoned Mike and said Lee Adams should be called immediately.

"I've already asked Susan Birkenhead," responded Mike, "and she's thrilled to do it." Again, I wondered if I should quit, but I'd met Susan Birkenhead and felt she was a fine lyricist (*Jelly's Last Jam*) in addition to being personable and attractive.

Then in 1996, Mike met Evan Hunter while playing golf on vacation somewhere in the Caribbean, and they hit it off. Now Chris Durang was out of the picture and Hunter, an author best known for stories about the New York City Police Department (written under the pseudonym Ed McBain) was to write the libretto. (For you trivia fans, neither Evan Hunter nor Ed McBain was his real name, which was actually Salvatore Lombino.)

Because all the elements were set, and because, as always, I longed just to compose, I quietly went along. We met daily to work on the show. Susan Birkenhead had a real lyricist's touch on songs and situations and was surprisingly "male-oriented" as far as the vagaries of stripping were concerned.

Our work went so well that in 1999, *Variety* announced that Timothy and Terri Childs and Jujamcyn Theaters had partnered to produce a new musical, *The Night They Raided Minsky's*, scheduled to bow on Broadway in March 2000.

Soon after the announcement was made, Mike Ockrent was diagnosed with leukemia and went into the hospital. Inside of three weeks, he was dead.

The last song Susan Birkenhead and I wrote, we performed at Mike's hospital bedside—tubes jutting from his arms—days before his death.

Stro was beyond distraught.

Was there a curse lurking here? This would not be like that time in 1968 when Bert Lahr died during the shooting of *The Night They Raided Minsky's* film, and shooting continued with a double. There was no double for Mike Ockrent. There was nothing for us to do but put this expectedly sad and unfinished melody away for now. The new millennium came and went without *The Night They Raided Minsky's.*

𝄢

Jason Alexander had been known for years by most of us around the New York scene as a "gypsy"—an actor or dancer who goes from show to show—before he became a famous TV star as George on *Seinfeld.* When *Seinfeld* ended its eight-year run, Jason started to sniff around for new projects.

I had been aware of Jason for a while when, in 1998, he called me to say that he (along with his friend James Weissenbach) had the rights to *Marty,* the much-loved teleplay by Paddy Chayefsky, which had been turned into the 1955 movie starring Ernest Borgnine in the title role. Jason wanted to do it as a musical with himself in the title role.

This was not the first time I had been approached about this property. In the past, I had only felt so-so about it, and no one had ever been able to acquire the rights from the playwright's family. Because of Jason's newly minted fame, he was given those rights.

Rightly so, Jason thought Lee would be the perfect lyricist (he was a great fan of *Golden Boy*), and even though we hadn't worked together in a while, Lee reread the script and agreed to do it. I was thrilled to be working with him again.

Anita Waxman and Elizabeth Williams were to be coproducers (both handsome and successful ladies), and Aaron Sorkin was asked to be the librettist. I was particularly excited about working with Sorkin, whose last play (and subsequent movie), *A Few Good Men,* was among my favorites.

As we set to work in Los Angeles, two things quickly became abundantly clear. First, Aaron wanted to write what I call a "garbage can" kind of play—that is, a song here and there perhaps but basically, a play—while Lee's and my backgrounds pointed elsewhere—to a full musical with dialogue integrated with music, set pieces, and the whole deal.

The second issue concerned Aaron's personal life. Aaron would turn up to work with us at very odd times, sometimes hours late and, once, not at all. Frequently, we had to call the hotel where he was staying to see if the staff could find him; or if we were supposed to be working in New York but Aaron wasn't there, we had to call his wife in Los Angeles and, without alarming her, ask if she knew where Aaron was. Each time, she had no idea, and it rapidly became obvious that his problem was larger than punctuality. It wasn't until *People* magazine reported that he had a drug problem that it all came together.

Jason Alexander suggested we soldier on with Rupert Holmes as the librettist. Rupert was the librettist, composer, and lyricist of *The Mystery of Edwin Drood*, for which he won three Tony Awards. He's damn good at all three but, happily, a fan of Lee's and mine, so he was fine with us doing our work while he stuck to the libretto.

We had also gotten Mark Brokaw as our director (after we worked on the show for a while with Robert Longbottom, who left us to do *Flower Drum Song*). Brokaw, a very highly thought of director, was lean and serious with one exception: He usually wore a short-sleeved Hawaiian shirt. Was he gay? Was he Hawaiian? Would he add gay fancy to some of Lee's and my "hetero" tendencies?

Somewhere along the way, Jason got another TV series and wasn't available to star in the show. With Jason out of the picture, someone suggested John C. Reilly as Marty. Reilly was best known at that time for films such as *Boogie Nights*, *Magnolia*, and *The Perfect Storm*. And despite having just finished shooting the film version of *Chicago* (for which he would get an Oscar nomination), Reilly, like Dick Van Dyke before him, claimed he couldn't sing. Still, he and I met and went through a couple of jazz standards, and it was clear right away that he had the pitch, the rhythm, and the range for the role. I trusted my judgment as I had with Dick.

And I was right.

When we opened in Boston in November 2002, John's performance brought tears not only to my eyes, but also to almost every audience member for the rest of the run.

The local reviews ranged from superb to constructive, but (and this was a very big BUT), the *Variety* review—the only one to reach New York—said that John was *too* perfectly cast, and wasn't it a shame we couldn't find someone more different than the character so that the results might have been more "invigorating."

My personal reading of this was that they were suggesting a black actor who was perhaps more hip-hop or rock, but I'm overly sensitive to the prevailing winds.

Even so, Gerry Schoenfeld called us all to the Shubert Organization offices and said he wanted to produce the show himself. He refused, though, to work with Waxman and Williams, its original producers, with whom he was angry for some reason.

In any case, we all become entangled in the Shubert web.

Gerry offered us a theater that sat about 1,100 people but which apparently couldn't support any more than ten-and-a-half human beings on the stage if the show was to profit. We had a small show as it was, and Mark Brokaw didn't want the cast size to get any smaller. Without someone like Mike Nichols on board, Gerry could be very tough. So we lost that theater.

Days later, Gerry decided that he didn't want to produce the show at all. He qualified this by saying that he *might* do it if

1. "no one uses an Italian accent" (which was odd as most of the characters were Italian American), and

2. it was guaranteed that there would not be a set that represented the front of a house in Brooklyn, which was something he had "seen in other shows."

With these odd and unmeetable demands, it was clear he just wanted out.

So, after all that anticipation and excitement, *Marty* never made it to Broadway.

It was dizzying, but fortunately, my Yamaha, my faithful friend and servant, sat quietly waiting.

But would there be a new show waiting for me?

Coming Attractions

DID YOU HEAR ABOUT the two musicologists at
  Mozart's grave?
One said, "Isn't that Mozart's *Haffner Symphony* I hear?"
"Yes, but why is the music playing backward?" asked
  the other.
"He's probably de-composing," said the first.

𝄢

Well, I may not be de-composing yet, but, with the turn of
a few pages I'm eighty years old. Not too many pages back, I
was eight.

Tonight, I've come from seeing a play, the first act of which
begins with the reminiscences of an old Irish woman sitting in
an old comfortable chair in an old Irish farmhouse. The play was
originally performed at the Abbey Theatre in Ireland, where it
received good notices. It is literate, and the young actors who
perform with the old woman are professional and pleasing to
look at. I have no desire at all to follow what anyone is talking
about, and yet, looking around, I see everyone is engrossed.

I leave at intermission, puzzled and sad.

I couldn't finish reading the newspaper this morning
either. Massacre in Darfur, another hurricane in Florida, a

critique of a new play that was "too much like another play this reviewer has seen," an opera in which "the soprano's high notes tended to become thin" (while she herself apparently *wasn't*). I couldn't get through it all. There seems to be a growing distance between me and, well, everything.

Is this what eighty is? What T. S. Eliot meant about the world ending with a whimper?

I think of Mozart. He had to finish his *Requiem Mass*, for he had begun to sense that it was his own requiem he was writing.

He was in his thirties.

It has been said that when he did die, soon after he'd finished the requiem, it was a cold day, and as it began snowing, the people accompanying the hearse turned back. *No one* went to his grave with him.

No! I want to write another musical, full of dancing girls, and smart jokes. I want it to open on Broadway in a big theater, and I want to arrive there on opening night with all my friends. I've read that that was how Cole Porter went to his openings: with all his pals, full dress, walking down the center aisle, laughing and nodding to all.

Why not?

♪:

I never expected to grow old. Dying, yes—*big fucking deal*. But growing old? My father grew old. I hated him for having to walk slowly and needing me to help him put on his coat.

I put on my own coat. I write music every day. I own a dog that I'm not crazy about but that gives my wife permission to make baby talk—a small enough price to be left alone to compose. We have a fancy apartment with a rehearsal studio, two fireplaces and an assistant who brings me music paper and a maid who hangs up everyone's coat when they come for a meeting. I've made more money than I can spend.

Still, I'm irritable 32 percent of the time.

Tonight, these are the thoughts that fill my head. I'm thinking all this as the television in the background blares *American Idol*, a TV program on which the singers make three notes out of one as they perform. It's not something I watch, but my children were here for the holidays, and they seemed to enjoy it, so I figured I'd give it a try.

I want to scream at the TV, "Will you shut up?" but I just get up and walk into the other room. I can't stop the cacophony inside my head. I'm buzzing with all the music in the world—in elevators, in concert halls, on CDs, at the dentist, in supermarkets; jazz, bebop, klezmer, gospel, country, baroque, Bartók, Berlioz, 12-tone, heavy metal. I'm overwhelmed, and all the while the words of my old theory teacher, Elvira Wunderlich— "honor your art"—echo in my ears.

Oscar Hammerstein wrote a song called "When I Grow Too Old to Dream." It was my father's favorite, but I always thought that made no sense. How can you grow too old to dream?

My back is hurting, and I've been prescribed pills to make me relax. I feel panicky, so I take two for good measure.

Oh, hell. Had I taken two already? I take another two. My memory, you know.

And then, suddenly, over the blaring of the television in the other room, another sound cuts through, and I hear the Mozart *Requiem*. I swear. I have a vivid imagination, but I know I hear it—softly at first, then crescendo-ing until it drowns out *American Idol*.

This is it, I think to myself. *I'm coming, Wolfgang!* At about measure 100 of the "Sanctus," I hear chimes, and I marvel that I've never heard them before in the *Requiem Mass*, then I realize it's my doorbell. *Bing bong.*

Death?

I go to the door (this must be a dream because Barbara is still in the other room, listening to *American Idol,* and she doesn't seem to be hearing anything but that), and you won't believe this: There are two men dressed in black on the other side of the door: one with a top hat, and one with a derby. I recognize them. They are Barnes and Noble. (I have seen their pictures on T-shirts.) They've come for me.

The "Sanctus" of the *Mass* is taking my breath away.

Barnes speaks first. "It's time for your book."

Noble says, "Now! Now! Finish the book! We have to reduce the price 25 percent in one month."

The voices echo as if in a cave.

I wake up in a sweat, thinking, *Those pills! What a dream!* My T-shirt is soaked through. The dream is already slipping away, and the familiar grayness of depression takes its place. I would seem to have everything: a few hit shows, money, a loving family. It should be others who are depressed, envying me. But the Gray Ghost of my mother is always there.

And then the thought strikes me: I never said good-bye to either of my parents. In each case, I had been alone with them just before their deaths, but at the final moment, I ran from their bedsides, never saying "good-bye" or "I love you."

Maybe, finally, it's time to tell Mom and Pop "good-bye."

I don't even know where they're buried.

"Good idea," says Barbara in the morning when I tell her I want to find the cemetery. "Why don't you find out and go and see them because you've become a pain in the ass for a while now—you and your damn memoir!"

And that's what I do.

My assistant looks in the New York City Bureau of Records and finds out where they're buried: Mount Judah Cemetery near Union Field Cemetery, Ridgewood, New York. I make an appointment to visit ("any day but the Sabbath"), and I hire a limo. (Mom would have found that excessive, which is exactly why I think it suitable.) My driver's name is Jean; when I tell him why I'm going there, he says, "She'll be happy," but I don't think he understands.

After the usual discussion about the spelling of our name ("-ouse," not "-auss") with the man at the gate, I'm directed to the gravesite. I walk there, and find the headstones:

"Ira Strouse, Husband"—doesn't mention anything about "Father"—"July 30, 1893–1956" and "Ethel N. Strouse, wife"—nothing about "Mother"—"February 26, 1904–March 25, 1962."

I try to summon up a reverent feeling and find the perfect speech to deliver, but I have nothing inside. Instead, I touch the cold, hard ground and say, "I love you, Pop. I love you, Mom. Good-bye."

I realize that, in a funny way, my visit out there isn't so much about *them* as it is about me. I have said, "Good-bye, I love you"—something I was too confused, terrified, and empty to have said back then—and I feel like I'm a better (or at least a smarter) person now.

I turn away and walk slowly back to the car. Jean is leaning against its side, and as I approach, he says gently, "You made your folks very happy today."

I am too exhausted to say anything. I simply nod, and slip into the backseat.

♮:

The music is overpowering. "Put on a Happy Face" segues into "Applause." Peter Duchin's band is really cooking.

Barbara and I pause at the entrance of the great hall at the Museum of Natural History, looking in on my book party, which is now in full swing.

It's like a dream.

In fact, I can't help but wonder if it is.

"You know," Barbara says, "I'm not sure having the book party under the great blue whale was such a great idea. Those wires holding it up look very fragile." Barbara is suspicious of everything.

"I lived my early life here, and the great whale never budged," I assure her. "Those wires will hold up forever—or at least through the book signing."

Imagine me telling Barbara not to worry and her believing me. Yep—this is surely a dream.

We saunter in and survey the scene. There's Iris Blasi dancing with Ilie Nastase. Dick Hyman and Hyman Spotnitz are going at it, and over there, there's Hillel Swiller with Phyllis Diller.

Suddenly, Rhoda Herrick, an old friend who had said she wanted to give this book party for me, is standing on a platform waving her hands for quiet. Peter Duchin cuts off the band (damn, they were in the middle of "A Lot of Livin' to Do"), and everyone stops dancing.

"Everyone, welcome. I hope you are having a good time," Rhoda begins.

There's mild applause, and she goes on. "I think it's time for us to meet the author, Charles Strouse."

There's milder applause.

"Charlie!" she's now calling. "Charlie, where are you? Let's bring him up here. Charlie?"

I'm standing in back, holding Barbara's hand. "This isn't how I want the book to end," I whisper. "Let's get out of here!"

As we run down Central Park West (except I'm not so great at running these days), I say to her, "I learned something at the cemetery today!"

She says, "That's great. Can we get a taxi?"

And I say, "Better yet, let's get that horse and carriage!"

Barbara looks at me strangely. "Are you crazy? That's at least forty dollars."

"Mom's gone," I explain. "She's really gone. I said 'good-bye' at the cemetery."

And so, we run after a carriage, and I shout to the driver (who looks very much like Jean, my limo driver), "Around the park!"

And he says, "You're right. That *is* no way to end the book. Hop in!"

I'm mesmerized by the *clip-clop, clip-clop* sound the horse is making when Barbara says to me, "What is that you're whistling?"

"What? Was I whistling?"

I notice that as I'd been listening to the horse's hooves, they'd become like a sort of mantra, erasing my previous gloomy thoughts, as I whistled a tune I haven't yet written for a new musical I haven't yet begun.

"You're right!" I yell to the driver over the clop of the horse's hooves. "This wasn't the right ending. It's just the beginning!"

"You've got to end it on a high note," he shouts back. "Remember how you did it in that show about the redheaded orphan?" The horse turns its head back and whinnies.

Barbara says, "What the hell is going on?"

The driver turns back around. "Congratulations! I read that *Marty* just got its financing."

"Thank you," I say. "And did you know *Annie* is opening in China?"

"Of course I did," the driver says. "My horse told me."

Barbara, getting into the spirit of things, adds, "And *Bye Bye Birdie* is going to have a revival on Broadway!"

"I hadn't heard that," the driver says, grinning back at us.

And suddenly—you're not going to believe this—my cell phone rings! Right at Sixty-eighth Street, near the carousel, which is turning and playing a hurdy-gurdy version of "A Broadway Musical," a show which had a dismal ending although I still liked some of the songs from it. The voice on the other end of the phone is that of Casey Nicholaw, the director of *The Drowsy Chaperone*.

"Guess what?" he says. "This may be a dream, but my news is real. It's happening! *Minsky's*—the show that got derailed when Mike Ockrent died—is going to be produced by Bob Boyett, the richest man in all Christendom. Bob Martin, who wrote *The Drowsy Chaperone*, will do the book."

The coachman turns to Barbara and me. "I knew that," he says. "You're booked into the Ahmanson Theatre, Los Angeles, opening a little after Christmas 2009, and then New York!" Then, almost as an afterthought, he sings, *"Brrrrr-oadway!"*

𝄢

I wake with a start. I'm still in the limo on my way back from the cemetery. We're not even back in Manhattan yet. I rub my eyes and glance over at the seat next to me.

Buddy is there, smiling.

Neither of us say a word as we drive back to Manhattan. We don't have to now.

The car stops in front of my apartment building, and I get out of the car. When I turn back, Buddy's gone.

But I smile, because he's not really gone. The fat kid with the dark circles under his eyes will always be around.

He's part of the music.

𝄢

Well, that's it for my Requiem.

Eighty is not a bad time to end the book. My advance wasn't that big to begin with. (*"But your ego was,"* I can just hear Lee saying.)

I believe I've hit the main points: the musicals I've written, the celebs, my children and my wife, thoughts about other composers and art in general (*boring*), all the fun I've had, the heartache, my mother and father and David and Lila, too.

Oh, yes . . . and Buddy.

It hits me: Life should be like musicals: along with the sentimental ballads and the sadness hiding in the shadows, laughs, lots of laughs, and dancing always. I think I understand that now.

You can write the pain (God knows there's enough of it), or you can let loose the joy.

Why did I remember half this stuff? *Because it's a memoir, pal.*

But it's not. It's a musical comedy.

Nadia Boulanger was right: It's all something to write a song about.

Shows and Awards

Bye Bye Birdie
Opened April 14, 1960, at the Martin Beck Theater, and ran
for 607 performances.

Produced by Edward Padula in association with
 L. Slade Brown
Directed by Gower Champion
Book by Michael Stewart
Lyrics by Lee Adams
Music by Charles Strouse

All American
Opened March 19, 1962, at the Winter Garden Theatre, and
ran for 80 performances.

Produced by Edward Padula in association with
 L. Slade Brown
Directed by Joshua Logan
Book by Mel Brooks
Based on the novel *Professor Fodorski* by Robert Lewis Taylor
Lyrics by Lee Adams
Music by Charles Strouse

Golden Boy
Opened October 20, 1964, at the Majestic Theatre, and ran
for 595 performances.

Produced by Hillard Elkins
Directed by Arthur Penn
Book by Clifford Odets and William Gibson
Based on the play by Clifford Odets
Lyrics by Lee Adams
Music by Charles Strouse

It's Bird . . . It's a Plane . . . It's Superman
Opened March 29, 1966, at the Alvin Theatre, and ran for
129 performances.

Produced by Harold Prince in association with Ruth Mitchell
Directed by Harold Prince
Book by David Newman and Robert Benton
Based on the comic strip "Superman" by Jerry Siegel and
Joe Shuster
Lyrics by Lee Adams
Music by Charles Strouse

Applause
Opened March 30, 1970, at the Palace Theatre, and ran for
896 performances.

Produced by Joseph Kipness and Lawrence Kasha in
association with Nederlander Productions and
George M. Steinbrenner III
Directed by Ron Field
Book by Betty Comden and Adolph Green
Based on the film *All About Eve* and the original story by
Mary Orr

Lyrics by Lee Adams
Music by Charles Strouse

Annie
Opened April 21, 1977, at the Alvin Theatre, and ran for
2,377 performances.

Produced by Mike Nichols, Irwin Meyer, Stephen R.
Friedman, Lewis Allen, Alvin Nederlander Associates,
Inc., the John F. Kennedy Center for the Performing Arts,
and Icarus Productions in association with Peter Crane
Directed by Martin Charnin
Book by Thomas Meehan
Based on the comic strip "Little Orphan Annie" by
Harold Gray
Lyrics by Martin Charnin
Music by Charles Strouse

A Broadway Musical
Opened December 21, 1978, at the Lunt-Fontanne Theatre,
and closed the same night.

Produced by Norman Kean and Garth H. Drabinsky
Directed by Gower Champion
Book by William F. Brown
Lyrics by Lee Adams
Music by Charles Strouse

**Charlie and Algernon (originally produced in London as
Flowers for Algernon)**

Opened September 14, 1980, at the Helen Hayes Theatre, and ran for 17 performances.

Produced by the John F. Kennedy Center for the Performing Arts, Isobel Robins Konecky, the Fischer Theatre Foundation, and Folger Theatre Group (Louis W. Scheeder, Michael Sheehan, Producers)
Directed by Louis W. Scheeder
Book and lyrics by David Rogers
Based on the novel *Flowers for Algernon* by Daniel Keyes
Music by Charles Strouse

Bring Back Birdie
Opened on March 5, 1981, at the Martin Beck Theatre, and ran for 4 performances.

Produced by Lee Guber, Shelly Gross, and Slade Brown
Conceived and directed by Joe Layton
Book by Michael Stewart
Lyrics by Lee Adams
Music by Charles Strouse

Dance a Little Closer
Opened May 11, 1983, at the Minskoff Theatre, and closed after 1 performance.

Produced by Frederick Brisson, Jerome Minskoff, James M. Nederlander and the John F. Kennedy Center for the Performing Arts
Book, lyrics, and direction by Alan Jay Lerner

Based on the play *Idiot's Delight* by Robert E. Sherwood
Music by Charles Strouse

Rags

Opened August 21, 1986, at the Mark Hellinger Theatre,
and ran for 4 performances.

Produced by Lee Guber, Martin Heinfling, and Marvin A.
Krauss
Directed by Gene Saks
Book by Joseph Stein
Lyrics by Stephen Schwartz
Music by Charles Strouse

Nick & Nora

Opened December 8, 1991, at the Marquis Theatre, and ran
for 9 performances.

Produced by Terry Allen Kramer, Charlene Nederlander,
James M. Nederlander, Daryl Roth, and Elizabeth I.
McCann in association with James Pentecost and
Charles Suisman
Directed by Arthur Laurents
Book by Arthur Laurents
Based on characters created by Dashiell Hammett, based on
The Thin Man motion picture
Lyrics by Richard Maltby Jr.
Music by Charles Strouse

WEST END OPENINGS

I and Albert
Opened November 6, 1972, at the Piccadilly Theatre, and ran for 120 performances.

Produced by arrangement with Donald Albery, Lewis M. Allen, and Si Litvinoff in association with Theatre Projects and Richard Lukins
Directed by John Schlesinger
Book by Jay Presson Allen
Lyrics by Lee Adams
Music by Charles Strouse

Flowers for Algernon
Opened June 14, 1979, at the Queens Theatre, and ran for 28 performances.

Produced by Michael White in association with Isobel Robbins Konecky
Directed by Peter Coe
Book and lyrics by David Rogers
Based on the novel *Flowers for Algernon* by Daniel Keyes
Music by Charles Strouse

OFF-BROADWAY AND OTHER

Shoestring Revue
Opened February 28, 1955, at the President Theater,
New York.

Music by Charles Strouse

Shoestring '57
Opened November 5, 1956, at the Barbizon Plaza Theatre,
New York, and ran for 110 performances.

Music by Charles Strouse

Medium Rare
Musical revue produced in 1960, Chicago.

Music by Charles Strouse

Six
Produced Off-Broadway in 1971, and ran for 8 performances.

Music, book, and lyrics by Charles Strouse

Charlotte's Web
A musical first produced in 1973, based on the novel by
E. B. White.

Music and lyrics by Charles Strouse

By Strouse
Produced Off-Broadway at the Manhattan Theatre Club,
1977, and ran for 156 performances.

Music by Charles Strouse

Bojangles
Workshop production in 1993 at the Barksdale Theatre
in Richmond, Virginia.

Music by Charles Strouse

Upstairs at O'Neals
Produced at O'Neals nightclub in 1982, and ran for 308
performances.

Music and lyrics by Charles Strouse

Mayor
Produced Off-Broadway in 1985, and ran for 225
performances.

Music and lyrics by Charles Strouse

Annie Warbucks
Produced Off-Broadway at the Variety Arts Theatre in 1993,
and ran for 200+ performances.

Music by Charles Strouse

Can't Stop Dancin'
Musical revue presented in 1994 at the Marymount Theatre, New York.

Conceived and directed by Charles Strouse

A Lot of Living!
Musical revue presented in 1996 at Rainbow & Stars.

Lyrics by Lee Adams, Sammy Cahn, Martin Charnin, Alan Jay Lerner, Richard Maltby, Stephen Schwartz, Charles Strouse, and Fred Tobias
Conceived and staged by Barbara Siman

Real Men (working title of work-in-progress)
A revue-style show presented in January 2005 at the Coconut Grove Playhouse in Miami, Florida.

Music and lyrics by Charles Strouse

Dancing with Time (working title of work-in-progress)
Presented in April 2005 at the Trinity Repertory Company in Providence, Rhode Island.

Book, music, and lyrics by Charles Strouse

Marty

A musical based on the 1955 film *Marty* by Paddy Chayevsky starring Ernest Borgnine, performed in 2002 at the Huntington Theatre, Boston.

Music by Charles Strouse

FILM AND TELEVISION

Bye Bye Birdie

A motion picture released April 5, 1963, by Columbia Pictures.

Produced by Fred Kohlman
Directed by George Sidney
Book by Michael Stewart
Screenplay by Irving Brecher
Lyrics by Lee Adams
Music by Charles Strouse
Starring Dick Van Dyke, Janet Leigh, Ann-Margret, Bobby Rydell, Maureen Stapleton, Jesse Pearson, and Paul Lynde

Alice in Wonderland aka *What's a Nice Girl Like You Doing in a Place Like This?*

A one-hour animated TV special based upon the Lewis Carroll book, released in 1966 by Hanna-Barbera Productions.

Produced by Bill Hanna and Joe Barbera
Directed by Charles Shows
Script by Bill Dana
Lyrics by Lee Adams
Music by Charles Strouse
With the voices of Sammy Davis Jr. (Cheshire Cat), Zsa Zsa
    Gabor (Queen of Hearts), Mel Blanc, Janet Waldo, Don
    Messick Howard Morris, Hedda Hopper, Harvey
    Korman, and Bill Dana (the White Knight)

Bonnie and Clyde
A motion picture released in 1967 by Warner Brothers.

Produced by Warren Beatty
Directed by Arthur Penn
Screenplay by David Newman and Robert Benton
Film score by Charles Strouse
Songs by Charles Strouse and Lee Adams
Starring Warren Beatty, Faye Dunaway, Gene Hackman, and
    Estelle Parsons

The Night They Raided Minsky's
A motion picture released in 1968 by MGM/UA Studios.

Produced by Norman Lear and Bud Yorkin
Directed by William Friedkin
Screenplay by Norman Lear, Rowland Barber, Sidney
    Michaels, and Arnold Schulman
Based upon the novel by Rowland Barber
Lyrics by Lee Adams

Music by Charles Strouse
Starring Jason Robards, Britt Ekland, Norman Wisdom,
   Forrest Tucker, and Elliott Gould

All in the Family, **1971–1979**
Theme song, "Those Were the Days"

Lyrics by Lee Adams
Music by Charles Strouse

Just Tell Me What You Want
A motion picture released in 1980 by Warner Brothers.

Produced by Sidney Lumet and Jay Presson Allen
Directed by Sidney Lumet
Screenplay by Jay Presson Allen
Film score by Charles Strouse
Starring Alan King, Dina Merrill, Ali McGraw, Peter
   Weller, and Myrna Loy

Annie
A motion feature released in 1982 by Columbia TriStar
   Studios.

Produced by Ray Stark
Directed by John Huston
Book by Thomas Meehan
Screenplay by Carol Sobieski
Lyrics by Lee Adams
Music by Charles Strouse

Starring Carol Burnett, Albert Finney, Ann Reinking, Tim
Curry, Aileen Quinn, and Bernadette Peters

Lyle, Lyle Crocodile
A 20-minute animated film produced in 1984 by HBO.

Produced by Michael Sporn
Directed by Michael Sporn
Script by Maxine Fisher
Based on the 1962 children's story *The House on East 88th
Street* by Bernard Waber
Starring Tony Randall, Liz Callaway, Devon Michaels, and
Heidi Stallings

(Also staged as a musical in Chicago and Milwaukee with a
book by Charles Strouse and Thomas Meehan, as directed
and choreographed by Barbara Siman)

All Dogs Go to Heaven
An animated feature film released in 1989 by United Artists
Studios.

Produced by Don Bluth, Gary Goldman, and John Pomeroy
Directed by Don Bluth
Screenplay by David N. Weiss
Music and Lyrics by Charles Strouse
With the voices of Burt Reynolds, Dom DeLuise, Melba
Moore, Ken Page, Irene Cara, and Loni Anderson

Alexander and the Terrible, Horrible, No Good, Very Bad Day
An animated TV musical produced in 1990 by HBO.

Produced by Gabor Csupo
Directed by Allen Foster
Screenplay and lyrics by Judith Viorst
Based on the book by Judith Viorst
Music by Charles Strouse

A Child's Garden of Verses
Released in 1992 by Family Home Entertainment.

Produced and directed by Michael Sporn
Script by Thomas Meehan
Based on the book by Robert Louis Stevenson
Orchestrations by Michael Starobin
Music and lyrics by Charles Strouse
Starring Paul Austin, Jonathan Pryce, and Heidi Stallings

Bye Bye Birdie
Produced for television in 1995 by Hallmark Entertainment.

Produced by Tim Bell and J. Boyce Harman Jr.
Directed by Gene Saks
Book by Michael Stewart
Lyrics by Lee Adams
Music by Charles Strouse
Starring Jason Alexander, Vanessa Williams, Chynna
    Phillips, Tyne Daly, Marc Kudisch, George Wendt, and
    Sally Mayes

Annie
Produced for television in 1999 by Disney/ABC-TV.

Produced by John Whitman
Directed by Rob Marshall
Book by Thomas Meehan
Teleplay by Irene Mecchi
Lyrics by Martin Charnin
Music by Charles Strouse
Starring Kathy Bates, Alicia Morton, Victor Garber, Alan
   Cumming, and Audra McDonald

NOTABLE AWARDS

1961   Tony Award for Best Musical, *Bye Bye Birdie*
1961   London Critics Best Foreign Musical, *Bye Bye Birdie*
1965   Tony Nominee for Best Musical, *Golden Boy*
1969   Grammy Award for Best Original Score for a Motion
   Picture, *Bonnie and Clyde*
1970   Tony Award for Best Musical, *Applause*
1970   London Critics Best Foreign Musical, *Applause*
1977   Tony Award for Best Original Score, *Annie*
1977   Drama Desk Nominee for Outstanding Music, *Annie*
1978   Grammy Award for Best Cast Show Album, *Annie*
1981   Tony Nominee for Best Original Score, *Charlie and
   Algernon*
1983   BAFTA Film Award Nominee for Best Original
   Song, "Tomorrow" from *Annie*
1985   Inductee into the Songwriters Hall of Fame

1986 Drama Desk Nominee for Outstanding Music, *Mayor*

1987 Drama Desk Nominee for Outstanding Music, *Rags*

1987 Tony Nominee for Best Original Score, *Rags*

1992 Tony Nominee for Best Original Score, *Nick & Nora*

1996 Emmy Award for Outstanding Individual Achievement in Music and Lyrics, with Lee Adams for "Let's Settle Down" from *Bye Bye Birdie*

1999 Winner of the ASCAP Foundation's Richard Rodgers Award for lifetime achievement

2002 Inductee into the Theater Hall of Fame

Acknowledgments

TO MY TALENTED, brilliant, and funny children, Ben, Nick, Victoria, and William, who are still showing me what is really important in my life.

To Iris Blasi, supportive, loving, smart, and always there.

To Barbara Hogan, more than a friend.

And also thanks to Linda Konner, Carolyn Rossi Copeland, Stephen Cole, Mary Kickel, and Magda Herbut.

To the performers who brought my music to life.

To the theater producers who made money from my shows.

To those producers who didn't: sorry.

Index

Eb   Fmi7   Gmi7 C7

WHY WEAR A PUSS THAT'S SO-UR?

Fmi7 C7   Fmi7   Bb7   Bbmi7

Slower; PUT ON A HAP-PY FACE

F7   Bb7   Eb   Ab

MAKE LIFE WORTH-WHILE. SHAKE OF

F7   Bb7sus Bb7 Eb

CI-DED TO SMILE ——! PICK OUT

Fmi7   Bb7   Fmi7 Bb7

TICK OUT THAT NO-BLE CHIN—!

Fmi7   Bb7   Bbmi7